CHARLTON'S GROUND

Dan Cassenti

ANAPHORA LITERARY PRESS

QUANAH, TEXAS

Anaphora Literary Press
1108 W 3rd Street
Quanah, TX 79252
https://anaphoraliterary.com

Book design by Anna Faktorovich, Ph.D.

Copyright © 2018 by Dan Cassenti

All rights reserved. No part of this book may be reproduced in any form or by any electronic or mechanical means, including information storage and retrieval systems, without permission in writing from Dan Cassenti. Writers are welcome to quote brief passages in their critical studies, as American copyright law dictates.

Printed in the United States of America, United Kingdom and in Australia on acid-free paper.

Edited by Destany Atkinson

Published in 2018 by Anaphora Literary Press

Charlton's Ground
Dan Cassenti—1st edition.

Library of Congress Control Number: 2018907740

Library Cataloging Information
Cassenti, Dan, 1977-, author.
    Charlton's ground / Dan Cassenti
    232 p. ; 9 in.
    ISBN 978-1-68114-460-3 (softcover : alk. paper)
    ISBN 978-1-68114-461-0 (hardcover : alk. paper)
    ISBN 978-1-68114-462-7 (e-book)
1. Fiction—Historical—General. 2. History—United States—19th Century.
3. Social Science—Slavery.
PN3311-3503: Literature: Prose fiction
813: American fiction in English

CHARLTON'S GROUND

Dan Cassenti

For Lucy

Acknowledgements

I would like to express my gratitude to Destany Atkinson for a wonderful editing job. Charlton's Ground would not have been published without the support of the Harford Writers Group. In particular, I would like to thank Kate Lashley, Karin Harrison, Larry Garnett, and Katherine McGuire for their insightful comments and edits.

Chapter One

May 1841
A South Carolina Plantation

Charlton brought the book to his nose with his dark-skinned hand, inhaling the scent of Belle, his master's daughter, and smiled. She had excused herself, saying she would come right back, and he already missed her.

While he waited, Charlton read aloud the words of the fable. When he finished, he closed the book and looked up to see eleven-year-old Belle. The sunlight shining against her blonde hair cast a glow, which made Charlton squint and smile.

"Did you like the story?" she asked.

The seven-year-old boy scrunched his face. "I don't know. Why'd the princess not like the pea? I just want one mattress, it could even have a big rock under it."

Belle laughed. "Oh, Charlton, you're funny! You see, the queen would never know she had found a real princess, if she couldn't feel the pea. That's just what the story's about. Do you understand?"

Charlton nodded, knowing he didn't. "Belle, I start my job tomorrow." She looked at him with bright eyes and smiled, urging him to continue. "Pete, the older boy who brings the water to the fields, showed me how and now I got to do it by myself. I used to help Mama around here and she let me go off on my own and I read the books you gave me, but I can't do that no more."

"Well, Charlton, I been taking care of you for as long as I can remember and I know you're going to do so well. Just remember that bringing the water to the fields is a big help to everyone. They need it and you're going to give it to them." They smiled, then Belle hugged Charlton, and he swore to himself that he would marry her someday.

***

After bringing enough water to the fields on the first day, Charlton struggled carrying the water on the second day. Charlton's aching muscles gave out and he dropped a full pail of water. He fell to the ground and allowed the dirt-packed water to soak his shirt.

Henry, a white hired hand, saw him collapse and rushed over. Seeing him, Charlton gasped harder to get some sympathy. Instead, Henry kicked Charlton just below the ribs. The pain shot through him and he screamed. Henry crouched low and started yelling. "Get up! Get up, boy. Look what you done! You see that?"

Charlton groaned. The white man grabbed him with his dirty hands, hoisted him up, and dropped him back down into the deepest puddle of mud the spilled water had created. Charlton screamed again and mud filled his mouth.

"You see it now?" The hired hand pushed Charlton's face in the mud until Charlton forced out a nod. He grabbed a fistful of Charlton's shirt and pulled him. Charlton's face broke free from its muddy seal with a sloshing sound, and he gasped for breath. He coughed the mud from his throat.

"I'm watching you, boy! You take a break like that 'gain or spill any more of that there water, you'll get worse." Henry tried to push Charlton back into the mud with the heel of his boot. Charlton caught himself before he got soaked again. Henry stomped off without looking back.

Charlton gritted his teeth and sprang up from the ground. His face flushed. The hulking figure of the hired hand stopped him from defending himself. He thought about how his weak, small body would prevent him from taking on this brute. Charlton eyed the empty pail. *Maybe carrying that pail will make me strong enough next time.* He picked up the pail with his stiff muscles and bruised body. He couldn't fill it all the way to the top again that day, impeded by the aches in his side and arms.

The slaves in the field suffered; the sun beat down on their bodies. When Charlton arrived with water, they rushed to him, pushing each other out of the way to get to him first. They spilled much of the water in their haste.

Charlton struggled to deliver water to the workers. The cramps in his side nauseated him. The mud streaking his face and the obvious limp brought no sympathy from those who suffered themselves. Shame filled his eyes when alone at the well as he drank water to replenish what he lost from tears and sweat.

When the sun set that evening, the field workers rushed to the well, except Ole Joe, the oldest among them. Ole Joe's body somehow held together despite the deep creases in his face and neck. He covered himself at all times except for his head, but every once in a while someone caught a glimpse of flesh underneath his collar and regretted it. Penetrating, tangled ridges coursed downward. Everyone who saw the patch of skin knew it kept the same pattern all the way down.

Ole Joe almost always kept to himself, but he sometimes told a story, and when he did, the slaves gathered around him. Charlton often stared at Ole Joe while the slaves ate. He wanted to ask him how he could look so relaxed braced up against a tree or a large rock.

Charlton didn't notice Ole Joe that day, at first. When he saw the onslaught of slaves rush the well, he felt worse than ever and fled to the slave camp where he buried his head in his hands, crying.

Ole Joe sat alone. Charlton continued to cry as Ole Joe sighed, slapped his knees, and sauntered over to him.

"You're making it hard to eat you knows. What with your crying and all."

"I'm sorry." Charlton struggled to get enough breath to form the words. He peeked between his fingers as Ole Joe plopped down beside him.

"That's fine, you just tell Ole Joe what's on your mind. Why you cry like that?"

Charlton steadied his breathing. Ole Joe had a calming effect on him. He took a couple more moments to regain control. "You work the fields, so you know."

"I don't knows nothing."

"Didn't you know that I didn't bring the water fast enough? They all hate me. They're all at the well on account of how slow I am."

Ole Joe smiled, took out an old flask and tipped it back in his mouth to show it still had water in it. "That's why I brings my own."

Charlton smiled and laughed, something he didn't think he'd ever do again much less that night. "Where'd you get *that*?"

"I stole it. A long time ago...from Old Master."

"Who's Old Master?"

"Boy, don't you knows nothing? That was New Master's daddy. He's dead."

Charlton stared at Ole Joe, unsure how to respond. As far as Charlton knew, the master had always run the plantation. "Did you used to work for him?"

"Of course I worked for him. How you think he got the name Old Master? You talk like a white man, but you sure are slow."

"I'm sorry," Charlton said and put his head back down in his hands.

Ole Joe patted Charlton on the back. "That's enough boy. I'm the one who sorry."

Charlton looked at Ole Joe and saw a man of wisdom. He wanted to hear his stories. "What was Old Master like?" Charlton asked.

A grin came to Ole Joe's face. "Ohhh…Ole Master? He one mean and cruel man. Believe me, boy, you gots it good round here 'pared to that."

"What'd he do?"

"Not much. He just beat us with no mercy, let his men whip us when we ain't done nothing wrong, cut our food on the hardest day, then cut our water on the hottest day. I knows this one time, one of us got up and died before the Sunday of the next week, he work us so hard. Old Master, he cut our water when someone stole his flask and it was so hot, I near enough sweat out half my body."

Charlton's back stiffened. "You mean that flask?" he asked, pointing at Ole Joe's pocket.

"Yeah, but don't you be looking at me that way. I didn't steal it."

"But, you said…"

"I *knows* what I say, boy, but I kind of fib to you. I stole it from the man who stole it. I didn't steal it from the Ole Master's pocket or nothing. The whites, they let me keep it on account of they don't know where it come from no more."

Charlton dropped his shoulders as Ole Joe continued. "That man who stole it, he knows what he did was wrong, but he didn't say nothing 'bout it 'cause he not want be killed."

"Old Master *killed* our people too?"

"Right in front of my eyes once."

Charlton's eyes widened. He had never heard about killing a slave. "What-what happened?"

"Well, Tom, he my buddy from way back, he got it in his head, he going to escape. He might've made it too, but someone squeal on him the night before Tom leave. Master set up with a shot gun behind that tree." Ole Joe pointed to a gnarled oak across from the slave quarters. "I was looking through a crack in the wall to see my friend off. He say he going to come back for me, so I want to see him off. All a sudden, the air fill with a loud bang and Tom, he fall to the ground and he not get up ever 'gain. Then, Old Master, he come from behind the tree carrying the gun over his shoulder and smiling like he done shot a bear. He walk right up to Tom, kick him in the side to make sure he dead and call over his shoulder to his men and they pull Tom over to where they want his grave. The gun woke the whole lot of us and we go out there and see. Oh, they be sobbing and crying but none of it bring poor Tom back. The whites care nothing 'bout that. They make us dig his grave and dump him in. His bones still buried under there today."

Charlton and Ole Joe sat in silence while Charlton tried to ease his eyelids back to their normal height. Finally, Charlton spoke, "I hate Old Master."

"Well you should, boy, but no sense in it now, he's dead. He a cruel man. I guess you don't believe that story of that killed baby neither 'cause you look pretty shook."

"What killed baby?" Charlton's heart began to race once more.

Ole Joe paused a moment, looking ashamed. "I'm sorry. I thought all 'round here knew. Never mind I say nothing 'bout it."

"I can't never mind now. You have to tell me."

Ole Joe let out a "tsk," lifted his hands, and slapped them down on his bent knees. "Everyone here think that New Master, he kill a baby for being too small."

"What?" Charlton asked, his eyes wide again. "Why would he do that?"

"He didn't and that's what I'm trying to tell you." Ole Joe took a deep breath and let it out, slow. "I knew New Master when he was a boy. He a coward, but he smart too. He know his daddy cruel and he know he lost his men and his women from being cruel. He cut off the water and our people die. That don't do no good for business. A master, he want all the help he can get. The year the people die, the crop don't come in good. New Master know being mean get you nowhere."

"Then, why did the master kill the baby?" When Ole Joe gave him a disapproving look, Charlton said, "Why does everyone think he killed the baby?"

"Cause he smart. He keep us working hard by making us think he cruel. Killing a baby 'bout as cruel as it get. He make our people hate him, but he make us *fear* him too. We work better that way."

"What did he do?"

"We always keep pigs in a pig sty. New Master, he got Paul to tie up one of the runt pigs in a bag and then throw that bag right in the water. The ones who hear the splash and the squealing, sound to them like the baby. True enough, the baby he taken from his mama he sold to a trader. New Master, he know what he do. He make money and get the fear. He no fool. This the first time I tell anyone 'bout it. We ought to fear New Master."

"How do you know what you're telling me?"

"I tend the pigs in those days. New Master, he let the runt live 'til the baby born, then he kill it. It got to be what happen. The baby not that small anyhow." Ole Joe trailed off, the silence broken by the sound of the men and women returning.

Even at his young age, Charlton began to understand the master and knew that Belle had him wrong. The master didn't want to take care of his slaves. He wanted to use them to help himself, but one thing didn't make sense about the Master, and Charlton hoped that Ole Joe had the answer. "Ole Joe?"

"Hmm?" Ole Joe asked, breaking out of his spell.

"Why does New Master let me play with Belle?"

"Belle? Oh yeah, New Master's child. Well, I…" Ole Joe looked up and hesitated long enough for Martha to charge forward. Charlton didn't know how long his mother had watched, but he didn't like that she interrupted when he could have gotten the answer to his important question.

"It getting late, Ole Joe. You're kind for taking Charlton under your wing, but he got to eat and then go rest," Martha said.

"Yeah ma'am, I guess he ought." Ole Joe rose, dusted off his overalls, and looked relieved to put an end to the conversation, yet still reluctant. He leaned over Charlton, clapped him on the back a little too hard for Charlton's aching muscles and said, "You keep up the fight, boy. You keep lifting that water bucket and you get strong, day by day."

Charlton watched Ole Joe saunter over to his spot to finish his supper. He turned back to face his mother, "Mama, I'm sad."

Martha lowered herself to the ground and without a word wrapped one arm around his shoulders and with the other leaned his face against her chest. Charlton sobbed against her.

Chapter Two

July 1842

Charlton found himself moving with ease through the grounds of the plantation carrying two water buckets, each filled three quarters of the way to the top. Though he still felt the tug of the weight on his arms, he managed to keep them on the cusp of aching. He thought that by the start of the next week he could fill them even higher.

His thoughts drifted to Ole Joe and the first night they ate together. An extra spring in his step emerged as he thought of the family that had started that day. Ole Joe took shape as a father figure to Martha and a grandfather to Charlton. He regaled them with stories night after night and seemed to enjoy the attention almost as much as Charlton enjoyed listening to him.

Charlton caught sight of Ole Joe and moved to avoid him, as usual. Though they spoke each night, Ole Joe always carried his flask and chastised Charlton whenever he approached with the buckets. Charlton accepted early that their relationship resumed with the setting sun. He turned toward the greatest bustle of activity and saw frowns and eye rolls. As always, they gave him the same impression: they liked to see him for the water, but held something against him, though he couldn't figure out what. He always acted respectful and polite to them and Belle had taught him well enough, he did not think they disliked him for a lack of manners on his part.

That night, Ole Joe and Charlton arrived in line to receive their supper at the same time. It looked like some kind of stew with meat and potatoes. His mother prepared the food, but never got to pick the ingredients. Charlton shrugged and stopped thinking about it. "Charlton," said Ole Joe with a nod of his head.

"Joe," Charlton said in a like manner.

"How you doing?" Ole Joe slapped Charlton on the back.

"Tired," Charlton said. "What about you?"

"Same. I saw you out there a lot, boy. You been working hard and you knows these folks 'preciate it."

Charlton's puzzled look at Joe's statement didn't faze Joe, but they moved forward through the line in silence. When they arrived at the spot where his mother sat eating, Charlton let Ole Joe settle down and then couldn't wait any more. He launched into a question he had meant to ask for a while. "Ole Joe?"

"Hmm?" Ole Joe asked with his mouth full of stew.

"You know how you told me about how that little baby that everyone thinks was killed, wasn't?" Charlton asked.

Martha tsked, but didn't try to stop the conversation.

"Yup," Ole Joe said after swallowing.

"Well, I was wondering. If Master sold him like you said, then how'd he live? Every baby needs their mama's milk. If Master sold that baby, didn't he need his mama?"

Ole Joe raised an eyebrow and looked over at Charlton's mother who continued to eat her supper. "You really going make me answer this aren't you? Ain't this your place?" he asked her.

"I ain't answering. You the one always filling his head with these stories. 'Sides I want to hear your answer," said Martha with a grin.

"All right then. You see, son, it true a baby need a woman's milk," Ole Joe said.

"Then, that baby died!" Charlton said.

"Now, hold on there, you got to listen. Babies, they need a woman, but it don't have to be the mama. That baby just nurse on someone else."

"Really?"

"Yeah, boy, you think I fib?"

"No, I guess not."

Ole Joe leaned toward Charlton and lowered his voice. "You knows how I know it?"

"No," said Charlton and his mother at once.

"'Cause New Master, he nursed by one of our own."

"What?" Charlton and Martha asked in unison.

"Sure 'nough. That boy's mama, she all dried up. Ole Master, he grab a woman from her cabin in the middle of the night and we don't see her for near 'bout a year. When she get back to living with us, she told us, she nurse the baby 'til he eat real foods. She say it the best time, seeing as she get to stay in the house and only tend to that baby. Think on it. New Master get his say over us 'cause he white, but he only live 'cause of one of our own." Ole Joe clapped his hands and rocked back and forth laughing. Charlton and Martha soon joined in with him. With a few words, Ole Joe knocked the master off his fake pedestal and made him an equal to Charlton's people. Charlton felt a surge of power as he laughed at the master.

After dinner, Ole Joe lay on his stomach with his elbows digging into the soft ground as he propped up his head with his hands and gazed at Charlton. "What on your mind, son?"

"I wanted to know if the master loves the mistress."

"Boy, you sure do know how to ask 'em!" Ole Joe let out a guffaw, which caught the attention of a few heads. Charlton settled in for a good story.

"The white man, he a strange creature. Our people, we choose our other half by the one that light our heart on fire. The white man? Well, he choose a wife by the one that make others jealous."

"What's jealous?" Charlton asked.

"That mean, you have something and someone else, he want it too. New Master didn't pick New Mistress 'cause he love her. New Mistress, she the most beautiful white woman of all. She turned the heads of all the white men and they all want her. She didn't give them no mind though. She keep to herself, always looking down her nose at all them. You see, she what they call standoffish."

"What's standoffish?" Charlton asked.

"She not want to be with any of those men. She like to just let them stare. She decide to just do what she do. Her mama, though, she not too keen on letting New Mistress flitter her life away and spin herself into an ole maid. So, New Mistress forced to make a choice when she got old. New Mistress's mama held a ball for her and all the white men who want her come down to the house and beg her to marry them.

"Everybody in town know Old Master not long for the world and so New Master going to come into the land when his daddy die. He been following New Mistress around watching her, but never talking. He say, so all in the house could hear, that when he go to that party, he tell her what no other could. She marry him and he just leave her alone. All those other boys, they tell her she get shiny things and they dote on her. He tell her he won't care nothing about her and what she do? She choose him. Those two don't love each other. They don't like each other. They don't even hate each other. They just don't care none at all. You ask me, I rather be married to someone I hates than to marry someone I don't give a care 'bout. You ask me, the only one New Master ever cared 'bout his daughter."

"How do you know all this?" Charlton asked. Both he and Martha stared at Ole Joe anxious to hear the answer.

Ole Joe returned Martha's stare, then shifted his gaze to Charlton. Back and forth he continued like this, as if debating whether he should tell them. At last, he said, "'Cause the cook was my wife and she heard the whole thing. Look, I got to go sleep now. I'm real tired. Good night."

Ole Joe seemed to age ten years as he got up with a groan and shuffled over to his quarters. Martha squeaked out a good bye and looked at Charlton wide eyed. They never talked about Ole Joe's past. He only told stories about others. They didn't know what to say, even to each other.

Charlton wanted to pursue him, but reconsidered. Even at his age, Charlton knew that he had provoked a painful memory in Ole Joe and he needed privacy. He decided to leave him alone for now, and apologize in the fields in the morning.

Chapter Three

Charlton woke to the dawning sun streaming through the tiny cracks in the wall and heard the cowbell used to wake the slumbering slaves. He slipped on the overalls that doubled as a blanket for his feet, and climbed down the ladder from his cot. Lack of sleep from worrying over making Ole Joe upset made Charlton slow and sluggish. His mother talked to him afterward about how remembering lost loved ones brought back as many painful memories as good ones. This did nothing to ease Charlton's guilt.

He looked around for Ole Joe in the breakfast line, but couldn't find him. Ole Joe sometimes ate breakfast on the way out to the field, anyway.

Charlton gobbled down his breakfast and headed to the well before the overseer prodded the lingerers. He made three trips to the field before he saw Ole Joe in a corner of the cornfields. He decided that Ole Joe's isolation made it the perfect time to offer his apology.

Since he carried heavy water, Charlton looked for the quickest way to Ole Joe. Although the path around the field could reach Ole Joe, Charlton wanted a faster one, so he chose to walk through the corn, though it would make seeing difficult with crops taller than his eyes. He stood on the hill scanning the cornfield to figure out the best path to reach Ole Joe.

As he made his way, Charlton staggered around to get the two buckets through the rows of corn without knocking them over. He didn't succeed in keeping all the stalks upright despite his care and brushing up against them made hearing anything else, difficult. The sight of the cross-path that allowed horses and riders through the field sent a rush of relief through him and he quickened his pace, unaware of the sound of a horse galloping toward him.

He saw Ole Joe through the stalks just beyond the path. Ole Joe saw him too and raised his hand. Charlton took it for a greeting and jogged into the middle of the path. He looked up in time to see a black spotted horse coming toward him and the overseer looking down at the floor of the cart he sat in. He froze. Then he felt a sudden force against his chest and stomach. Charlton fell into the corn.

Charlton gasped for breath. His chest and throat burned and a spot on his arm seared with pain where a stone and a stalk of corn broke skin. After a while, he heard the voice of the overseer.

"Damn it! Damn it! Damn it!" the overseer said.

As the air filled Charlton's lungs, he scampered deeper into the cover of the corn to avoid detection. It occurred to him that Ole Joe hadn't come over to check on him. The sound of Charlton getting knocked over by a horse should have brought Ole Joe running.

"You blasted, Negro, get up!" the overseer said. Charlton shot up to his feet, but realized the overseer didn't mean him, and he sank back to the ground.

Ole Joe lay five feet down the path from where Charlton crouched looking like a crumpled heap of clothes and skin with one foot twisted in the wrong direction. The overseer stood over him and delivered a swift kick to Ole Joe's side. Ole Joe did not respond. Charlton wanted to run to him, but fear kept him from moving. The overseer didn't seem to notice Charlton, so he remained still and watched in horror as the overseer approached Ole Joe, not shouting any more but twisting his head with his lips jutting out. The overseer pushed his scarred boot under Ole Joe's shoulder and turned him over. Instant revulsion and disgust appeared on his face. The overseer turned and gagged. Charlton thought the overseer might vomit. What did Ole Joe look like? Did he die? How could a man lay so quiet with his foot twisted in the wrong direction?

When the overseer composed himself, he rushed back to his cart, which had remained attached to the horse. He snapped the reins and rode out of sight. Charlton stood still for a moment longer.

Charlton felt every stone and twig under his boots as his feet pulled him closer to his friend. He cried when he saw the reason for Ole Joe's twisted foot. His leg lay squashed, his trousers sunken around the spot, soaked in blood.

Charlton's eyes darted all over Ole Joe. Both of his arms had snapped. On the left arm, Charlton saw bone for the first time as one poked out of the skin below the elbow. He stared, unable to look away. The bone looked so skinny and fragile. He wondered if all bones looked this skinny. Ole Joe's upper right arm lay broken and bent.

As he moved closer, Charlton lost all hope that Ole Joe would awaken. The back of Ole Joe's skull had sunken into his head. A horrifying mixture of white and red liquid made a dirty pink puddle on the ground next to Ole Joe's head. Charlton no longer wondered what filled a person's head. He promised himself he would never think of it again.

Charlton got a salty taste in his mouth. He gagged, frightened that some of the pink liquid had gotten into his mouth. It took a while to realize he tasted his tears.

He forced himself to stare at Ole Joe so that he could stomach the sight of the broken man when he approached him to say goodbye. Charlton got closer and knelt to the side where Ole Joe looked almost normal. "Joe, you, you died for me didn't you? You... you... pushed me out of the way and I lived and you died and I... I... I..." He sobbed and struggled for breath, gasping when the sobs ended.

He turned to his friend and began again, "You was like my papa and now you gone and all I have is Mama and Belle." Charlton wheezed and the tears burned two salty streaks down his cheeks.

"I should be down there. Why'd you save me? You should've let me die instead."

The tension in Charlton's neck pulled against him, but he lowered his head down to Ole Joe's still intact chest and buried his eyes in the surprising softness of Ole Joe's overalls and whispered "thank you" over and over.

He arose with a start when he heard the beat of distant horse hooves. He stood, whispered "good bye" to Ole Joe, grabbed the buckets, and took off into the rows of corn.

With the buckets empty, he traveled lighter and reached the spot on the hill where he could look down upon the place where Ole Joe's body lay and duck behind a tree if the overseer looked his way.

The overseer stood over Ole Joe with a shovel in his hand. Once he had dug the grave, he went to Ole Joe and searched his body in a cautious, hesitant manner. His hand found something as his head jerked upright. He pulled out the flask Ole Joe had stolen years ago. He sprang from the ground and dashed over to his horse, putting the flask in a saddlebag.

Charlton knew the workers in the fields already missed him, but he wanted to see Ole Joe get buried. After what seemed an eternity, the overseer finished digging a shallow grave and went back to Ole Joe when something seemed to catch his eye. The overseer walked to the place where Ole Joe had pushed Charlton and knelt on to the ground.

Charlton followed his gaze and his eyes widened at the glare coming off the puddle of water that spilled when Charlton fell. The overseer moved further toward the corn.

Charlton hid behind the tree, his heart pounding faster and faster. He felt overcome by fear. He had gotten lucky that the oblivious overseer hadn't seen him at the time of the accident. Had the overseer figured it out? Would he discover that Ole Joe had gotten trampled in the process of saving the water boy? How else did so much water find its way down there?

Charlton's thoughts turned to what might happen next. The worst that could happen to the overseer would be getting dismissed and thrown off the plantation for killing a hardworking slave. He'd find another job, though. Charlton would get much worse. He doubted Belle could save him. If anything, the master would have an excuse to keep her away from him. After causing such a terrible accident, Charlton could lose Belle, but that would be the best that would happen to him. Charlton faced a certain beating too or worse, getting sold to Mr. Beauregard, a nearby slave master who everyone knew mistreated his slaves.

He watched as the overseer removed his filthy hat and started scratching his head. He stared for a long while with his mouth gaping open. Charlton let out a sigh of relief as the overseer shook his head, pushed his hat back on his balding head, and returned to the body.

The overseer snatched Ole Joe's unbroken leg and yanked on it to drag the body. As the overseer got up to a steady pace, Ole Joe's broken arms flapped around him. One hand flipped over and settled with the palm down. The fingers dragged in the dirt as if trying to stop the rest of the body from getting dumped in a hole.

When Ole Joe rested in the hole, Charlton turned away, picked up his buckets, and headed back to the well to refill them. He couldn't watch anymore and worried that someone would stumble upon him. He could still get in trouble for Ole Joe's death and knew he could not risk it. Besides, he knew he had to get back to the fields with water. He would get punished for sure if he didn't, and Charlton had taken all the punishment he could for one day.

The slaves in the field glared at him when he brought them water, but he ignored their protests.

Numbness overtook Charlton the rest of the day. His legs and arms did the work without thinking. Whenever the memories approached, he allowed the tears to course down his cheeks and then wiped them away, willing himself back into numbness.

After what seemed like an eternity, the sun set. Charlton trudged back to the well and dropped his buckets on the ground next to it. He had no idea what he would tell his mother. The uncertainty tied a knot in the pit of Charlton's stomach.

With dinner already cooked, Martha sat waiting for Charlton when he arrived back at camp. He held back from waving to her on his way to her spot, then slumped on the ground next to her. "Child, what's the matter?" she asked.

Charlton stared at her. His eyes welled up as he remembered the puddle next to Ole Joe's head. He couldn't speak. He didn't even bother trying. Martha's eyes widened as she looked around for Ole Joe as if he could help her through the situation.

Charlton took his time, then signaled for his mother to follow him. He wanted so much to tell her what happened so she could comfort him, but he knew he couldn't talk about it so close to other listening ears. He imagined what Ole Joe would say if he could, "Don't be no dang fool. You keeps it to yourself. You want New Master to find out and beat you?"

He saw the terror in her face as he beckoned her away from the camp. When they got far enough away, Martha said, "Child, you got to stop scaring your poor mama. What upset you?"

Charlton gulped. His throat felt raw and painful. He said, "Mama, I'm sorry. It's Ole Joe, he…" Charlton stopped and took in two deep breaths, letting the pain slip past him.

"He what? He what, Child?"

Charlton stared hard, trying to focus and said, "He's dead, Mama." Then, his heart raced and he told the story faster than he had ever talked. Martha listened. She didn't gasp or cry, but Charlton knew her heart sank at the news.

After Charlton finished explaining the gruesome burial, Martha asked, "Did he see you, Charlton?"

Charlton stared back at her. "Of course, he saw me, Mama! He saved my life!"

"Child, not Ole Joe, I'm asking 'bout Mr. Bentley. Did he see you?"

"No, Mama, he didn't."

"Then, you're safe. Charlton, I'll miss Ole Joe. He like a father to both us, but you so smart to call me away like that. No one. No one should ever hear of this."

Charlton peered at his mother. Tears streaked her face, yet even in the grip of sadness, she thought of Charlton's safety first. Charlton felt his love for his mother grow even greater.

They ate, and every now and then looked around as if wondering what happened to their friend. Ole Joe's name came out of the chatter around the fire over and over again. No one knew where he had gone or if age had gotten the better of him and his body lay in a field somewhere dead and stiff.

***

Charlton thought he would spend a restless night, turning and tossing, but the events of the day proved too much for his young body and mind to bear. As soon as his head rested on the bundle of hay, he drifted into sleep and awoke when the cowbell rang the next morning. When he got outside, he saw the master himself. White hired hands directed the men, women, and children over to where he stood on an old tree stump.

Charlton only glimpsed the master a couple of times, so he took this opportunity to examine the master. The master needed the stump; he stood shorter than some of the hired hands even with the lift. He wore a tidy beard and mustache under a bulbous nose and two beady brown eyes. His dull brown hair sat matted and parted on the left side. The impression of a rounded belly forced itself through the dark blue of his buttoned vest, over ordinary blue pants and shiny black boots. His expression showed a quiet contemptuousness and impatience. He displayed his evident displeasure at wasting his time waiting for his slaves to organize themselves around him.

Charlton's heart beat faster as he considered his own fate. Despite his best efforts, maybe the story did get to the master and he would name Charlton in front of everyone. Charlton glanced at his mother whose wide eyes shifted her gaze all over the scene.

When the white hired hands had finished their count, the master spoke like a Southern gentleman. "Yesterday, Mr. Bentley reported that one of the oldest among your people was caught stealing from me. The culprit was Joe, whom my father owned before me. We knew him to be a scoundrel, but he was a hard worker and we were fooled into thinking that he was one of our best. Mr. Bentley caught him with this."

The master held up the old flask. Charlton's eyes twisted into an angry squint as his gaze shifted between the master and the overseer who stood nearby. "This belonged to my dear departed father and that scoundrel made off with it without any remorse. Mr. Bentley approached Joe and tried to talk sense into him to return our beloved possession and instead Joe tried to escape. Mr. Bentley chased him down and delivered justice and for that we owe him our gratitude."

Charlton's stomach twisted in rage. How could these men wrap themselves in such a disgusting lie just to avoid the disgrace of a white man? Despite his love for Belle, at that moment he despised her father.

The master puffed up his chest, looked down at the people gathered around him, and slashed his index finger through the air as he spoke. "This was not just a crime made by one of you, but by all of you. If the oldest among you thinks that he can steal when he pleases, then you all must think that. I will not tolerate stealing. If anyone among you, *an-y-one* steals from me or my family again you can expect swift punishment, like Joe received. I will have respect on my plantation!" With that, the master jumped off the stump, and strode back toward a horse and carriage.

Chapter Four

April 1848

Charlton leaned against a giant oak tree and looked over the dozens of slaves in the field. His water buckets lay at his feet. He still carried them, even at fourteen years old, due to a lack of a boy old enough to take over the job on the plantation. Yet he had more responsibilities, such as collecting firewood.

A couple of the hired hands lay sprawled out to the side of the tobacco crops. The sound of the hired hands' light-hearted voices carried up the hill to where Charlton stood. He reflected on how their skin tone allowed them to lounge while the others worked, but dropped the thought. The hired hands taking a break meant they would not harass his people.

He pushed himself away from the tree to head down the hill and deliver the water, when the wind drove Belle's excited voice into his ears. He smiled as he ambled toward her voice.

The sight of a girl developing into a beautiful young woman met his eyes. Charlton noticed how grown up she looked. She bounded toward him repeating his name as her blond curls trailed her.

They stopped just short of each other, Belle making up more of the ground than Charlton did. "Hi Belle," Charlton said with a grin that grew larger.

"Hi Charlton. I have wonderful news! Here, come with me." She reached out and grabbed his hand. Charlton peeked over to make sure the hired hands couldn't see him, knowing that one report of this behavior to the master would send him into a fit. He exhaled when he couldn't see them. She pulled Charlton into a run down the other side of the hill and away from the fields. Her school satchel swung by her side in an excited manner. Charlton reveled in her pull on his arm.

When they reached the first trees in the woods, Belle sat down on a large rock. Charlton took a seat in some dried leaves.

Belle stared into Charlton's eyes for a long moment demanding that he ask about her news before she revealed anything. Charlton laughed, then asked, "Well, what is it?"

Belle let out a squeal of delight and said, "Charlton, everything is going to be fine." Charlton's face took on a puzzled expression.

"Oh, Charlton, it's so unfair that you were born into slavery. You're my best friend. I get so sad thinking about how you get treated so poorly by Father's hired hands and, and, well, I just couldn't bear the thought that you would be in this situation forever."

Charlton hung his head and pushed a pebble around with the toe of his boot. Belle had broken an unspoken promise between them that they would never talk about his condition. His heart beat quicker, as it welled up with a mix of love for Belle and a little disappointment. He stared into her eyes as Belle paused. She gazed down at him with an unmistakable glint.

"Charlton, I have reason to believe it will not last forever. Why, you'll be as free as I am!"

"How can that be?" he asked.

"Because, well, because of this." Belle rummaged in her satchel and produced a book. The title read, "History of the United States of America."

"My tutor taught me all about it today. She said that all young ladies must know the history of our country for intellectual discourse in polite company, but listen, America's greatest patriot was Thomas Jefferson."

"What's a patriot?"

"A patriot, dear Charlton, is a man who truly loves his country and would do anything for it."

"What did Thomas Jefferson do for his country?"

"The best that he could do, he wrote The Declaration of Independence."

"He wrote a book?"

"No, it was just a few pages, but you see it got the people in the country together and they decided that they did not want to be ruled by England anymore. You see, England is some other country way over the sea and they owned America and were very mean to us. Then, when Mr. Jefferson wrote those words, people realized that they didn't want to listen to England anymore and they would have their own country. Teacher called that our founding and when that happened we were free."

"But, Belle, what does that mean for me?"

"Well, you know the words he wrote were really important and they said what the country is supposed to be like and that is what I am talking about.

"I'm not saying this right. Oh, Charlton, you look so confused. I'm sorry. Here, read this." She reached over and handed him the book, which had the corner of a page turned down where she opened it. She pointed to a part of the page.

Charlton read the words next to her finger, "We hold these truths to be self, uh to be self. Belle, I can't read that word." Belle squatted next to him, reading over his shoulder.

"Self-evident. That means that everyone knows it."

"Thank you. Self-evident that all men are created equal. How can that be?"

"Those are just what the words say. Charlton, you're just a boy, but when you're a man, and you will be a man someday, you won't have to work here if you do not want to. You could leave because, if all men are created equal than you will be equal to anyone else. Don't you see? That's the law because Thomas Jefferson wrote it."

"What about the men who work here? Why don't they leave?"

"I thought about that and I think they all decided to be here. Where would they go if they left? But, Charlton, you're so smart, you can leave and you'd do so well. I just know you would."

"You want me to leave?"

"Oh, Charlton, not really, but if that would be best for you, then yes, I would miss you, but I would want you to leave. I hate Father's hired hands. They're so mean and stupid. It'd hurt my heart to see them treat you more cruelly like they treat the other men."

Charlton yearned to believe her, but something about the words didn't sound right to him. Jefferson said nothing about women, but the hired hands and, worst of all, the overseers treated the women with equal cruelty. He heard only a few gripes among the men, but with Paul around they didn't feel free to speak about their misery. Charlton couldn't believe that any of them would stay if they could leave.

Belle maintained her position crouched close to Charlton, so close he felt her breath on his neck. He wanted so much to turn into her, but didn't dare. The two friends remained in place for a few moments, then Belle moved back into position on the rock and asked, "Charlton, you don't believe me do you?"

Charlton collected himself before answering. "I want to believe you, but it just doesn't make sense. Why would any one of the men stay here if they didn't have to?"

"Maybe they don't know it."

"Then your father isn't telling them. Why would he do that?"

Belle stuck her lower lip out, grimaced, and let out a puff of air. A wave of self-loathing overcame Charlton. His only friend in the world showed nothing but support and caring for him and he could only muster doubt at her hopes for him. He knew she thought no ill of her father and yet now he tried to force her to think of the master as a liar or that she had misplaced hope.

"He must not know!" Belle said. "And I'm going to tell him!"

Charlton's whole body tensed with her words, forcing him to stand. "Belle, don't do it!" he said. He spoke with such force that Belle flinched.

"Well, why not? Doesn't he deserve to know?"

Charlton took a moment to calm himself before speaking. "Well, yes, he does, but um." He didn't know what to tell her that wouldn't hurt her feelings. If he told Belle that she got Jefferson wrong, then Charlton would have to dash her hopes for his freedom. If he said anything against her father, she would get angry with Charlton. Either way, his freedom and the master's desires stood opposed to one another. Belle would never accept that truth as long as she loved both her father and his slave.

"See? That settles it!" Belle said as she made a move to bound back home.

Charlton stopped her. "Belle, don't!"

With her back still turned to him, Belle threw her arms down and stamped her feet. "Why not?" she asked with her teeth clenched.

"Because, because if you do, then something bad is going to happen. I don't know what, but he isn't going to like to hear that. What if he gets mad and says that I put you up to it?"

Belle turned around and Charlton saw her tears. Charlton hated causing her pain. The tears never dropped. Instead, Belle's face took on an understanding that broke Charlton's heart even more.

"I know, Charlton. I know you don't trust my father. I know why, but I don't think he knows how mean the hired hands are to your people. He's a good man and he'll listen to me. Will you have me not fight for you? I love you. You're my best friend."

Charlton wondered how he, of all his people, achieved this love from Belle. He could do nothing but try to hold the tears back and nodded his assent.

Belle's face lifted at his approval. She came back, threw her arms around him, and kissed him on the cheek. Then, she bounded down the hill and toward her house while Charlton stood helpless.

Chapter Five

Charlton's eyes opened as he lay in his cot unable to sleep. Since Belle came to him late that day after school to tell him about Jefferson, he did not get to have the relief of knowing what happened when she confronted her father. He couldn't stand the wait any longer and he shut his eyes tight, trying to force sleep on himself. He whispered to himself some encouragement, but none of it slowed his beating heart. After countless moments of thoughts bouncing around in his head, exhaustion wore him down and sleep offered itself.

***

Clouds in the afternoon sky blotted out the sun and kept a chill over the plantation. As Charlton yanked up his second bucket, a shrill voice came from behind him. "Oh, I am so mad!"

Charlton's frayed nerves tensed his back and made him lose his grip on the rope. The bucket made a clunking sound as it bounced off the wall of the well, then made an enormous splash. Belle startled Charlton often, but this time she did not bother apologizing. Charlton's nerves sparked a little more in anticipation of her news.

He turned around and looked at Belle. He peered at her, trying to get a sense of what had happened. Relief came when he realized that her father had not forbidden her to see him.

"Well...?" Belle asked with an exaggerated frown.

"Well, what?"

"Aren't you going to ask me what made me mad?"

"I guess your father didn't agree with you?"

"Yes," Belle said and she spun away from Charlton and plopped on the grass, folding her head in her arms.

Charlton sat down next to her and asked, "Do you want to talk about it?"

Belle raised her head and looked at Charlton with tears forming in the corner of her eyes. Charlton stared off down the path to the fields to avoid seeing them.

"Well, Mama, she called me for dinner and, Daddy, he was at the table. We said grace and all I could think was that I really needed to tell Daddy about what I learned in school. Charlton, I thought I was going to burst at the seams! It took him forever to ask me what I learned in school and he always does that. So, I started talking really fast about all I'd learned. He acted like he didn't understand me. How could he not? Everyone knows about the law. So, I had to explain it again, but I slowed down. Then, I finally got him to understand, but then, he told me that I was mistaken. He said that was only for our people."

"Aren't we all people?" Charlton asked.

"Well, that's what I asked him. You should have heard the mean remarks he made about your people. He told me 'they're not smart' and 'they're not God's chosen people' and…"

"What's that mean?" Charlton learned about God from some of the stories he read, but he never thought that God would only choose to give freedom to people with lighter skin color. Whatever led to slavery, God couldn't have done it because the stories spoke of his love for all.

"Well, I didn't know what that meant either, and I asked him and he wouldn't answer me. He told me that I was not respecting my elders and that if I knew what was good for me, I would stop talking about this at once. I've never seen Daddy acting like this. I was so scared." Her lips trembled, then she embraced Charlton and cried into his shirt. He stroked her hair, while hatred for her father pressed on him.

She disengaged and Charlton felt Belle's piercing blue eyes staring up at him. She needed reassurance and he didn't know how to give it. "It could've been worse."

"What do you mean 'worse'? Worse than that?"

"Did he say anything about me?"

"No."

"What if he thought that I caused all this trouble? Wouldn't he have told you that we couldn't be friends anymore?"

"He wouldn't do that, Charlton. He knows that would make me so sad. You don't know what he's like. He shouldn't have said what he did last night, but he loves me more than that."

"You don't know what he would do." Charlton wanted to make her understand; to tell her all the stories Ole Joe told him. He yearned to tell her that her father had lied about Ole Joe's death just so he could threaten his slaves. He thought that she should know about how he made everyone believe he murdered a baby, but still ended up selling the baby away from a new mother. Charlton knew that he had escaped having Belle taken from him and wanted to make sure she didn't tempt fate again.

As Belle stood silent, Charlton couldn't figure out if her mind began to permit her to see her father's bad side or if it still blocked her way. Charlton decided to speak again rather than let her lose faith in her father. "Belle, I love that you want me to be free, but I just can't stand to see you get so sad. Why don't you just forget about it?"

Belle shed more tears. "I can't."

"Why?"

"Because I want you to escape, Charlton. I want you to get out of here and then I can get out of here and then we can be friends forever. We can live up North where people like you aren't slaves, but are all free."

Belle's words cast a spell on Charlton. He would do anything to go with her to the North. They both sat in silent contemplation.

Belle spoke first. "You know, Charlton. Maybe Daddy doesn't know what the law says."

"You already tried that. Why do you think it will be any different the second time?"

"I never told Daddy the exact wording. Don't you remember it said, '*all* men are created equal' not some and not certain men. So..."

"Please don't tell him again. He told you not to talk about it."

"That's true," she said. "Well, why don't you tell him?"

Charlton laughed. He could expect no less than a beating for trying to talk to the master uninvited. No way would he get out more than a sentence or two before he got dragged away. Belle looked at him with offense at his laughter.

"I'm sorry," he said, "but I could never tell your father that. He wouldn't hear of it."

Belle agreed. After several moments, she said, "So, you don't talk to him. You write it."

"What?"

"You *write* it! You get a stick and you write it in the dirt, right in front of the house. Daddy won't miss it and then he'll know."

"But, Belle, I'm not supposed to know how to write."

"But, you do know how to write Charlton, you do."

"Well, if anyone sees me write it, I'll be in big trouble and so will you."

"Then, make sure no one sees you. Go in the middle of the night."

"How will I see?"

"By moonlight."

"I don't know. Someone might see me."

"Charlton, this is our chance. Don't you understand? If you do this we can be together. Mama and Daddy are already talking about how I need to have a coming out party. Do you know what that is?"

"No." Charlton held his breath while every muscle in his body tightened.

"It's when they dress me up all pretty and I have to meet all the young men in the county. Do you understand, Charlton? Soon, they're going to make me get married and then I won't be able to see you anymore. I know that already. You have to do something!" Charlton tried to swallow down the lump in his throat.

"Please help me, Charlton. I know you're younger than I am, but if I could just know that you were free, then I could put off getting married. I could be mean to all the men at the party and I could refuse to marry them and then, when you get to be a man, you can leave here with me and…"

Charlton straightened. Would Belle give him what he wanted more than anything else? He stumbled over his words, then asked, "And what?"

Belle took a deep breath, looked around her, and said in a hushed tone, "and we could get married."

Charlton's heart soared and the two friends embraced. To fulfill his most ardent wish, he would do anything she asked.

"So, you'll do it?" Belle asked with her chin resting on his shoulder.

"Yes."

Belle disengaged from the hug and gave Charlton a peck on the cheek. "I'm so happy, Charlton! Let's make a plan. I'll give you my schoolbook and it'll tell you exactly what to write. You get away from the cabin when the moon is bright and get a stick and write the words, 'We hold these truths to be self-evident that all men are created equal.' I memorized it and then you go back to the cabin. When you wake up Father will have read it and then he'll know that he has no right to keep you here after you've become a man and then, well, you know the rest."

"Yes, Belle. I will."

"Good, then it's settled," Belle said and righted herself with a flourish, then slumped her shoulders. "No, it's not settled. Charlton, if anyone finds out you wrote the words, you tell them I made you do it."

"But, I want to do it."

"Charlton, you and I both know that you're doing this because of me. If they suspect a thing, I don't want them to hurt you. You tell everyone that asks you that I told you to make the marks on the ground. The law says that you'll be free when you become a man, but it also says that you're not supposed to be able to read. Do you understand?"

"Yes."

"Then tell me what do you say when someone asks if you can read and write?"

"I don't know how to read. You told me to write the words."

"No, Charlton. You don't know about words. You don't know about letters. You only know about marks. You tell them that I told you to make the marks."

"But, Belle, you'll get in trouble."

"Yes, but they won't hurt me. They'll hurt you, Charlton. I don't want them to hurt you. What do you say if someone asks if you can read and write?"

"I tell them that I don't know how to read or write. You told me to make the marks."

"Good!" Belle said and gave him another peck on the cheek. "We won't regret this, Charlton. This will work. You'll see." With that, she bounded off and skipped home.

Charlton got back to the rope and started pulling to drag the bucket back up again. He slowed when rain poured down. The rain would help the field hands from needing his services, which gave him the time to think.

He had no doubt that Belle misinterpreted the law, but it didn't matter. His best friend wanted to marry him and now he would do whatever she wanted. Charlton had to write the words, so he could show Belle that he would take a big risk for her. If she saw him do that, then maybe she would wait for him to escape. He knew he could suffer the same fate as Tom from Ole Joe's story, but he needed to try. If he died trying to escape, then he would have died for a noble quest, like in the fairy tales he read. Dying for love meant doing his best to make Ole Joe's sacrifice worth the price.

Charlton performed his job with renewed vigor. Even though the men and women in the fields had little need for the water, Charlton kept up a steady pace around the fields. He brought water even as they ignored him when he offered it.

***

The sun shone bright the next day. The sky took the deepest blue that Charlton had ever seen. His heart pounded when he saw the sky. If it lasted long enough to welcome the moonlight and Belle delivered the book, he would write the words that would prove his love for Belle that night.

Belle came to see him in the afternoon, after school. She found him coming down the hill near the woods and beckoned to him.

As he approached, she ducked into the woods to give them some privacy. Charlton found her sitting on the rock. "I have it," she said. "But, you need to turn around while I get it out."

Charlton followed her request and heard her wrestling with her school clothes.

"You can turn around now," she said.

Charlton spun around and saw her offering a blue, cloth-bound book to him. He took it with a shaking hand. Belle placed her hands on his outstretched hand and said, "Oh, Charlton, you're trembling. Don't worry, it'll be fine. You'll see."

"I know, Belle, I'm just excited." Fear and agitation kept his hand quaking.

"Well, you need to calm yourself. This will work. Now let me show you." She turned until they stood side by side and she asked him to hold the book out for her. She then flipped to the page, which had a down-turned corner and pointed to the spots where she had made vertical lines to indicate what Charlton should write. He pretended not to notice that her hand shook, too.

The passage stood beneath block letters under the title "Declaration of Independence." It read, "We hold these truths to be self-evident that all men are created equal".

"Daddy will read the words and he will know that the law says all men are the same."

"Don't you need this book?"

Belle looked all around herself. In a low whisper, she said "I said I lost it."

Charlton's jaw dropped in surprise. Did his friend lie?

"Oh, don't look like that," Belle said, as she gave him a playful swat on the arm. "My tutor had an extra one. You keep the book, Charlton. Just don't let anyone know you have it."

Before Charlton could voice any more concerns, Belle pecked him on the cheek and said, "I have to go now, but you remember what I said. If anyone asks you, I told you to make the marks. Do you understand?"

"Yes, Belle."

She gave him a glowing smile and jogged back to the house. He tucked the book into his waistband and let his shirt fall over it. Charlton headed back to his cabin and put the book in his usual hiding place. He had constructed his secret place with sticks, rocks, and discarded old clothes to make sure that rain and other weather couldn't get to his stuff.

The rest of the day sped by. He couldn't shake the thoughts of impending doom, yet he would still write the words.

The lumps in Charlton's throat kept him from eating much dinner. He tried to listen to his mother as she spoke a bit too fast. In no time, night had fallen. Charlton climbed into his cot, this time trying not to sleep.

Chapter Six

As Charlton lay in his bunk, time began to slow down. He didn't have to try to stay awake as his heart pounded, his stomach churned, and the lumps in his throat pained him. The breathing and noises around him penetrated his mind as he tried to distinguish the noises in the cabin from the chirps and peeps of the frogs and insects outside. His attention shifted from one man to the next.

Charlton paid the most attention to Paul. He couldn't tell if he slept or not. He needed to know this above all else before he left.

Charlton's fears crept into his head. Would he find the book in the darkness? What if he couldn't find it? What if the moonlight didn't shine bright enough for him to find the book, much less the trackway, the path that led from the road to the Big House? What if he stepped on a twig and everyone came running?

His mind turned to the words. Maybe he could remember the words and then he could leave the book in its hiding place. He thought about them while listening to everyone's breathing. The words involved truths, but what about them? He remembered struggling with the word "self-evident" and he had stared at it so long before that he could even remember how to spell it. *Was it "We think these truths are self-evident"? No.* Charlton's mind drifted back to the image he made in his mind. In it, old white people cradled the word "truths" in their arms. *That's right! They held them.* "We hold these truths to be self-evident."

Charlton remembered that he needed to write down one of the truths after the word "that." *What's the word that means, 'the same'?* Charlton made an unintentional snort when he thought of the word, "equal". His eyes grew wide at the mistake. Did he ruin his chances? He cycled through listening to each man's breath. Nothing had changed.

He continued trying to remember the words. His inner voice rehearsed the first phrase and then "equal" until he pieced together the rest. "We hold these truths to be self-evident that all men are created equal." His body lost some of its tension when he grew convinced of the sentence. He didn't need the book; it could remain hidden.

At long last, Charlton grew convinced that everyone, including

Paul, slept. He pulled off his coverings and sat up, then twisted his body around to avoid every creaky spot in his cot's boards. His body positioned at the end of the bed, Charlton let one leg drop to the ladder rung, then the next. He did this for each rung in succession, then placed his feet on the floor. Not one sound gave him away.

Charlton crept along the floor toward the door, nudged it open, and stepped outside. He took each of the two stairs down and landed on the ground. His hand stretched behind him to let the door tap closed.

After a few steps, Charlton paused to look around him. The world shone bright with mere moonlight. Shadows took out part of his view from time to time, but if he stuck to the middle of the path that led to the big house, he thought he might make it without stepping on a single twig. He moved across the ground letting each foot take the balance of his weight only when he ensured nothing below it would give him away. Each of his joints remained loose and flexible, ready to stop any noisy impact. His eyes darted from side to side, so dark adapted from the scant light dripping into the cabin that even details of the ground and surroundings revealed themselves. He made his way over to the master's house and onto the dirt and pebble path the horses and carriages took.

When he spotted the house he moved at an even slower pace—at once trying to assess the state of its occupants while trying to keep any noise from alerting anyone. Nothing moved in the big house as far as he could tell. Charlton crouched to the ground and began carving the words in the ground with his finger. He soon felt the pain of dirt and gravel traveling under his fingernail and embedding the earth deep beneath it. Besides the pain, he thought about how the dirt wouldn't keep his secret if it got any deeper.

His eyes trained on a spot near a tree lit by moonlight where a stick of the perfect length lay. Charlton smiled in spite of his dangerous position. He crept over to the stick. The crunch of his boots against the trackway made a louder sound than the chirping of the animals around him. He came to a complete stop, took deep, soundless breaths and started out again with more careful steps.

Charlton snatched up the stick and brought it back to the trackway. He began writing again and had no trouble getting the first words etched. His hand remained steady, deliberate, and careful through the rest of the message.

With the last letter spelled, Charlton stood back and admired his handiwork. The letters looked perfect, as if he tore the words right out of the book. He began to walk back to the cabin with a light heart, but as he progressed, the sleep he denied himself pushed at his eyes and he ambled forward growing desperate to reach his cot. All the excitement of anticipating what he would do reversed when he had finished the deed. His body had almost reached its limit.

When he reached the cabin, he looked down to the see the stick still in his hand. Too tired to do anything else, he dropped the writing stick beside the cabin promising himself he would hide it in the morning. He opened the door and forgetting his regimen, he let the floor creak, pulled a little too hard on the ladder, and fell into bed. Sleep overtook him before he could even pull a cover over himself or wonder whether he woke up Paul.

***

The cowbell used to wake the slaves rang sharp in Charlton's head. The pounding in his head continued well after it stopped. He wanted nothing more than to stay in his cot and sleep the day away, but he had to get outside to avoid a certain beating. The writing stick, with dirt penetrating its sturdiest end, lay unnoticed to the side of the cabin as he made his way to breakfast.

As Charlton ate he noticed his right index finger still had the dirt encrusted on it from his first attempt to write the words. He ate with his other hand while pushing and pulling at the dirt with his thumbnail. By the time he walked away from breakfast and toward the well, he glanced at his hand and grinned, confident that no one would see the evidence.

Charlton's first trip to the fields brought the rush of talk and gossip amongst the hired hands. They talked about how the master had a fit about some words written in his trackway, calling it "some devil's trickery." The ripples reached Charlton's ears and he did what he could to tamp down his reaction, but he wondered how he could hide his feelings when his heart made a deafening banging sound in his chest, when his lungs pushed out raspy breaths, and when his stomach growled with uneasy churning. Belle had told him about the Devil once and he knew if the master brought up the Devil, Charlton could face a terrible punishment.

When he got back to the well, he began pacing back and forth, searching his mind for any clue that would reveal his identity. With a jolt, the stick came back into his mind. "I left it by the cabin!" he said aloud. He clamped his hands over his mouth and whipped his head around, looking for anyone who overheard him. After giving himself a moment to let the renewed pounding in his head pass, Charlton sighed with relief seeing no one around. He thought about retrieving the stick, but it lay in the opposite direction from the fields and if he got caught trying to get it, he would reveal himself for sure.

Charlton gained control of himself by focusing on his job. He made another trip back and forth to the fields and began to calm down. If anyone suspected him of the "devil's trickery" he would have been snatched up by now. He repeated his well-rehearsed task again. As he leaned against the well while pulling up the second bucket, two massive arms that crushed his arms against his sides forced the air out of his lungs. Charlton gasped, trying to suck in air again, but an unsatisfying amount came to him. He kicked and struggled as the arms lifted him up and clear away from the well. Charlton's eyes popped out from his head as he watched himself turn onto the path that led to the master's house.

Charlton identified the dark, muscular arms as Paul's. In desperation, Charlton delivered a backward kick to Paul's right knee. Paul groaned, then crushed Charlton further. More air rushed out of Charlton's lungs. He let his muscles relax. Paul did the same, allowing the air to come back to him. He struggled no more. One way or the other he would get where Paul wanted him to go.

The up-and-down motion of his ride made it hard to focus on where they headed and when he tried, it made the pounding in his head come back. He tried closing his eyes, but his nerves got the better of him and his eyelids shot open after a couple seconds. His eyes found the master sitting on a stump gazing up at him with a creepy half grin. Paul released him and Charlton hit the ground with a thud.

Chapter Seven

Charlton lay flat against the ground for a second and then propped himself on his hands and knees. His right side had taken a stiff blow from a rock. He groaned when he felt the stabbing ache of exerting his stomach muscles around the fresh sore.

Instinct and fear took control of his body. He ignored the pain as he got up on his feet and tried to take off back down the path where he had come. His mind and body knew only that he did not want to confront the master. Paul stepped in his way and without so much as a shove, Charlton bounced off Paul's crossed arms and toppled over flat again. This time the rock found his left calf and created an instant welt. With a sinking feeling in the pit of his stomach and aching on both sides of his body, Charlton gave up the fight and lay still. Tears flowed from his eyes and formed little pools against the ground.

Charlton thought the attempt to run would make the master furious. Instead, the master started laughing at him. When the laughter fell away, the master spoke. "As amusing as I find this, boy, I did not bring you here to put on a show. Now, get up and look at me."

Charlton did not get up, though. He felt defiant at his treatment and stayed still. The master spoke Paul's name and Paul lifted Charlton up by the shoulder with such speed and ease, Charlton felt like an empty water bucket swung by the handle. Paul tried setting him on his feet, but Charlton let his feet go lax. Instead Paul pushed him down into a sitting position a few feet from the master's boots. Charlton felt no choice but to succumb to Paul's incredible strength.

"Now look at me or Paul will make you look at me," the master said. This time Charlton did not dare disobey. Charlton looked at the master, noted a strong, pungent odor on his breath, and saw him holding the writing stick. The master made scribbling strokes in the ground. Charlton kept his eyes focused on the stick, while it moved back and forth.

"Why do you look at this stick? It looks like an ordinary stick to me, boy. Why so curious about it?" the master said.

He knew that the master had already figured him out and knew he could not lie about it or deny it. Then, he thought back to his promise to Belle that if someone figured out he had written the words, he had to blame her and make sure they did not realize he could write. He resigned himself to confession, but he would have to convince the master that he didn't have the smarts to write words.

"I don' know what you say, Master," Charlton said. The master's eyes got wide in apparent anger, the reaction Charlton expected from his attempt to run away.

The master heaved the stick to the ground in front of Charlton's face. "Look at that stick! Look at it!" Charlton did not hesitate. He plastered his gaze on the stick. "That's enough! Now, you best not lie to me, boy, or I'll crack that stick right off the curls on the top of your head. How do you know that stick?"

He did not hesitate. "I use it to make them marks in the ground, like Belle told me. I do what she tell me, Master. I a good boy and I do what I told."

The fury that compelled the master fell away from him as fast as it had come. He eased back down to sit on his stump. Charlton saw it in the master's eyes. He showed the disappointment of knowing that his daughter had told the truth when she confessed what she had made Charlton do. Now he had to face the reality of a disobedient child who defied him on what he had instructed her to leave alone.

The master hung his head down as he began to speak. "I made a mistake, boy. A grievous mistake I intend not to repeat. When a father looks into his child's face and sees sincerity and longing, his heart melts and he has no choice but to give her what she desires. Oh, I knew it was a mistake, even then, but I was left with no choice. My daughter wanted it and I provided. The alternative was far worse. If I had gone through with what I discussed… Oh, not killing, I'm no fool, but to sell the baby when she would think I had it killed. Why, I didn't have the heart for it. Belle has a good mind, she will make a treasured wife to some lucky gentleman. I would not have her think her father a cruel man."

The master continued and though he had addressed Charlton to start, Charlton could tell that he spoke only to himself. "The mistake grew, but I had no way to stop it. Once begun, the mistake ran its course until now. Those words in the ground! A more embarrassing spectacle I have not experienced! It was my fault that Belle was under a mistaken impression. If I had given her a pet, maybe a dog or a pig, she would have grown just as attached to it, but she would not have seen it as human."

He gestured at Charlton with a casual sweep of his hand. "Look at him. Two arms, two legs, hair on the top of his head. He looks like a person. How easy to mistake him for one of us! How could I not see it?! God is not with his people, he's with ours. The Devil! Yes, the Devil is with his people! And he spun a lie in Belle's head, the accursed beast! He made her think that this boy and all his people have what we have. Rights? Hah! Freedom? Hah! What would they do with them if they had them? Drink themselves to death! Rape our women! Steal and put terror in the hearts of our children!

"These creatures! They need what we can give them: structure, purpose, and a guiding hand. We show nothing but kindness to them. How would they eat or have roofs above their heads, but for us?

"Belle is but a child still. How can she understand what she wants? She is kind too. She does not want these creatures to kill themselves with their freedom."

The master slumped on the stump, his hands cradled his chin and he appeared to have switched to thinking instead of speaking. For a long while, he sat in silence, saying the occasional muffled "Hmm…"

Charlton stood shocked. He did not understand all of what the master said, but he comprehended most of it. The master had given Charlton to Belle when he was born. Maybe Charlton came out the same size as the tiny baby who Ole Joe had mentioned. The master could not let his slaves think that he did not have the stomach to kill this one and now Ole Joe's story stood verified from the master's own lips. He had sold the baby to a trader and pretended to kill it. Charlton's thoughts churned while the master grew agitated again, speaking out loud.

"Devils they are! Whisper words to the innocent and casts demons in their heads!" The master quieted again pulling at his hair in big clumps while hiding his face behind his arms.

A hard lump formed in Charlton's throat as he thought back to the master's spoken attack on the ability of his people to take care of themselves. He knew that Ole Joe could have taken care of himself. He would have farmed himself a nice crop on a little patch of land. What did the master know of hard work? He sat in his house, letting others grow his crops for him. What did the master know that made any difference to making a living? Ole Joe told Charlton that Old Master had given the master his land when he died. Could the master ever hope to produce the same crops that Ole Joe did if he didn't have his slaves?

Belle had only mentioned the Devil once and only then as the most evil creature in the world. Charlton thought of the Devil as a ghost and decided that the master had ghosts dancing around in his head. They had no substance in the real world, but he still saw them.

Charlton looked with pity on the master as he sat unable to stitch his thoughts together. In Charlton's tired, frightened, and pounding head, his imagination started running away with him trying to picture what the master saw in his mind's eye.

God and the devil and a typical white man and a typical black man danced in front of him. God's skin shone white under a long white beard. He wore white robes and cloaks and the white man looked like the master dressed in a suit of white. God and the white man joined hands and circled together in a loving embrace.

Charlton imagined that the master thought of the devil as a black man, looking a little too like Ole Joe, except stooped over with deeper wrinkles and barely visible, sunken eyes. The devil joined hands with the black man, a muscled and clumsy faced stooge. Instead of putting him into a loving embrace, the devil grasped the black man's hands and spun him around in a swirling whirlwind. The devil let go of the black man and the black man sailed up in the air and landed on a white fence. His back folded over the fence and he lay still with a lazy smile spread over his face.

Charlton's frightful imagery continued as Belle's ghost with her shiny yellow hair and innocent face entered the scene. She could make no sense of it. The Devil approached her and whispered in her ear. A demonic smile spread across her face and she turned her back on God and the white man, who still embraced one another. Belle's ghost began to approach the broken black man.

The master broke out of his stupor and stood erect ending Charlton's vision. "That's it! I will not tolerate this anymore!" He turned to Charlton with furious eyes once again.

"You!" the master said, as he bolted upright, charging at Charlton and sticking his index finger in his face. Charlton flinched, backpedaled, tripped over his feet, and was on the ground once more. The master continued to shout into his face. "You will not sully my daughter's morals anymore! You will stay away from her! If you so much as wave at her, I will turn around and sell you to Mr. Beauregard as fast as you please!"

"Master, please!" Charlton said with tears pouring out of his eyes.

Charlton had doubted that the master could get more furious, but he stood corrected. The master trembled with anger, opening and closing his mouth as if he couldn't force the words to issue. Even Paul sat immobilized and looking frightened. "You… You… dare… to… talk back to *me*!" The master paced back and forth, his breathing erratic. Charlton's eyes grew wide with fright as a new mumbling gibberish issued forth from the master's mouth and the shaking got worse. Charlton prepared for the master to beat him to death in his rage. Charlton caught a glimpse in his imagination of himself lying on the ground in the same condition of Ole Joe after he got trampled.

To Charlton's amazement, the master seemed to take hold of his senses once more. His pacing slowed, the mumbling receded, and his breath regained regularity. All three behaviors stopped at once and the master stood with his face tilted into the sun and his eyes closed.

His eyes opened little by little, and the master resumed his seat on the stump. "Get up, boy," he said with calm. Charlton eased himself into standing to reassure the master that he would cooperate and make no sudden movements. The master continued as Charlton stood at attention. "Those 'marks' you made, they mean something false, but I am a gentleman and I understand such things that you will never understand. You are what they call a pawn. That means someone who is used to follow the bidding of another. Women, from Eve, the first woman, to now, have tricked the minds of men. Unfortunately for you, my daughter has tricked you as well. You were made to do her bidding and I am afraid that you were led astray."

Despite whatever kindness the master thought he showed, Charlton knew that he would prefer a beating to this.

"Do you know what being equal is?" the master asked.

Charlton surely did, but had to continue his play act. "Uh-uh. No, Master."

"Equal means that you and your people are no different from my people. This is what those marks in the ground meant. It is a lie. Your people are most definitely different from mine. Just look at your skin." Charlton shot a glance at his skin, which he admired as a solid shade of dark brown.

"You see how it is the color of mud? God long ago marked your people as the color of mud and mine as the color of the morning light because he loves my people and not yours. Your people have been marked as lowly creatures, and mine as your masters.

"Now before you start to feel sorry for yourself, I assure you that God still has mercy for your kind. He has compelled my people to take care of yours. You have food to eat and a roof over your head because of God's mercy. You and your people should thank us.

"Now," the master said as he clapped his hands together, "I cannot let you continue to see my daughter. It is for your own good as well as hers. My people and your people are not meant to be friends with one another. I am sorry that I ever allowed it. It was a father's indulgence and it will not happen again. I will see to it that it does not happen again. I will tell my daughter the same as I have told you. If she talks to you, waves at you, or so much as nods at you, I will ship you to Mr. Beauregard. I will have no choice."

Charlton took a look of calm surrender on his face, but remained sure that Belle would not pay any heed to this nonsense. They had met without anyone seeing them. She had lent him books and no one had discovered his hiding place. They could get around this problem. Besides, they had to meet to make a plan to run away together and then get married.

Charlton nodded at the master and seeing that, the master said, "Good. Paul, take him out of my sight and give him fifteen lashes." Charlton froze with terror. The whip had connected with him a number of times, but fifteen in a row would rip his skin to shreds.

"Yes, Master," Paul said and approached Charlton in a lumbering, but gentle way. The master turned and took the path back to his house while Paul walked behind Charlton back down the path. Charlton resigned himself to his fate hoping Paul would have mercy on him without the master's watchful gaze.

***

Charlton's back seared with pain from the whipping. He couldn't even hate Paul for it because he knew the man had held back the full power of his massive arms. Each blow cut a thin line of flesh out of his back, but nothing that would not grow back. He trudged into camp that night unwilling to let anyone read his pain. He did not speak of it to his mother, nor did he try to find Paul with his eyes.

He thought of Belle as he ate his bacon and cornmeal. He had done for her what she required and suffered for it. No doubt crept into his mind that she would fulfill her end of the bargain. She would find him when no one could see her and they would hide out while they made their plans for escape. A smile graced his lips as he ate. Martha caught his expression and kissed him on the top of the head.

When he returned back to the men's cabin after supper, he noticed that the landscape around it looked a bit odd, as if someone had rearranged it. Charlton understood that the master had instructed Paul to find the source of the words that Charlton had written. His eyes darted to the true hiding place and he breathed easier to find that Paul had left it untouched.

Charlton decided he would let Belle know that she could have her book back whenever she wanted it. Still he hoped she wouldn't want it. He felt the need to study it and learn from it. He wanted to absorb what Jefferson wrote most of all.

On his side, trying to fall asleep, Charlton couldn't keep the pain in his back, sides, and head at bay enough to let him rest. He thought back to the master's words and knew that if God gave his people that color it meant only that, they took on the color of the earth, which made the crops grow. What else could it mean other than his people gave life through their sacrifice? The sun gave off light, which made the plants grow too, but the sun didn't look white to him, it looked yellow, the color of Belle's hair. Clouds could take on the purest white color, but not the ones that gave the rain. The clouds that gave rain to the plants became gray or black. The white clouds did nothing but block the light from the plants. Charlton grinned at his observations, then let exhaustion overtake him.

***

Pulling at the bucket and dragging it out of the well took all of Charlton's attention. A week had passed without a sign of Belle. His wounds no longer pained him, but now his heart ached. He only had his job to keep him occupied, to keep him from thinking about Belle. If he let his guard down for only a moment, he'd start to whirl around again, looking everywhere for her.

On his Sunday off, Charlton couldn't take it anymore. He stood behind a tree and waited to see Belle emerge from her house on the way to her church. She exited the house first, even before the carriage and driver arrived.

Belle looked beautiful. She wore a yellow dress that set off her figure. He couldn't keep his eyes off her. Her curled hair twisted down her back in tight spirals. Her hands gripped tight to her side and Charlton felt his hand moving up and out as if standing next to her and ready to coax her hand out of the grip and to hold his. He focused on her face and saw only a blank expression. Charlton's breathing turned dry and uncomfortable and his mouth tasted like swamp water.

He looked around and seeing no one, he stepped out from behind the tree. Belle's eyes traveled to him and her lips made a perfect circle of shock. Charlton tried to give a reassuring smile, but she only looked down as two shiny glints coursed down her cheeks His smile disappeared and instead he tried a cautious wave.

Belle looked up again only to shoot her gaze straight back to the ground. Her hands clasped even more tightly to her sides and made her dress protrude out more on each side. She turned away from him to stare in the opposite direction. Charlton's heart sank into his stomach.

With nothing to grab her attention in that direction, Belle turned around, and went back inside her house. Charlton watched as she swung the door open, entered, and eased the door closed behind her. He stayed for a minute staring at the windows, but she did not even peek out at him.

The trip back to the cabin lasted a lifetime. The men and women relaxed in the shade and took up light-hearted conversation with each other. His mother didn't even notice him as she chatted with a group of women. Charlton felt more alone that he ever had. He kept walking, past the cabins and onto the path that led to the well.

When he reached the well, he folded against a grassy patch. He thought the tears would start then, but instead, a long stream of bile came up through his throat and filled his mouth with the same swamp water taste he had felt earlier. The bile made him choke and sputter until he spat it on the ground. The orange acid sunk into the earth, but a few drops stuck to the grass. He wanted to follow the acid down into the ground. If only the earth would swallow him too and let him rest in peace, but he knew the earth and he himself would never permit that. No, he would stay as the drops that clung to the grass, holding on to life, no matter what it did to him next.

Chapter Eight

October 1848

Charlton stared at the ceiling willing himself awake. Manhood approached. His mother stood at least five inches shorter than him. Men worked the fields. Boys did odd jobs like carrying around water buckets or collecting firewood, but the lack of a suitable replacement to Charlton had stood in the way of making him work in the fields. Charlton did not know the age of Phillip, the oldest child on the plantation, though the boy looked about old enough to take Charlton's role. When Phillip reached the age of seven, Paul would report to the overseer and Charlton would work in the fields where his freedom to roam the plantation during the day would end. He didn't know what he would do without that time. It gave him time to think, plan, and most important, keep track of Belle.

Charlton felt the pull of sleep, but he turned thoughts over in his mind to keep himself alert. He could do nothing about keeping updated on Belle, but he would have the time to roam and think if only he could get out at night. So, he trained himself to learn how to live with less sleep. Night after night, Charlton forced himself to stay awake for an ever increasing amount of time. Without physical means of keeping track of time, Charlton worked at learning the cycles of the sun and the approximate time of year. The rest he left to chance and whim.

The day came when he thought he had reached enough time to give himself a solitary walk to keep his mind sharp. That night, he snuck out of the cabin and got away from his confines. Every day that the weather held gave him another chance to escape into solitude. It crossed his mind on occasion to make his escape during that time, but he didn't know his way north to freedom. He would not leave his mother either, the only person who kept him tied to a life he hated.

Charlton listened to the rhythmic breathing of his companions until he decided that they all slept. No plantation rule existed for getting out of the cabin at night and the master had no one in place to keep watch. The slaves held themselves in check by exhausting labor and the urge to sleep. As long as Charlton walked within the confines of the plantation, he remained safe. Getting caught reading remained his only danger. In deliberate steps, he made his way out of the cot and into the night.

The night sky's stars twinkled a cheery canopy of lights on Charlton. The contrast of star against space struck him with a beauty that kept him fixated. With only a sliver of the moon left, Charlton did not attempt to read his history book. Instead, he enjoyed the beauty until a pang of longing for Belle squeezed his heart. His hand pulled around the empty space as if to hold her hand. He kept his fingers and palm spaced just right to hold her hand for a moment. A stabbing thought told him that he looked foolish and he crunched his hand into a fist.

Charlton sauntered forward and let his memories flood him. Belle had never uttered another word to him, let alone signaled any recognition of him since her tears the day after the master took her away from him. He tried not to think about that day or Belle, but the book reminded him.

He wondered what happened with the book situation. She had taken it. Did anyone ever ask her about its whereabouts? Charlton had no idea. He knew he would return it if she asked, though it provided him with a fountain of knowledge. He would give up all that in exchange for the chance to tell her that he still loved her no matter what her father made her do.

His memories of the last couple months drained his energy as he stumbled and sat on the ground. Suitors, like in the stories Belle used to read him, formed a steady stream of visitors to the big house. With Belle's education concluded, her warning to Charlton that she needed to grow up came true. As the water carrier, he could take detours to check on her and saw many of them.

At first, Charlton hated each of them. As time passed, he noticed a different suitor appeared every time and that brought the realization that Belle had rejected each of them. His spirits lifted as he figured she rejected them because she still intended to marry him.

A month later, Charlton saw the same suitor a second time. The young man had a thick crop of black hair, a nose with a noticeable bend, and a fidgety body. The first time, Charlton heard the rumble of carriage wheels and got within viewing distance of the big house and his behind a tree when the coach arrived with the suitor and an older man, perhaps his father. When the Master and Mistress went out to greet them, Charlton caught the name of the interloper when his father introduced him as Master Robert Cavendish. Robert bowed to the master and the mistress, shook the Master's hand, and kissed the Mistress's outstretched hand, but when the Master invited them both in the house, Robert lagged behind. As the adults moved into the house, Robert's eyes darted around his surroundings as if judging his inheritance. While looking, Robert spied Charlton peeking around the tree. His face took on an evil grin and he raised his hand high in the air and cracked an imaginary whip. Charlton stood his ground anyway and watched as the young master spit on the trackway as if marking his territory. Master Robert strolled into the house after the adults.

Charlton walked away from the big house unimpressed by Robert's chances at getting Belle. The next week he appeared again, worrying Charlton. The third time sent Charlton's mind into a panic.

Charlton paused from his work when he spotted Belle and Robert walking alone down the paths behind the house. Charlton had returned from the fields moments ago, so he thought he could take a break from his work and do a little spying.

They sauntered with a significant distance between them, while Robert talked and Belle listened. "You know, my father owns the biggest plantation in the county and I, Miss Armand, am his sole heir. My father bestows great confidence upon me too. We have a plantation manager that has been managing Father's holdings for the past twenty years and he has been ordered to give me lessons. I have learned so much from him that when I take over the holdings, I will manage them even better than my father. My mind is set on expansion. We have two hundred slaves, but I know we can do better.

"Well, take for instance, if we were to get married. Your father's holdings would be added together with mine. Together, we would have holdings to rival anyone in the great state of South Carolina."

Charlton stopped his careful trodding on the ground to hear Belle's reaction to this impudent suggestion. His heart lulled when he heard no words or even a muttering. He half expected her to say that her heart belonged to another. Belle didn't so much as break stride.

Charlton paused in his careful and stealthy pursuit of the young man and woman. His mind searched for answers on why Belle, who had shown him only tenderness and caring, would accept this hard and cold assessment. The Belle he knew would only marry for love. Instead, she smiled and told Robert, "Master Cavendish, that is so true."

The young master showed no appreciation for her concession. "Yes," he said.

Charlton stopped following them altogether and could not hear the words. All the words came from Robert. Belle strolled along without so much as a word, giving Charlton the impression that she had nothing but obedient respect for the unimpressive youth.

Silence overtook the scene. Charlton slowed his breathing while craning his neck to see the couple, in time to see Roberts pulling away from the kiss he gave Belle on her cheek. He half expected Belle to return a slap across his face. Instead, Belle looked down at her shoes and acted shy. She reached out her hand and took Robert's into it. They turned a corner in the path and walked out of Charlton's sight.

Charlton held out until they walked far enough to hear and collapsed to the ground. Tears rolled down his cheek and sobs issued from his mouth. To his core, he knew that Belle had forgotten about him and would marry another, but he had always ignored those ideas. Whether Belle faced pressure from her family to marry someone or not, she would give her heart to Robert Cavendish. Charlton told himself to let go of Belle, yet his heart could not stand the thought. He had to figure out a way to stop the marriage.

***

Several days later, Charlton sat outside with a full moon shining down on him. A couple days ago, while wandering forlorn thinking about Belle, he found a clearing among trees that allowed the beam of light from the moon to allow him to read. On any given night, cloud cover could stop him from reading, but on a clear night, he would get out of the cabin with as much silence as he could manage. Every morning and night that Charlton got out of bed, he paid attention to where he stepped and listened for the slightest noise. He did the same when he climbed up to his bunk, learning the ladder's tiniest noises. By the end of a week, he had mapped in his head the exact levels of force and the locations that would minimize the noise. Even without a rule on leaving the cabin, he did not want to get caught and face questioning.

Charlton turned himself to where he could read in peace. He looked at the spot where he had hidden his book and admired it. He figured out that the book needed a resting place far from the cabins. Too many people milled around there and might find it. Yet, he knew that meant the book would need to reside outside and the rain and wind would soon ruin it. So, he needed to find a way to protect it.

The solution lay in the geology of South Carolina. The soil consisted of a mix of dark brown and red colors. Sometimes the red dirt hardened together and took on a flat shape; these stones littered the landscape. Most of these stones would not cover a fraction of the book, while the rare stone would lay over the whole book. So, Chartlon kept track when he came across them and carried them to his reading spot. Once he had one for the top and bottom of the book, he used four others against the four side of the platform he created to allow rain to drain off the sides and away from the book. He found a spot with tall grass and built up a mound of rocks in the center of the area where he placed the pieces of his container. Anyone would notice it, but Charlton scattered dead grass and hay on top of it and looked at it from every angle to make sure it appeared natural.

Charlton beamed with pride recalling how he found the way to protect the book and it made him hungry to read it in the peace of the slumbering plantation. He looked around his surroundings with an air of owning the place.

He read the title of the book in a whisper. "*The American Manual, or New English Reader: Consisting of Exercises in Reading and Speaking, Both in Prose and Poetry; Selected from the Best Writers, to Which are Added, a Succinct History of the Colonies by Moses Severance.*" The print on the inside proclaimed publication in Cazenovia, N.Y, which he knew stood for New York. Charlton let the thought that occurred to him every time he saw it enter his mind again. How he wished he could touch the letters "NY" and through magic find himself at the publishing house in the North. He placed his finger on the words, closed his eyes, and drew them back open to see the same familiar surroundings. The same sigh as the last time he tried this magic escaped his lips.

He decided to read The Constitution, which came right after The Declaration of Independence. The book had many challenging words in it, and although he did not have Belle around anymore to check on their meaning, he found that he could figure out most of them if he used the words around the difficult ones. The words said that the Declaration of Independence separated America from England, but it did not have any laws in it. It gave reasons why England had done America wrong, but did not say what government should do.

The book had little to say on the history of America except for some of the events that occurred before it became a country and an account of the Revolution. The book included The Constitution and The Constitution of the State of New York, but had no explanation of these documents. A quick scan of The Constitution showed Charlton that it did have some rules in it. He hoped to find something to show that the master could not own slaves. If so, he could use that and then the master couldn't forbid him from seeing Belle. She could marry him instead of Robert Cavendish.

After a struggle with a lot of difficult words, Charlton flipped the pages until he came to a section labeled, "Amendments." In that part, he noticed the word "right" associated with a lot of different statements. Though, he didn't know what it meant to have "a right to bear arms" or "a right to a speedy trial," the text helped him to see rights with a lot more clarity than he had seen them.

Charlton thought some more about the word "right." When Belle taught Charlton she would tell him that he got an answer right or wrong. Sometimes, instead of "right," she would say "true." So, he figured that rights are truth and belonged to people whether government liked them or not.

Charlton's mind wandered over to his own condition. What rights did he have? He glanced down at himself and saw his two arms and two legs. He reached up and grazed his fingers over his nose, eyelids, mouth, and ears. What difference kept him from his rights and granted them to white people? Did skin color really matter so much that his darker tone kept him from his rights?

A chill passed through Charlton despite the night's heat. He knew to his core that he possessed the same rights as any white person, but the master denied him the use of his rights.

The master held Charlton and all his slaves in a kind of prison when they had done nothing wrong. Not only that, he forced them to work the land without keeping what they did or sharing the profits. Charlton realized the slaves on the plantation worked the land and without them nothing would grow or get harvested. The work that they put in should have some reward attached to it and yet they did not get to take the reward. The master denied them their right to the harvest.

Despite his trembling and his anger, Charlton felt the pull of sleep. He glanced up at the moon and saw that it sunk too low in the sky. He had stayed up a lot longer than he intended. He put the book back in its safe spot and started back toward the cabin; he would pick up on his thoughts the next day.

***

The day began in the same way it had the last several months. Charlton ate his breakfast wondering if today Paul would tell the overseer that Charlton could begin working the fields. He kept his weary eyes on Paul all through breakfast, half-listening to his chattering mother.

When Paul didn't speak with the overseer, Charlton realized that he would not switch jobs yet and he trudged over to the well to begin his old job.

Thick clouds had moved into the area while Charlton slept, blotting out the sun. Even the scant light kept an exhausted Charlton squinting and longing for a quiet nap. He, of course, didn't dare to do it. He knew that the moment he closed his eyes to rest, he would be out for a long time and the men and women in the fields would suffer for it.

About mid-day, Charlton passed close to the house, when the sound of horses pulling a carriage caught his ears. He sneaked over to a place where he could spy on the family and figure out the cause of the commotion.

Charlton made it to the location where he had spied so often without discovery. The coach had arrived, but the occupant waited for the coachman to open the door. The coachman put the wood frame of two stairs in front of the door, opened it and put out an arm to let Robert Cavendish out of the coach. This time, he wore an exquisite dark blue gentleman's suit, misplaced on his bony frame and under his slack-jawed expression.

Chapter Nine

The young man strolled over to the front door with a sweeping arrogance. He knocked and fidgeted with his clothes while he waited. Robert took on posture after posture as if trying on different stances to get the perfect one.

Alice, the house slave opened the door in the middle of this bizarre dance. He looked embarrassed when he looked up at her. He stifled the embarrassment he would have felt if the Master had caught him, instead of a slave. "I'm calling on your Master," he said to her in an abrupt tone.

"Yes, Master," Alice said and closed the door. Robert continued to play with his posture, appearing to will himself into an embarrassing with the master this time.

The master came to the door and looked away from the young man as he contorted himself one last time. "Why Master Robert! How good to see you, my lad. Would you like to come in?"

"Sir, I would much like to come in, but I must ask you first if I may speak with you in private. Perhaps out here on the porch."

The master appraised the boy with a careful glance up and down. "Yes, you may."

Robert looked surprised by the master's agreeable nature. Charlton thought for a moment the master would refuse. The young man looked nervous and jumpy. As the master looked down to step onto his porch to occupy the space where his caller stood, Robert remained frozen. "You must permit me," the master said.

Robert mumbled an apology and shuffled backward. He went back into a dance as he tried to regain his balance and avoid taking a spill off the porch stairs. The master caught Robert on his arm and pulled him back to steady. Charlton almost blew his cover in laughter at the sight of it. "Master Robert, are you quite alright? You appear to be unnerved."

"No! I mean, yes. I mean, yes sir, I am quite alright," Robert said. A smile crept onto the master's face.

When he had regained his balance, Robert stared into the master's face and the master stared right back into Robert's eyes. "Well…" the master said.

"Well what, sir?" the young man asked.

"Well, what did you want to talk to me about?"

"Oh yes, oh, I am sorry, sir. I just, I just…" Charlton could almost see the palpable nerves and racing heartbeat of the young man. He hoped Robert would vomit all over the master and thought that it could happen.

"I am very busy, my boy, so if you can't speak to me then, I must get back to my activities," the master said.

Robert looked around himself and spoke without eye contact, "Sir, will you grant me permission to ask for your daughter's hand in marriage?"

Instead of looking shocked, the master looked as if he had expected this to happen. His eyes grew cool to the young man. For the first time in his life, Charlton delighted to hear the master say, "Master Robert, I think that would be unwise."

The young man's hurt eyes met the older man's cruel ones. "But sir, why?"

"Why indeed. Be seated Master Robert," the master said as he gestured towards his porch bench. The shocked boy slumped onto the bench.

"And there we have it," the master said.

"There we have what, sir?"

"Look at you forlorn in that seat. I tell you that it would be unwise to let my daughter marry you. You are resigned to my answer. There is no fight in you, my boy. Well, Master Robert, how can I allow my daughter to marry a spineless, no gumption boy like yourself? You did not challenge me. No, you merely slumped in a bench at my orders."

"What would you have me do, sir? Stand up and challenge you to a duel?"

"Ha! That is a contest I would surely win. No, now what I want you to do is sit and listen. Since I told you that you should have fought, it is much too late for you to do so now."

Robert looked confused and acquiesced. He sat ready to receive the master's lecture, though straightening his posture.

"That is better," the master said dusting off his hands. "I will be candid with you, Master Robert." At that moment the scene froze for Charlton. Unknown to either of them, Belle's face appeared in the window above them. She took an active interest in the conversation outside. Charlton could still read her face. She knew about Robert's wishes and hoped her father would agree to the proposal. Charlton's only hope resided with the master.

Charlton leaned closer to hear every word and the scene melted back into action as the master continued. "My daughter is the most precious part of my life. I only ever had the one child and she has brought me joy and life itself. I could not bear for her to fall into a marriage with the wrong sort."

"The wrong sort!" Robert said as he braced himself to rise. Charlton hoped a duel would begin in the near future. "I will have you know that my father owns a plantation many times this size with many times the slaves and I am his sole heir!"

"Stay seated, Master Robert!" the master said with wild-eyes. The young man obeyed. "I am well aware of your father's holdings. You are not aware apparently, that I do not care at all. This is not about inheritance. I want more than a large parcel of land for my daughter. I want you to worship the very earth she walks upon."

The master began to pace as he did when he gave his speech to Charlton. "Oh, I liked the way you got up and showed some backbone, but you know who that was for, do you not?"

Robert shook his head. "That was for you. I insulted you. You will apparently fight for yourself, but not the woman that you intend to marry? Is this the type of person I should simply hand my daughter over to?"

The young man sat still, like a deer caught at the end of a rifle. "Answer me!" the master said.

"Yes," the young master said and then he painted the same devilish grin on his face that the master had worn earlier. A spirit the younger man had not shown before sunk into his demeanor. To Charlton's astonishment, the master appeared at once cowed as the cretin rose to his feet and also respectful. As the master and the Robert stood facing one another, Charlton envisioned a mirror reflecting across the years between them. The boy Ole Joe described stood staring at the older man he would become. Charlton's heart sunk as he realized at once that Belle pulled toward a young version of her father and that her father would offer his consent to the marriage.

"I do worship the ground Belle walks on. She is everything to me. I will shower her with gifts and books and whatever else she desires.

I will give her land worthy of her beauty and grace. I will admire her from afar and be her devoted servant. Is this what you want?"

"Yes," said the master.

"Then, will you offer your consent?"

"Yes."

"Then, let me break the news to Belle who has already given her answer," Robert said.

The master swung the door open to the young man who marched into the house. The master stood back and admired his future son-in-law, entered, and closed the door behind them.

Charlton sank against the tree. The tears did not come to his eyes as he expected, though he half wished he wailed as his heart demanded to drown out the cries of jubilation from inside the house. The cries made Charlton jump to his feet and he took off into the woods.

His desired to get lost in the woods. If he could get lost, he would only worry about getting out again, Belle and her broken promise could escape his thoughts and memory.

When could he see his dreams fulfilled? How could a good-for-nothing, cold, and selfish creep come out of nowhere and steal his dream and his love from him? How could the love of his life, who filled herself with caring and childish hope, turn around and consent to corruption? She would lose her humanity with Robert and yet strolled into the trap blind and ignorant.

He collapsed in a heap, his head missing a jagged rock by inches. He did not notice. If he had, he would have cursed his luck that the rock didn't break his head open just like Ole Joe's. When the inside of a person's head is on the outside, they don't have to think any more and Charlton desired this more than anything else.

He propped himself up to sitting only to fold himself at the waist with his fists pounding the ground and he howled, not caring if anyone heard him. The tears flooded down his face leaving salty burns in their wake. He cursed and sputtered, hating Master Robert Cavendish. He wanted to tackle him and bash his head against the master's until they both lay sprawled on the ground silent and wasted. His enemies conspired to ruin the love of his life, they deserved that and more.

And what of Belle? His mind turned to the girl who broke her promise to him. The old and young masters could not help their natures, both arrogant and hateful. Who could expect them to act any different? Belle, though, she should know better. The beautiful, innocent child who taught Charlton everything he knew should run from Robert Cavendish should run from him, not toward him. How could she make the same mistake her mother made?

The attempt to hate Belle died away in vain. Her innocence kept her from knowing any better than to throw her life away with her fiancee. The idea struck Charlton and his tears stopped. He understood that neither young nor old master deserved his hatred either. Their power over people, the society that surrounded them corrupted them as much as Belle would get corrupted. What other choice did they have? The government allowed them to squash the rights of Charlton's people, to work their fields without compensation, to be whipped when they did not perform up to the highest levels of work.

The pain dug into his heart more when Charlton realized that this would be the death of Belle. Her innocence and love of life would perish under the weight of a cynical and immature husband.

At that moment, Charlton grew resolute and rose from the ground. He would make his stand again. He would hit slavery back for what it did to him this day and all the days of his life. He would find out the date of Belle's wedding. He pictured the scene in his mind. The words of the Declaration of Independence would lay scrawled in the ground where the wedding carriage stopped. Belle would see them and remember her broken promise while two slave-owning families would get smacked in the face with the words. The more Charlton thought about the idea, the more he longed to see what would happen.

Chapter Ten

June 1849

The pale moon shone on the words in Charlton's schoolbook and the light reflected on his wide eyes. He absorbed up the word that he saw before him. The title read "Jefferson's Grave," perhaps the most boring section in the book. It described the site of Thomas Jefferson's gravesite, but the word "Charlottesville" enthralled Charlton. Jefferson's family buried him on a mountain overlooking the town of Charlottesville. *Could this have something to do with my name?*

When Charlton slept that night, he pictured himself standing by Jefferson's grave giving homage to the wise man who wrote about rights. He thought about the section so much, he dreamt about it the entire night.

In the morning, Charlton woke refreshed before the cowbell called him to breakfast. He gathered up his food and sat in the familiar nook he and his mother shared. Martha looked downright chipper. Taking advantage of her good mood, Charlton asked the question he had never thought to ask her and wanted so much to know now.

"Good morning, Mama!" Charlton said before she reached their spot.

"Good morning, Child! You sure do look happy today," said Martha.

"It is such a nice morning, Mama. I feel good."

"You happy, that make me happy too," Martha said with a bright smile. Charlton could see how much she meant what she said.

"Mama?"

"Yeah, what on your mind?"

"Mama, I just wanted to know so bad. Who named me?"

"Named you?"

"Yes, who gave me my name?"

"I gave you your name."

"Why did you name me Charlton?"

"Oh, that such a good question." Martha clasped her hands together. "You listen up, Child, and I tell you."

Charlton beamed at his mother and stuffed gruel into his mouth. He hoped his name meant what he thought it did.

"My mama, your grandmama, was a lovely woman. She die before you born, but she love me so much. I hope I love you as much as she love me. She have so much love in her heart cause she come from the greatest place. She work for master Jefferson at Montcello."

Charlton's heart raced. He had to know for sure about this. No mistake. "Do you mean Mont*i*cello?"

"Oh yeah, it was Monticello. That was Master Jefferson's first love. Oh, some say his true love was Sally, your grandmama's friend, but your grandmama say that never happen and she would know. No, the way your grandmama say it, Master Jefferson, he love Monticello most."

Charlton had stopped listening for a little bit. He didn't know until now, and he cursed his oversight. Thomas Jefferson believed in rights, yet he sounded like a slave master. Maybe the term "Master" meant the same as Master Robert, yet Jefferson must have been well past his youth when his grandmother worked for him. He had to know. "Mama, when you say Grandmama worked at Monticello, do you mean as a slave?"

Martha's shoulders slumped. "Charlton, child, I told you before, we slaves. Your grandmama, she a slave. We all slaves. You just got to accept that. Do you want me to tell the story?"

She didn't understand the effect this news had on him: her words had lost him his hero. How could the man who wrote about rights own slaves? At that moment, he hated Jefferson as much as he hated the Northerners. Southerners lived in ignorance, unable to understand rights, but Jefferson wrote about rights and should have known better.

His mother waited for his response, looking at him with disappointed eyes as he ignored her. "Yes," he said with a weary nod.

His mother eyed him for a second and then continued. "Your grandmama love the work she do, and love how Master Jefferson come himself on his horse to see how the work go. She beam at him all the time. The way she say it, she hardly keep to her work when he come. I want my child to be named after the place that set my mama's heart glowing whenever she 'membered it. So, I name you after Charlottesville. If you was a girl, I name you Charlotte and if you a boy you get Charlton. You a boy, so you Charlton. Your grandmama was very good. I miss her holding me." Martha got a faraway look in her eyes and a tiny tear came down her cheek. Charlton decided to ignore his disappointment with his hero's fall and tried to distract his mother.

"Mama, how did you end up here?" Charlton asked.

Martha shook her head, blinked, and refocused on Charlton. "What you say, Child?"

Charlton tried again. "How did you come to this place?"

"I born at Montcello, but I so young, I don't 'member it. Your grandmama sold here to the old master. He die 'fore she die, but she die not long after. She got real sick and I so sad, but our people, they take care me and then I had you."

"Why did Master Jefferson sell her?"

"Your grandmama, she tell me why. She say..." Martha pursed her lips. Charlton felt relief that she didn't ask why he wanted to know. He didn't want to lie to her, and he could never admit the truth. She would make him get rid of his book if he told her about it.

"I 'member! Master Jefferson no good with money. He always sell his slaves to keep his land. Your grandmama, she want to know what happen to him, but she go to her grave not knowing."

"He died," Charlton said before he thought better of it.

"How you know that, Charlton?" Martha pressed, her eyes wide with suspicion.

"I, uh, I guess he died, Mama. I don't know. He must have gotten really old. Like Ole Joe, he had to die sometime."

"You ain't fibbing me, are you boy? Did you hear that somewhere? You been snooping around Master's house?" Disbelief shone from her face, concerned for a son who took far too many risks. Charlton realized he could keep from fibbing because he didn't hear that Jefferson had died, he read it and he had snooped around the master's house, but that's not where he got the information.

He answered with honesty. "No mama I did not hear that Jefferson was dead from anybody and definitely not from snooping around the house."

Martha hugged him tight. "Fine, Child. I believe you."

The overseer shouted at the slaves. "All right, all right, get out to the fields. That's enough."

Charlton headed down to the fields with his mother. They did not talk about the past on the way.

He reflected on the work in the fields as he headed out to start the work day. When he used to carry the water to the fields, it took so much less out of him. With the water, Charlton could take a break and rest. When he dared, he could even go to his book and read a couple pages. The men and women in the fields would not question his absence because they never knew when he came and went with the expanse of ground that he had to cover.

Working the fields meant feeling the nip of the lash all the time when he didn't work fast enough or made a mistake. His fellow field hands all told him that the newest among them always got the worst of it and that he would learn and get hit less. Yet, it didn't seem like it got any slower. The marks wouldn't leave him for a few weeks, along with getting new ones.

Charlton felt a twinge of longing for his water-carrying days. Now Philip, a boy more than seven years younger than Charlton, carried the water. Philip had an odd shaped face with a large nose that came to a sharp point, wide-set eyes, and jagged teeth.

As Charlton picked up his scythe for harvesting tobacco, the words of some of the field hands came to his mind. "That boy look more like a rat than a human."

"I can't hardly stand the sight of him."

"Some time, I rather go thirsty than have to look at him."

Philip also struggled carrying the full buckets. The men in the fields grumbled about his slow pace all the time. Charlton's heart ached thinking of Philip's plight.

His mind drifted to the work in the fields. Mistakes resulted in the whip, and taking too many breaks could cause a sting of the whip and almost always more than one. One field hand, Patty could not hold it in long and always had to go relieve herself. The hired hands and the overseer often accused her of laziness and lashed her. She learned to dehydrate herself and ended up sick. The hired hands learned that hitting her when she fainted didn't get her back to work, so they made Philip pour his water over her. Charlton interpreted the look of anguish on Philip's face when he had to do this as more out of concern for wasting his water than out of concern for Patty.

The hired hands hit slaves who sat multiple times. They could kneel, stand, or crouch, but sitting resulted in punishment. The whites would punish lying down worse than sitting, but Charlton had never seen any healthy slave do that in the fields.

Even though he got whipped as much as when he first started, reaping, planting, and plowing had become so familiar he could he let his mind wander while performing his duties.

Today, he wished to think of anything else but Jefferson, the man he once considered his hero. After about an hour of ignoring his thoughts, the tedious field tasks left him too much room in his head. He went back to thinking of Jefferson and how much he hated him.

To push Jefferson from his mind, he thought about something more painful—Belle's upcoming marriage. When Charlton didn't let his overactive mind wander, he listened to the hired hands as they milled around speaking about the latest gossip from the big house.

By eavesdropping, Charlton learned that Master Robert's family had welcomed his engagement, though they insisted he not get married until his nineteenth birthday. His father, a fat, stodgy man who far eclipsed his wife's age, saw to it that Master Robert learned to run the family plantations and figured that then he would conclude his training. Charlton overheard the birthday would fall eighty days away from the time he heard it.

Belle taught Charlton how to count, so he marked the days on an old tree stump near where he hid his book. The wedding would take place in twenty days. In the early morning of that day, Charlton planned to write in the trackway the words Belle had compelled him to write, except more. This time he would tell the master and his household, "We hold these truths to be self-evident that all men are created equal, that they are endowed by their Creator with certain inalienable rights."

Anger at Belle drove Charlton just as much as concern for her and what she would become. He wanted her to admit that her father's threat to sell Charlton hadn't caused her to break her promise. Although the threat may have stopped Belle from seeing Charlton at first, he knew time would have made her father give her more freedom.

Belle could have seen Charlton without anyone knowing. She could have joined him at night and roamed the countryside hand-in-hand. One day they could have traveled so far that it wouldn't have been worth coming back. She could have said goodbye to slavery, her corrupt father, and her useless mother and to the South, all the while posing as Charlton's owner. When they reached the North, life would have gotten difficult, yet they would love each other, something she would not find with Master Robert Cavendish, for as soon as he divested the name "Master" for his youth, he would wear it again in the face of the people he oppressed.

The crack of a whip shook Charlton from his thoughts. He heard a female voice yelp, but could not tell who got hit. He kept focused on his work while the aggressor watched over his section of the field.

When enough time had passed, he felt it safe to let his mind wander and thoughts crept into his head again. If Belle became Belle Cavendish before he had a chance to reach her, Robert would break her like Charlton imagined the master broke her mother. Even with anger still directed at Belle for her betrayal, it gave him a queasy feeling in the pit of his stomach to think of what she would become. He pictured Belle a little older with her pale skin blinding his eyes in the sunlight as she looked over the oppressed people toiling in the fields. Instead of the powerless child whose father refused to listen to reason, she would have some say over the treatment of her slaves as the mistress of the plantation, yet she would remain quiet as they got whipped and punished for having the wrong color of skin.

The way he visualized it, Charlton saw no tears running down Belle's cheeks. Without his words in the trackway to remind her of her affection for him, she would sink into the corrupt views of the South. She did forget him because she never tried to see him, and she didn't stop Robert from breaking her promise to Charlton, but the words would change everything, serving as a reminder on the day she stepped into a new life as mistress of a plantation.

He knew she would not change her mind and run away with him when she read the words. She would still go through with the marriage, but she might plead with her husband to refrain from handling his slaves with cruelty. If Robert meant what he said about worshipping Belle, then even a person like him might listen to her.

Could he save some people from the lash? Could he help out others he had never met? As if called by his thoughts, Charlton felt the sting of the lash on his neck. He brought his hand up to the mark and he felt sticky wetness where the lash landed. He shot a glance up at the hired hand who stared him down.

"Don't you stare at me, boy! When I catch you being lazy, I'm going to let this fly. Now back to work or I'll give you another," the slack-jawed redhead said.

Charlton felt the urge to lunge at the man and grab him around his throat. He would choke him until the man stood on the edge of fainting and then he would grab that whip and beat him with it until his own mother wouldn't recognize him. Instead, Charlton picked up his scythe and turned back to his work.

Chapter Eleven

The bustle around the plantation marked Belle's wedding day. Had Charlton not marked the tree, he still would have kept up with the timing by measuring the intensity of the excitement. It showed in the hired hands who gossiped about the latest panic that kept the mistress snapping at everyone, and crying as plans for the big day got the best of her. It even reached the slaves who took a break from the hard work as the distracted taskmasters let minor indiscretions slip.

Charlton both dreaded and longed for this day. Relief spread over him when a thick morning fog broke and the clouds rolled back to reveal a shimmering sun. He needed a clear night to see his way to the trackway and write the words.

The day before the wedding passed in a flash, and in no time Charlton had to bid his mother good night and noticed that an air of sadness surrounded her. He supposed a lot of the people heading to their cabins felt the same way. After all, the master's daughter's wedding marked the end of leniency from the distracted overseer and hired hands.

The anticipation of what would happen, and his practice at staying awake, made it effortless for Charlton to fend off sleep. With his heart pounding so loud in his chest the noise alone would keep him from sleeping.

After enough time of hearing the snores and breathing of the men, he snuck out the usual way, but this time headed to the house. Lanterns glowed from the windows when he got there. He hadn't considered this. With only so much time for preparations left, sleep would have to make way for activity.

Following what seemed an eternity, the last of the lights extinguished. Still, Charlton waited a while to make sure all activity in the house had ended. At last, he crept to the middle of the trackway near the steps. He would write the words close enough to the house so a horse and carriage would not wipe them out.

The words flowed out of him this time. He knew how to write in the dirt better now, but it also came from the confidence that writing the words would help his childhood friend and maybe save future pain and suffering of his fellow slaves. These words would do good; he had no doubt about that.

After completing the words, Charlton left the stick lying at the end of the line and he snuck back to the cabin. The knowledge that the master would figure out who wrote the words kept him awake deep into the night. He doubted whether he did the right thing, and thought about what punishment would await him. His racing heart kept him alert long into the night.

***

He awoke not to the cowbell, but to a woman's scream. Charlton hopped out of bed and without putting on his boots rushed outside the cabin and in the direction of the scream. Stopping short of the house so as not to make his presence known, he dropped his body to the ground to listen to the voices.

He recognized Belle's sobbing.

"Stop this at once!" her mother said.

Belle switched from sobbing to repeating the word, "no" over and over again while the mistress repeated "Dear Lord, Dear Lord, Dear Lord…"

Charlton's reeled with a flurry of uncontrolled emotion. The confidence in his decision to write the words did not waver, yet he could not believe his ears. He thought she would read the words, maybe get a little sad and reflected on her relationship with him. Not for a second did he anticipate this intense of a reaction. Could he have ever loved someone and still do this to her? Yet his love for her had made him do it.

The pattern changed over at the house; the mistress had recovered somewhat. "Stop this right now!" she said with such force that it took Belle out of her refrain. Charlton wanted so much to look, but he dared not and stayed close to the ground.

In the silence, the concerned mother softened her tone and asked Belle, "Whatever is the matter, dear?" Belle's mother said in a softer tone.

Charlton heard no answer.

The mistress proceeded to ask, "Those words? They don't matter, let's forget them. We have a wedding in a few hours."

"Mother, I, I can't marry Robert. I just can't," Belle said, a sense of calm in her tone.

Charlton lifted his head off the ground and he smiled.

The mistress gasped. "Why ever not?" Her plans had crashed before her eyes and Charlton knew she demanded an answer not only to hear it, but to destroy it.

After a prolonged silence, Belle said, "Because, Mother, he does not love me!"

"What do you know of love?" the mistress asked. "You're just a girl; you don't know."

"But, I do know Mother. I…"

Charlton flinched as a door slammed against a wall. He heard the master bellowing. "That's enough! What is the meaning of this?" Silence filled the air, leaving Charlton to assume the master had read the words in the trackway.

"That Goddamned bastard! He's behind this. I'll kill him! You! You get that boy!"

"What boy?" a gruff voice asked.

"The boy… Oh, for God's sake. He's fourteen or fifteen. He's a real dark skin."

"Yes, sir, I knows the one."

"Daddy, please…!" Belle said.

Charlton marveled at the distress in her voice.

"No, I will not desist. This will be your first wedding gift. The boy is too important to you. This ends today."

The decision came to Charlton with even greater clarity than when he deciding to write the words. He stood and gazed at the scene. The mistress looked horror struck. The master had stopped blustering as he scraped the words out with his boot. Belle looked desperate, her eyes darting around the landscape. A burly hired hand stomped off toward the slave cabin. Other hired hands milled around the family.

Belle saw Charlton first. He raised his hand in greeting and smiled. She cried, "Charlton, run! Please run!"

Charlton's smile widened as all eyes fell on him. The master had it all wrong. Charlton offered the wedding gift to Belle, not the master. If the master killed him, Charlton's death would give Belle a lesson in the cruelty of slavery she would never forget. All the compassion she would lose by marrying Robert would return to her heart. Belle could be saved and Charlton stood ready to die for that.

The master glared at the boy who would squash his greatest business deal. He whirled on his hired hands, "Well? Get him!"

The hired hands stood dumbfounded looking in turns at each other and at Charlton. Charlton felt laughter rise up from his chest and it exploded out. He stood his ground as a boy, skinny, awkward, and facing several white men empowered by law to do whatever they wished to him. Despite this, he laughed at them and made their anger worse as it ratcheted up driven by their fear. They stood and stared at him with disbelief.

Charlton marveled at the scene, forgetting about the burly hired hand. Two meaty arms surrounded him. He didn't struggle, instead, he went limp -- forcing the white man to drag him.

The large man struggled to keep a grip on him. He dragged Charlton a bit, then a brush or roots would catch Charlton's feet and pull him loose. The hired hand would curse, stop, pull Charlton up a bit, and start again. The white man kept demanding that Charlton straighten, but he refused to make that man's job easier. His bootless feet bled as they dragged over stones, sticks, and roots, some catching in his skin before getting ripped out by the force of the dragging, but he could handle the pain for Belle's watching eyes. He wondered how that gravel of the trackway would feel against his feet.

He never got the answer. The other hired hands awakened from their stupor and lifted his blistered, bruised, and bleeding feet into the air.

They moved Charlton quicker and soon the hired hands holding his feet and midsection dropped him at his captor's command. Charlton's lower half flopped to the ground as the burly hired hand kept his grip on him. He winced as his bloodied feet hit the ground.

Charlton shifted his gaze to Belle, who covered her face as she cried. She wouldn't look at Charlton. Maybe she had gotten used to not seeing him or maybe she had seen his feet and couldn't bear to take in his pain. Charlton didn't know and couldn't think of how to reassure her.

He looked around and spotted the mistress, but her gaze avoided him as well. She stared into the distance. He did not see the master.

The master emerged from the house carrying something Charlton had never seen before, but he recognized it from one of Belle's picture books. He carried a sword. Charlton had no doubt that he would die today, yet no fear crept into his heart. His death would mean so much for Belle. He delighted in knowing that the master would lose a slave who would otherwise toil year after year with no reward. The master would no longer possess a slave who he condemned yet needed to live his comfortable existence. What of Charlton? He would either meet with Ole Joe in an afterlife, or his mind and body would find peace. Either way, Charlton would have a better existence than the one he had lived and would always live.

Belle looked up and horror spread over her face. "Daddy, please, what are you going to do?"

Charlton wanted the master to kill him. Would Belle get married on the day that her father killed the friend he had tried to make her forget and the boy to whom she first promised her hand in marriage?

"Keep her back!" the master ordered.

The mistress stood between Belle and her father. Belle did not resist but looked on helpless.

The master walked over to Charlton with slow and steady purpose. Charlton bowed his head so the master could make a clean slice through his neck.

The master met the eyes of a hired hand standing close by and said, "Make him look at me!"

The hired hand grabbed Charlton by the hair and pulled his head so his eyes would meet the master's hate-filled gaze.

"Boy, this is the second time you did this. I was a fool and gave you another chance. You will not have a third because today you will pass from this life into whatever afterlife God gives your people."

Belle gasped. "Mother, please. Please don't let him!"

The mistress looked from her daughter's desperate eyes and to her husband who stood transfixed waiting for his family to stand down so he could strike. "John, dear, please put down your father's sword. It was meant for the glory of war, not the slaughter of an unarmed boy," she said.

The master whirled to face his wife. "Yes, my dear wife, this was meant for the glory of war and this boy is my enemy. I will stop him from ruining this wedding!" He turned back to Charlton and raised the sword.

The hired hand released Charlton's head and stumbled backward. Charlton eased his head lower.

Belle continued her plea. "Father, if you kill him, I will never marry Robert. I will run away from you and Mother and you will never see me again. If he lives, I will marry today, but if I ever hear he dies at your hand or your order, I will run away from Robert."

The master stopped and stared at Belle. Charlton raised his head and admired her tangible courage, but he wanted her to fail. If the master struck, then Charlton would have assurance that he saved Belle.

"You cannot mean that," the master said with a trembling fear in his voice.

Charlton knew the master wanted to strike, but Belle had the power to stop him, not only now, but for as long as Charlton's natural life lasted.

"I do mean it, Father. I cannot allow this."

The master's eyes darted from Belle to Charlton. Charlton decided to goad on the master. "Strike," Charlton said.

The master's gaze grew fierce and wild just as Charlton had hoped. "Strike me, master, and all your troubles go away. Strike me." Charlton saw the fury rise even higher in the master's face, so he stopped goading him and lowered his head. The burly hired hand loosened his grip allowing Charlton to kneel on his own. He backed away to let the master strike.

Charlton's gaze lifted while his head remained lowered. He watched as the master let out a cry, raised the sword, and swung down toward Charlton's head.

He heard Belle cry, "No!" and everything went dark.

Chapter Twelve

A throbbing head jostled Charlton from unconsciousness. Every heartbeat brought him new agony. The pain took all his focus until he could accept it. His burning, dry throat came next, then the scratched skin of his face, which rested on wood planks. His hurt feet grabbed his attention. They remained battered, bruised, and bleeding from the dragging.

When he had calmed himself, the memories and what they meant pushed their way into his mind. He lived. This thought brought more torment. His life meant Belle's death because of her promise to the master. When they checked his heartbeat and found him alive, they must have informed Belle and she went to her grave by marrying Robert. She would die over time with each whip crack on the back of one of Robert's slaves. He knew she'd accept each, as every mistress must, and deaden her innocent sensibilities until nothing remained of her spirit.

Charlton tightened his muscles as he tried to curl up on the floor and bring himself comfort. Instead, the motion stopped midway as his body screamed at him to stop.

Once again, Charlton accepted his wounds. He pushed at his muscles with the most deliberate and slow motion that he had ever performed, to roll over and rest on his uninjured back. When he accomplished it, the new position brought him less anguish. He refused to risk the disturbing memories, but he did want to know his location. His eyes opened.

A small enclosure, with enough room to lay flat in two directions surrounded him. The wood boards that made up the walls let in the orange glow of an approaching evening, which revealed a dirty, worn floor cutting all around him to join walls with hooks and bars on them. Everything about the place indicated the hired hands had dumped his body in the toolshed, removing all the tools first, so he couldn't hack his way free.

He brought his hand to his face and felt the welts that had scabbed over in some places. He remembered his feet getting torn apart from the dragging, but what would explain the damage to the skin on his face, knees, and chest? Realization overtook him all at once. The white men must have mishandled him after he got hit and now he had far more injuries than he could recall.

Charlton decided to explore the rest of his head. He chose to start with the base of his skull, so he rotated his head up. Before he could get his hand underneath, his head seized and he groaned in agony. The throbbing resumed with renewed vigor. His vision blacked out as he released his neck muscles. A moment later, his vision returned. Charlton reached his hand toward the top of his head and felt sticky wetness. An examination of his hand showed dark red liquid with black and brown speckles spread across his fingers. He brought his hand to the same spot and discovered mounded flesh.

Charlton eased himself onto his elbows, then his hands to get into a sitting position. His head ached with each movement, but he pressed forward. He pushed his feet under himself and stood. Struggling against imbalance, he gained his footing and winced from standing on his damaged feet. He walked over to a wall, looked through the slats, and saw the tools scattered around the outside of the shed. A wave of weakness passed through him, but he took a ragged breath and crept over to the door. A gentle push told him they had locked it from the outside.

A tin cup and a piece of bread with a couple spots of mold lay next to the door hinge. Charlton tore off the mold, ate the bread, and drank the water. His stomach grumbled for more of both. Exhaustion forced him to lay down and let sleep overtake him.

***

After a fitful night of waking with every turn of his body, Charlton rose with the sun. No one came to get him. The hired hands retrieved the tools, but did not unlatch the shed. Charlton didn't bother asking them to let him go free. They wouldn't listen unless the master instructed them to do it. He waited.

At last he heard footsteps. The latch jiggled and Paul stood before the open door. He dumped Charlton's boots and a pair of socks on the floor and said, "Put them on and come with me."

Charlton obeyed. He eased the socks on as careful as possible, wincing every time they rubbed his wounds. The boots went on harder and standing hurt the most.

Paul did not grab him this time. He said, "Follow me." Charlton stumbled out of the door and obeyed

When he finished, Paul began a steady walking pace without looking to see if Charlton followed. Charlton could have run and Paul wouldn't have noticed. Charlton didn't even consider it. He had nowhere to go and his body wouldn't let him. It took all his willpower to keep up with Paul on his battered feet.

Charlton wanted to ask for their destination, but every time he tried to utter the question, he found his voice too shaky to speak. The pain overwhelmed him. His steps caused pain in his feet and stiff muscles exacerbated the throbbing in his head. He had learned to keep the pain in check while still in the toolshed, but keeping up with Paul meant something else altogether.

They entered the same clearing Charlton had gone to with Paul the last time the master had met him. The master sat on the same stump this time too. The master looked first to Paul, and then to Charlton. His glare projected the purity of hatred he felt for Charlton.

"Sit down," the master said to Charlton. Charlton felt a twinge of defiance in his legs. He did not want to follow any of the master's instructions, but a driving motivation to get off his feet won out and he plopped on the ground in front of the master.

"You, boy, have caused me untold grief." The master stared down Charlton. Charlton sensed he wanted to see him bow his head or show some kind of remorse. Charlton refused the unspoken demand. He felt no remorse, but pride for the trouble he had caused the master.

The master cleared his throat. "My daughter is married. You did not ruin the wedding." The news did not surprise Charlton though he still hated hearing Belle had committed the act. Charlton lowered his head and stared at the ground.

The master snapped his fingers. "Ah ha! I knew you were trying to ruin the wedding! I cannot figure how you knew the day to do it, but I knew you wanted to ruin it. Oh, you escaped death twice yesterday. Not only did my daughter save you when I was ready to send you on to the next life, but she saved you again later that day. When her husband heard what you did and how you almost stopped the wedding, he was ready to kill you himself. Now that would have been a beautiful sight to see." The master got a faraway look in his eye and grinned. Charlton looked up and saw the master's deep admiration for his son-in-law.

The master's grin faded as he stared off into the distance. "My daughter stopped him and threatened him with the same as she told me. You, boy, are one lucky son of a bitch. You cast some kind of voodoo magic on her 'cause she is confused as can be."

The master stared at Charlton and waited. Charlton understood that the master wanted an apology or a sign of remorse, but he offered neither. He wanted the master to break his promise, so Charlton could save Belle. An apology meant reducing his chances of saving Belle. The angrier the master got, the better for Charlton's goal.

The master waved his hands at Charlton, stood up and turned around. He muttered something under his breath that Charlton missed. He jerked around to face Charlton. In spite of himself, Charlton flinched, sensing the master would strike him again. Instead, the master used an even tone and asked, "What makes you insist on writing those words?"

Charlton refused to play the role of the obedient slave acting out the wishes of others like he did the last time he spoke with the master about his writing. He knew the same lie would not work, but he could also not bear the thought that the master would get more evidence of the obedience of his race. If the master wanted to ask this question, he would answer it. He looked the master in the eye and with confidence he said. "I'll tell you the truth, Master." Charlton paused because the master stared at him with wonder, having never seen this kind of behavior from a slave. Charlton basked in the moment at shattering the master's expectations.

"I lied when I first wrote the words. Belle told me to lie, and I did it for her. You think me and my people have no rights, but we do. You just stop us from using them."

The master marveled at the slave who looked him in the eye and spoke with confidence and intelligence. He glanced around at Paul who stood looking as perplexed. Charlton knew Paul had heard him speak in the same way, but he figured Paul saw a rare weakness in the master who would have torn into such insolence in any other slave. Charlton knew he took the master off guard with his speech. "I also wanted Belle to see it and not get married." The words snapped the master out of his stupor.

He stood up and stomped over to Charlton. The master raised his hand, palm up, and said, "Look me in the eye and tell me that again."

Charlton followed the master's command and stood up looking

the master straight in the eyes. "I wanted Belle to see it and not get married."

The master's hand flew into Charlton's face. The slap stung the blisters on his chin and the scabs on his cheek. The impact caused the throbbing in his head to resume. Then that master grabbed Charlton around the neck with both hands. "I ought to kill you right now!" the master said his face turning a light shade of red.

"Go ahead. Belle will run away and I'll die happy," Charlton said in a rasp. The master's eyes bulged and his grip tightened enough that Charlton started to panic. He grabbed the master's hands but with great effort he stopped himself from trying to pull them free.

The master released his grip and stepped back. Sweet air swam into Charlton's lungs. He couldn't believe how good it felt to breathe even though a part of him wanted the master to kill him.

The master cursed and kicked at the stump. Charlton felt embarrassed for the master. He looked behind him to see Paul's bewildered expression.

After what seemed like an eternity of waiting, the master stood up and said, "Ah ha!" He stomped over to Charlton, looking into his eyes. Charlton looked straight back. "So, you want to die?"

"Only if you do it," Charlton said. Charlton didn't want to die, but it would comfort him to save Belle.

"Oh no, I will not kill you. I will send you to a place that is worse than death. You think you have it hard here, but Mr. Beauregard works his negroes to the bone. My negroes work hard because they get the whip sometimes; his whips are always cracking against their skin. His negroes die all the time, mine get to an old age, his die young. I swear you will regret crossing me."

Charlton's heart beat faster. The master had come up with a plan where he could have his revenge on Charlton, but not kill him. Mr. Beauregard could kill Charlton through cruelty and overwork. Charlton had to stay at the master's plantation.

The master smirked, studying Charlton's face as he stared back at the master with wide eyes. The master clapped his hands together and said, "Paul!"

"Yes, Master?" Paul said.

"Take this boy back to the toolshed. I have a bargain to arrange."

Charlton turned to see Paul walking toward him. A plan formed in his head like a mouse approaching a crumb in the middle of an occupied room. He needed it, but didn't know if he could take the risk.

"I wouldn't do that, Master." Charlton stood.

The master, who had turned his back on Charlton and began walking in the direction of his house, turned around. "What do you mean?"

"If you sell me to Mr. Beauregard, I'll tell him that I can read and write and I'll tell him that you taught me how," Charlton said. "I know my people are not allowed to read or write and Belle told me that if one of your people teaches one of mine to read and write, they'll be going to jail. Do you want to go to jail?"

"You filthy little liar! How dare you? You can't even read! No slave can! You wrote those words from memory. When Mr. Beauregard finds out you're lying he'll whip you something severe."

Charlton knelt on the ground and traced his finger in the dirt, spelling the words, "I can write," and stepped back to let sunlight beam over the evidence.

The master crouched down to get a closer look as if his eyes had deceived him. The master looked up from the words, at Charlton, back down, and up again. Paul backed away, waiting for his instructions.

Charlton decided to push the master a little more. "When Mr. Beauregard finds out I can read and write, he'll say you have to pay him so he won't tell anyone. You'll have no choice but to do it and he'll keep me alive in case you ever stop paying him."

The master stopped his pacing, shook his head, and grunted. He looked at Charlton with narrowed eyes. "I didn't teach you to read and write. Belle did."

"You want her to go to jail? I guess that's the type of father you…"

The master rushed on him and again wrapped his hands around Charlton's throat again. Charlton did not struggle, despite the panic building up in him. He hoped the master would finish him, yet he craved air to breathe. The master screamed in his face. "Do not say it! Do not *say* it!"

The master released his grip on Charlton's throat. Sinking to his knees once again, Charlton felt the relief of air filling his lungs. He would prefer the master to kill him, but didn't want to get choked again.

"Paul! Put him in the toolshed!"

Paul scooped him up in his arms and walked at a brisk pace toward the toolshed. When he fell clear of the master's view, he slowed, put Charlton back on his feet, and stopped. "Boy, what's wrong with you?"

Charlton tilted his head at Paul. "What do you mean? He can't sell me or kill me now."

"I never seen the master so mad. You're a dang fool to say those things. You stay here, the master, he order the whip on you all your days."

Charlton hadn't considered this. The master couldn't sell him and he couldn't kill him, but he could create the living hell that Mr. Beauregard created for his slaves. Would his chances to slip away at night end too? The master might keep him under a tight watch.

Charlton paused long enough that Paul got tired of waiting. He nudged Charlton on the back and said, "Come on, we better get moving." Charlton complied, though he stumbled on his battered feet, wincing at the sensation.

When they arrived at the toolshed, Paul opened the door and stood back to let Charlton enter. Charlton stepped inside and turned to face Paul.

"You better get used to this. I don't know when the master let you out."

"I understand," Charlton said. He turned around so Paul wouldn't have to shut and latch the door in his face and heard the door close and latch behind him.

Charlton didn't mind getting locked in the toolshed that night, except for the little food and water he could expect. He knew he needed to stay off his feet, and getting dragged into the sun again might make his head explode and pound more than it already did. He needed time to heal and getting put back in the field would not do that for him. He lay on his back and took a long nap, exhausted from his exertion.

Chapter Thirteen

Upon waking, Charlton wondered if he had dreamed of the encounter with the master because everything appeared the same as when he first found himself there. His head pounded, his feet felt raw, twilight fed through the boards of the toolshed, and bread and water sat in the same place. Worst of all, confusion invaded his mind in the same fog he had experienced the previous day.

His throat offered proof he had not dreamed it. The air coming into his body burned like tiny grains of sand scraping their way to his lungs. Finger-sized bruises pushed against his neck where the master had squeezed him.

He had little time to feel sorry for himself though. He needed to make sure he used what little light he had to pick the mold off his bread. Charlton crawled over to the bread. Not getting on his feet helped him move faster and with less pain. He stared with incredulity at the piece of bread. It sat fresh and spotless. "Thanks, Paul," he said aloud.

He frowned. The others hated and feared Paul, but Charlton knew he had a good heart. Though Paul remained the master's right-hand man, he only did that to survive. Charlton couldn't blame him for deciding to take on the role. If he could make his life easier on the plantation he would do the same.

That thought led to the memory of his conversation with Paul after he saw the master. Charlton shivered thinking about what would happen to him now. Rumors of the treatment that Mr. Beauregard ordered against his slaves had reached him. Charlton had not lived up to the tales that Belle had read to him about heroes sacrificing themselves for the love of their maidens. Instead, he accomplished nothing but making his own future worse. Charlton scowled. He wanted to cry and wail, but with little water in the last two days, he could only muster a tear from each eye. His swollen throat would not permit him to wail.

Charlton decided to stop thinking about it. Despite his stomach's hungry protests, he took little bites of the bread to try and savor it.

With the fading light he had no other choice than to try and sleep, but with the long nap and so many thoughts swirling in his head, sleep eluded him. Could Belle stay the person he loved or would she become complacent? What kind of a life would she have? What kind of life would he have? Would the master have him whipped every day, like Paul said? Had Charlton only avoided the torture of Mr. Beauregard's plantation to run straight into torture at the master's plantation?

Worry and panic set in. Charlton lay as still as he could so that he had the best chance to fall asleep, but the thoughts about what his life would be like after the encounter pressed on him more than anything else. He could do nothing about Belle; he figured that since she moved to her husband's plantation he would never see her again, so he would not see her transformation, but he would suffer the pain of the master's anger. He shuddered with fear and worry. Though, he tried to relax again by whispering words of comfort to himself, it always led back to the same thought, *I need to get out of here and under the moon where I can think straight.*

After hours of no sleep in the faded moonlight that snuck through the wall, exhaustion overtook Charlton. The sun came up, but he did not notice, even when the hired hands came to collect the tools around from the shed. Mid-day, Paul jiggled the latch, but he did not stir. Only when Paul shook him on the shoulder did he jerk awake.

Paul jumped and they both shouted. After he got his breath under control, Charlton realized Paul might have thought him dead. *If only*.

"Boy, you got to get out and relieve yourself, then you got to get back in," Paul said. "Master say so."

Charlton slipped on his boots, dazed enough not to realize that the night and morning off his feet had healed them. He only noticed when he stood on his feet and felt only mild pain. His head pounded less too. He even risked touching the bump and realized that not only did the touch not make him seize, but it had shrunk.

The short-lived satisfaction from healing gave way to the realization that Paul had said he would have to return to the toolshed. How long would the master keep him in there? He didn't know if he could spend another night in the confined space without losing his mind.

Charlton took his time going into the bushes to relieve himself, he sighed with relief after two days of keeping it in. Paul lingered near, keeping the spot where Charlton went in view. Charlton figured Paul didn't want to explain to the master why he lost his charge in his few minutes of freedom. Still, he gave Charlton enough space to feel like he had some measure of privacy.

When Charlton finished, he looked over to see that Paul had brought a battered tin basin, a bucket, some soap, a tall tin cup, and a bowl with a spoon and some substance in it. "Wash up," Paul said, motioning to a basin filled with water. Charlton grabbed the soap and poured some water into his cupped hand, then rubbed them together and rinsed off with some more water. Next, he poured water into his cupped hand and brought it to his head wound to rinse the blood out of his hair. He rinsed his hands with a little more of the water. Then, he splashed the rest on his face, which felt cold and refreshing.

He took the half-filled bucket and poured water into the cup. He guzzled the water, and filled it again. The bowl held cold oatmeal. Charlton wouldn't have enjoyed this any other time, but savored the taste of the oats after having only bread the last two days. The amount didn't ease all of his hunger pangs, but he felt grateful to Paul for the trouble.

He looked up at Paul and grinned. Maybe Paul respected Charlton after he stood up to the master or maybe Paul revealed a side of himself he always had, but never showed. Either way, Paul seemed like a good person despite what the other slaves felt about him.

"Thank you," Charlton said.

"Yeah," Paul said.

"Paul?"

"Yeah, what?"

"How long is the master going to keep me in there?"

"I don't know. He never told me."

"It's hard to be in there."

Paul looked almost sympathetic, but said nothing.

"I have to go back in there, don't I?"

"You drink the rest your water first."

Charlton nodded and hid a smile. They sat in silence while Charlton took his time filling his cup and drinking its content three times.

When he could stall no longer, Charlton sighed and walked back into the toolshed. He turned to face Paul who leaned against the open door. "I be back with your supper," he said and closed the door on Charlton and latched it.

This time no exhaustion or need to sleep would save him from boredom and loneliness. He paced around his confines to give something to do, but his feet, still in need of full healing, groaned under the weight of his body. He tried to lie on his back and sit up and down, but moving his head like that made him dizzy and uncomfortable. Giving up on everything else, he braced his hands under his head and stared at the ceiling.

The inside of the toolshed took on greater familiarity to him than his mother's face. Every time he looked around, the walls seemed to have crept closer together than the last time he looked. He noticed his heartbeat next. It seemed to beat faster and faster. He put his hand over his chest and felt it. *Yes, it is getting faster! Am I dying? Will Belle blame her father when I die? No, he'll swear to her it wasn't him. He'll show her my body and see that I healed from the injuries. She'll believe. I can't die.*

His breathing deepened and got faster. He struck his chest with the palm of his hand to try to make it slow down, but it would not cooperate. He wanted to scream at it to slow down. "Slow down! Slow down! Please, you're killing us!"

This commotion only made things worse. His breathing came in and went out harder. He gasped and felt the burn of the air going down his healing throat. He tried to calm himself by laying still on the floor. His heart wouldn't explode. He knew that.

In a moment, he took control of himself. He realized that if he panicked, the master would win. He had put Charlton in this toolshed, knowing that keeping him here without contact with others would drive him mad. It gave him a sense of calm to realize that he could beat the master by controlling his emotions.

The day went by with Charlton going through moments of deep thought, panic, and calm. No matter how much he reminded himself that he could beat the master and then calming down, he always seemed to go back into panic mode. The day crawled forward. Charlton wished he could pop out of existence and come back when his time in the toolshed concluded. The monotony of his day only broke when he needed to urinate through the floorboards. He almost wished he had to do it again.

When twilight began, relief came over Charlton and he stopped panicking. He knew Paul would keep his promise to take him his supper. That would get him out of the toolshed for a little bit. Waiting for Paul made Charlton conscious of time even more though. He seemed to wait forever and wondered whether Paul took his time on purpose to hurt him.

Minutes later, Paul unlatched the door and found Charlton waiting for him. Paul looked startled at the sight of Charlton. The intense desire to push Paul out of the way and dash out of his prison was surpassed by Charlton's will to show no sign his confinement affected him as much as it had. Paul looked irritated, then gave way and said, "Come on."

Charlton stepped out and went to the bushes to relieve himself. Paul had the basin again, a bucket of water, slivers of soap, a cup, and supper in a tin bowl with a spoon. This time he brought a large serving of stew. The irritation at Paul's delay vanished when Charlton saw the large helping of food.

Charlton washed himself and ate his supper in silence. He kept trying to think of things to say to Paul, but Paul gave off no emotion as he sat, so Charlton chose not to bother him.

When he finished, Paul stood up with his arms crossed.

"I have to go back in there don't I?" Charlton said.

"Yeah, Master say so. Master whip me and make another do it anyway, if I don't make you."

"I understand. It's just, well, do you know when I get to go back to the cabin?"

"Master no say. You best not think of it. Come on."

Charlton obeyed. Paul closed and latched the door and Charlton heard him grunt and march away. Alone again, he couldn't believe with all his loneliness, he neglected to take the chance to talk to somebody when he had it.

Charlton curled up and went to sleep with little effort. It helped that he lingered so long with supper that the light of day had almost vanished.

He awoke to the pitter-patter of rain. He opened his eyes and saw dawn had arrived at some point but the grayness of the scant light and the rain sounds let Charlton know that the cloud cover lay thick in the sky. He peeked between the slats in the toolshed and could not see the tools. The work on the plantation had already begun.

Paul got to the door soon after Charlton started wondering when he would come. He had the same things with him as before and Charlton went through the same motions. Once again before locking him back into the toolshed, Charlton asked, "When am I getting out?"

"Don't know," Paul said and closed the door in a single, gentle motion. Charlton heard the click of the latch.

Trapped again, Charlton occupied himself by listening to the rain. Its drumbeat against the roof changed from fast to slow and back again.

He let himself get lost in listening, forcing out the thoughts of Belle, his future life, and the panic he had felt the day before. He hoped the rain would convince the master to let him go back to the slave quarters. Otherwise, the tools would sit out in the rain with no chance to dry.

An idea popped into Charlton's head and he couldn't stop thinking about it. *Why has Mama not come looking for me?* She could have followed Paul. Martha did odd jobs around the plantation much of the time. She worked the fields too, but she also did laundry for the slaves and the white people and kept the slave quarters tidy so their people would not get sick. She could have slipped away any time. Did she not care enough to look for her son? He decided she couldn't risk getting caught, but something about the explanation didn't sit well with him.

Time slogged forward. Charlton shifted his attention to the rain patterns whenever they changed, but they lost the power to captivate him. At the end of the day, the hired hands, a mule, and a cart arrived with the collection of tools. Charlton heard them unlatch the door.

"Come on out, boy. We're using this here shed now," an older man with a thick beard said.

Charlton hesitated, but the white men didn't wait. Two of them looked at each other and with a nod from each rushed Charlton, grabbed him by the arms, and hurled him out the door. Charlton fell to the ground, mud splattering all over his overalls, shirt, and boots. The field hands laughed and worked to put the tools back in the shed. Charlton scrambled out of the way and got up to leave, but stopped when he saw Paul blocking his way, holding a whip.

"Master want you whipped 'fore you go back," Paul said.

Charlton nodded and followed Paul. About midway back to the cabins, Paul stopped. "I ain't whipping you. You look bad 'nough. No one'll know."

Charlton couldn't speak as tears of gratitude flowed from his eyes. They continued on their way.

Chapter Fourteen

Though his feet still hurt, Charlton wanted to run past Paul to the slave quarters, the need to see his mother pressing on him. The days in the tool shed took Charlton away from his mother for the first time stretch of days in his life. The sight of him alive would bring her great comfort.

Dinner sat in the caldrons with spoons sticking out ready for stragglers to serve themselves. With the rain, many of his fellow slaves ate inside while others stood under the overhangs of the cabins. Charlton couldn't spot his mother, but since the cook would take the food away at some point he got his bowl, spoon, and cup from his bunk, and went back outside to dish himself some stew and fill his cup with water.

Once he had his food and water, his eyes scanned the sides of the women's cabin. None of the women stood outside. As he spooned stew into his mouth and the rain plinked against his clothes, washing him of the mud, he scanned the other buildings. Not seeing her, he walked around the cabins to look at each overhang that she could have used. He scraped the bottom of his bowl and finished the search.

Charlton figured three days without him must have driven her to eat in the women's cabin. When he arrived, he banged on the door. "Mama? Mama, it's Charlton. I'm all right. I'm here. I have a story for you that you won't believe. Mama?"

The chatter inside the women's cabin died down when he rapped on the door, but no one answered. Charlton didn't dare enter; the unstated rules never allowed men to go into the women's cabin. Men and women who got married could live together in smaller cabins, but single women stayed in the women's cabin and single men in the men's cabin. No one broke the rules.

He thought it over. *Could the Master have locked her up too, except not let her out? That would be completely unfair. I wrote the words not her. But the master's never been fair, so why would he start now?*

The men's cabin offered no insight to his mother's whereabouts either. Even Paul refused to respond to pleas, shaking his head and shrugging his shoulders instead.

If the master did have his mother locked up, Charlton had no idea where he would have put her. Maybe he had an empty room in his house and a cage where he held slaves he wanted to punish.

Defeated, he went out into the rain to scour the region again, searching behind the main cabins and around the couples' cabins, all to no avail. With no other choice, he gave up and sulked off to his bed, falling into a deep sleep after hours of staring at the ceiling and wondering if he'd ever see his mother again.

***

The morning brought a lonely breakfast. Charlton half hoped his mother would show up among the breakfast crowd, but again she did not appear. He forced himself to eat, trying hard to distract himself from the hired hands' watchful eyes. He knew the master had instructed them to keep the whip on him. The muscles in his legs tensed, urging him to run away. Regret at writing the words sank into him undeniable and unrelenting: it didn't help Belle to get out of her marriage and it might have hurt his mother.

Distraction at his mother's disappearance kept Charlton from concentrating on his first day back. He looked up from his work on the off chance the master might have released his mother from her prison. A sting fell on his arm and he bolted upright.

"Get back to work!" the overseer said with a sneer.

Charlton eased back into a crouch, but the overseer whipped him again, this time on the neck. When Charlton yelped, the overseer said, "Faster next time, boy!"

The overseer or another hired hand stuck to him all day. Charlton couldn't help looking for his mother from time to time, even though the lash came down on him every time.

At dinner that night, Charlton had to admit the master's plan to make him miserable worked on the first day. Exhaustion from lack of sleep made the sores from each crack of the whip, and his other injuries, sting even more. Worst of all, his mother still hadn't made an appearance. Again he went around and asked the others about her, but none could answer.

After getting his food, Charlton plopped on the ground to eat his dinner. He looked around to see the other slaves eating and chatting with family and friends. Except for the time when Charlton and his mother brought Ole Joe into their circle, they had only each other for companionship. He questioned this isolation now. He wanted so much to spend time after the workday with his mother that he didn't give much thought to the other slaves. Now, in his loneliness, he wished that they had ventured out more and made friends. The other slaves treated him with indifference and wouldn't answer his questions about his mother, though he knew one of them must have witnessed what happened to her.

***

The following days carried on in the same way. Charlton's stomach churned with worry about his mother. He endured more whippings while he toiled in the field, and ate his meals alone. Every night, panic built up inside him as he lay in his bunk staring into the darkness until a restless sleep overtook him.

On the seventh day, Charlton approached Paul at dinner, who sat alone and took his time eating

"Can I sit here?" Charlton asked, indicating the spot of ground across from Paul.

"Makes no difference to me," Paul said.

"Thanks. I have a problem and I thought you could help me."

Paul gestured to the patch of grass in front of him and continued eating. Charlton took a seat with reluctance. A man and woman eating nearby stared at him from the time he approached Paul. Charlton could hear the question their expressions asked. "Why is that boy speaking to the master's bootlicker?" Charlton spoke a little louder than usual to ensure the onlookers this conversation came out of desperation.

"I know you said you don't know where my mother is and I believe you, but…" Charlton paused to see Paul's reaction. Paul nodded his head, so Charlton continued.

"Paul, I don't know what happened to her. Nobody knows or they won't say." Charlton looked up at the eavesdroppers, who lowered their heads. A boy looking for his mother made for a good reason to talk to Paul.

Paul stopped eating and stared at Charlton, sympathy in his eyes. Charlton detected a sense of guilt in the man. Did Paul have anything to do with the disappearance of his mother? He decided not to make an issue of it.

"You have to understand. I need my mother. She's the only one who cares about me. If I died tomorrow, the master would be happy but no one else would feel anything about it at all."

"What you want me to do? I don't know where your mama's at," Paul said. Charlton studied him. He looked sincere, though a little nervous. Charlton guessed that he made a mistake when he thought Paul had guilt, it looked more like worry of getting in trouble with the master.

"I know, but you can talk to the master. You can get him to talk," Charlton said. He eyed Paul who shook his head. Charlton persisted. "Paul, I have to know what happened." Charlton leaned closer to Paul and talked in a more hushed tone. "I think he's got her locked up somewhere, just like he did to me. I made the master mad and well, you see, if he locks up my mother, then he can get even with me, but that's not right. My mama didn't do anything wrong. I have to find out." Charlton stopped, silenced by Paul's raised hand.

"You don't know what you ask. Master'll whip me for asking about your mama."

"But, the master likes you!" Charlton said too loud. The eavesdropping couple snorted.

Paul snorted too. "You know nothing 'bout it. Master don't care 'bout whipping me. Look." Paul turned and lifted his shirt to reveal fewer whip marks than others, but some clear ones. Paul had not kept his job without some cost.

Paul faced Charlton again. Charlton said, "I think the master will talk to me though. He hates me and will want to see me beg. I think he'll like it."

Charlton paused to let Paul consider, but Paul started shaking his head. "I can't do it."

"Why not?"

"What if you wrong, then Master beat me just for asking?"

"He won't. When was the last time the master beat you?"

"Been a while."

"He couldn't get by without you." Paul still looked unsure. Charlton continued "All right, look, just don't ask him straight out. Tell him that I've been pestering you about where my mama is and I seem really upset. The master will get the idea that he can tell me to my face that my mama is locked up. I think that's one thing the master would love to see. He won't hit you when you bring it up."

"You say I should do that, but Master don't talk to me like none of that. He tell me what to do and I do it. You think we friends, we not friends."

Charlton paused. He did think Paul and the master got together and talked like he would to Ole Joe. Why did he think that? When Charlton gave it more thought he realized how foolish the idea seemed. As Charlton gazed at Paul who stared at the ground, he had no doubt of the sympathy Paul felt for him. Yet, Paul dished out whippings to his fellow slaves without mercy. Why did he seem to care so much for Charlton, a boy who had disrespected the master?

Using Paul's sympathy to his advantage, Charlton put his head in his hands and pretended to cry. He tried to keep the volume down, but the thought of his mother alone and caged brought real, fitful tears. He felt a heavy hand on his shoulder.

Paul whispered, "All right, all right I'll be asking Master the next time I can."

Charlton looked up from his hands. "You will?"

"Yeah, the next time I can."

"Thank you, Paul!" Charlton said and dared give Paul a hug around his massive neck. Paul froze, but then patted Charlton on the back. Charlton could tell Paul wanted nothing more than to get Charlton's arms off of him. He disengaged.

"Best be going to bed now, boy. You going to need your rest."

Charlton nodded his head, unable to speak out of gratitude and the deep sadness he still felt. He climbed into bed well before anyone else and sunk into the straw. Paul's offer eased his mind well enough that he fell into an easy sleep.

***

The next day Charlton awoke to the cowbell, rested and refreshed from the first good night's sleep he had had since the night before he wrote the words. He got his food to eat by himself again. In the field, he received the same constant attention and punishment he now expected.

Hours after the day's work began, he caught Paul out of the corner of his eye. Paul almost never came to the field unless he needed to whip someone for more than just the typical fieldwork mistakes. Paul signaled to a hired hand, walked over to him, and told him something.

The man nodded in agreement. "Henry get that boy there, the master want to see him."

The burly field hand that had grabbed Charlton on Belle's wedding day stood in front of him. "Come on." Charlton obeyed without protest.

Charlton walked over to Paul who nodded at him and gestured him to follow. Charlton felt an excited lightness in his step as they headed to the same clearing where he had met the master days earlier.

They walked in silence until Charlton spoke. "Are we going to see the master?"

"Yeah," Paul said.

"Did you ask him?"

"Yeah."

"Did he hit you?"

"No." Paul stopped walking and tilted his head toward Charlton with a small grin on his face. Charlton had never seen anything like a smile on Paul's face and guessed no one since his childhood had seen one either. He had encouraged Paul to do something he didn't think that he could, and so Paul considered it a gift. He hoped the master would now give him the gift of information.

"Come on, Master's waiting," Paul said, wiping the grin off his face and turning back to the path.

The path seemed to go on too long; Charlton wanted so much to finish walking. When they reached the clearing, the master sat on a rock with his boots stretched out before him, crossed at the ankles.

Chapter Fifteen

When the master saw Charlton step into the clearing, he folded his hands onto the back of his head, and a contemptuous smile spread over his face. "Come closer, boy. Don't be shy. Sit." The master gestured to a patch of grass in front of him. Charlton sat more unnerved than ever.

"So, you want to know what happened to your mother?" Charlton nodded unable to speak.

"She's dead," the master said, his smile only spreading. Charlton stared ahead, willing the turning back of time to when he hadn't heard this news.

Memories flooded his mind. His mother smiling over him when he tripped and telling him everything would be all right. The kindly face that held his head in her lap as she stroked his hair. The woman who ate every meal with him and never failed to bid him good night. Tears washed over his face; he could not stem their tide even as the master basked in the glow of his sorrow. "You *killed* her?" Charlton asked in a trembling whisper.

The master let out a laugh. "Oh, *never*. I've never killed one of my slaves. You know how much money I would lose to do that? No, *I* did not kill her. All I did was sell her to Mr. Beauregard. That dirty old man!" The master chuckled. "You see, he wouldn't do business with me. Not since the last time when one ran away after two weeks and well, Mr. Beauregard spent a lot of money to hire slave catchers just to bring back a dead negro."

Charlton wrestled tears out of his eyes. Anger and hatred at the master. Shock and sadness at the loss of his mother.

The master continued. "For you, this story only gets worse, boy, so listen closely. I must admit you got the best of me, but you leave it to your master to find a way to break you no matter what threats you make against me. I knew you had a mother on my plantation. I am well acquainted with your kin since I unwisely gave you to my daughter. How do I best the boy who tried to destroy my family, but could not be sold and could not be killed? Why, sell his mother! It was ingenious.

What do you have left here, boy? Nothing. I want you to remember that I am the master here, not some worthless negro boy!"

Charlton stared, not at, but through the master. He began to envision his future life, which only made the tears flow faster. The master relaxed again and continued his story.

"I invited Beauregard here and pointed out your mother who was laundering the clothes. He took a real shine to her, he did. I never understood it. To me, your people have always been unclean. God branded you with the color of dirt to mark you as unclean, but Mr. Beauregard still fathered lots of children among his negroes, and that's the truth."

Bewilderment struck Charlton. The master's words made no sense to him and this frightened Charlton because his mind worked unlike others. He absorbed Belle's lessons with little effort and could recall them months afterward. Yet, now his mind failed him. The master continued. "Like I said, the last time I sold him a negro, he ended up running away and then Beauregard had to hire a posse to go find him. They brought back a corpse." The master snapped his fingers. Charlton flinched. "That's right!" A smug grin spread across his face and he leaned closer to Charlton. "You know who that corpse was don't you, boy?"

Charlton shook his head, but he didn't want to hear the answer. The sense of foreboding struck him again. He had learned of his dear mother's death and yet his heart pounded in his chest at learning the identity of a long-dead slave. His body trembled against his will. The master noticed and allowed a long pause before speaking. "Why, I do believe it was your father. Isn't that right, Paul?"

Charlton's eyes snapped over to Paul who looked shocked. Their eyes met for only a moment, then Paul dropped his gaze to the ground. "Yeah, master, that's right."

The idea of continuing to live after hearing this left Charlton feeling cold. He wanted his next blink to end his life right then and there. What he dared never ask his mother, the master shoved into his head against his will. How could he continue; forced to work for a man who brought both his parents into death?

"Hey!" the master said. Charlton's head snapped back to the master. "I'm the master here, you look at me when I'm talking to you, boy!"

After taking time to regain his control, the master told the story he hadn't intended to tell. Charlton stared at him like the time he witnessed Ole Joe's trampling. He couldn't look away but dreaded everything he observed.

"Your father was a hard worker. I remember the overseer telling me so. He was small, but strong. You were born small like him; too small for my liking. I got rid of a child bigger than you before. Well, I wasn't going to let a runt your size stay here; I had to get rid of you too. Then my daughter, bless her heart, stepped in my way and I gave you to her. Not to own, mind you, but to take care of you. She cared for you like you was some kind of precious pet. Kind of turned my stomach, but a promise is a promise." The mention of Belle turned Charlton's stomach a little too.

"Your father knew you was a runt and he set his mind to protecting you. He had the nerve to strike poor Paul here. Oh, Paul could have crushed him 'neath his thumb. Instead he turned to me and told me what happened. I hated to lose Sam, but he had to go. Whether Paul could stand up for himself or not, rules are rules around here."

Bitter, angry tears rolled down Charlton's face. His father, Sam, went to his death for protecting his child. What else should he have done? If the master thought someone would steal Belle away and murder her, would he have done any less? And Paul had told on his father? Paul, who had shown glimmers of kindness, helped cause the loss of his father. He decided never to trust Paul again.

"Stop your sniveling, boy!" the master said. "You're pathetic crying over a long-dead negro. Your father went from a fair-minded plantation to a place where he was worked over by the whip all the day long. Bet he wished every day that he had behaved himself. He stole away in the middle of the night. He thought running away would do him good, but it didn't. He got chased down by dogs and men 'til they found him. When they did, he still had the fight in him. He broke the arm of their leader with a tree branch. They taught him the last lesson he would ever learn. They beat him until he was good and dead. Beauregard had them dump the body on the ground and the smell of his rotting flesh was all the other negroes needed to understand the consequences of running away. They finally buried him somewhere. But, Beauregard's negroes sure learned a lesson that day, let me tell you."

The master sat back, chuckling to himself and shaking his head as if in answer to some remembered harmless prank from his childhood. Charlton stared, speechless at the callous way the master treated the death and humiliation of a fellow human being; and not just any human being, but the father of the boy who listened to the story. The master's thick and pungent evil permeated all of Charlton's senses. Where the master remembered a dirty and unworthy creature getting what he deserved, Charlton heard for the first time the story of a brave and heroic man defending his newborn son from murder and rewarded for his loving act with losing his family and then his life. Charlton seized with a surge of hatred for the men who killed his father including the slave catchers, Mr. Beauregard, and most of all, the master who chuckled to himself at the memory.

Charlton kept his eyes fixed on the master trying to betray no emotion. The master took notice of Charlton and stopped chuckling. "Well, I didn't call you here to talk about your father. Your mother is the subject of our story today. Now I want you to listen closely to this story, and I want you to know just how no good your mother was.

"You may have noticed my anger the last time we talked. I do not tolerate such insolence in my negroes, and you thought you had me. After you left, the idea occurred to me. Your mother, of course, had to go too. She was the way to punish you. I keep my negro families together when I can. It makes you work harder and it keeps you from running. You were another problem. I wanted you to run away cause then I could have you hunted and if you happened to get killed in the process, then all the better for me. Even Belle understands a negro might get shot down when escaping, but no, you wanted to stay." Charlton's heart sank. For the briefest moment he blamed himself for his mother's death. She wouldn't have been sold had he not challenged the master. Yet, the master made the decision to sell her. He cast off his guilt and continued listening.

"Beauregard was willing to deal with me when he saw her. I got a reasonable price and he carted her off kicking and screaming. Oh, she created quite the scene. White and negro alike stopped and stared at her." Charlton thought with bitterness at all the slaves who denied knowing what happened to his mother.

"Beauregard's son just paid me a visit to tell me the story and that he won't have business with me no more. Can't say I blame him." Charlton tilted his head to one side and took on a quizzical face.

"Boy, you have no idea what you're asking for, but I'll tell you. Beauregard took a shine to her. The way his son say it, he took her again and again."

"Took her?" Charlton said more to himself than the master. He understood the word, but the master didn't say where Beauregard took her to again and again. Paul grunted and let out a couple of mumbled words. The master eyed Paul as a warning, but said nothing to him.

"Yes, I said took her. Beauregard beat your mother, tore off her clothes, pushed his manhood up inside her, and satisfied himself. She must've put up one hell of a fight too. His son heard her screaming for hours. Beauregard liked it when his women put up a fight." The master chuckled to himself again and stared into the distance.

Charlton's mind raced in a confusing blur trying to process all the master said. The women slaves had a great deal of modesty and always got out of their cabins fully clothed. Charlton had no idea what a naked woman looked like, but he knew what the master meant by Beauregard's manhood. He shuddered.

The master continued. "Now that old bastard is dead. I hope he had his fun." Charlton perked up at this news. Had his mother gotten revenge for the terror she endured? "You listen up closely, boy. You're a slave and you ain't going to be more than that your whole life. I see the way you're looking at me. You got the sin of pride in you. What Beauregard did, he had all rights to do. Your mother saw it differently. While Beauregard lay passed out as naked as the day he was born, your mother found a plank of wood and beat that sleeping, defenseless man. She hit him and hit him, screaming as she did so. His sons had to break down the door, as it was locked. When they got in there, Beauregard had no face to speak of. She had clean beat it right off of his body. When his son came in, he dropped his last meal on the floor. He tells me the blood was everywhere, but the head was nowhere." Charlton could not hold the tears back any longer. They poured out of his eyes. He hated Beauregard and reveled in his death. Yet the details of the hardship his mother endured plagued his thoughts.

"Do you know what a savage is, boy?" Charlton sat sobbing, unable to answer. "Answer me!" The words startled Charlton into a headshake.

The master relaxed again and crossed his feet in front of him. "Let me tell you then. A savage is a creature that looks human but is really an animal. That's what your mother was. She was a savage. Someone who had a hunger for spilled blood. That man *owned* her. He could have done what he did and worse. She had food. She had a roof over her head. She had clothing, well at least before he took them off her, and she had all those comforts of life from her master. How did she repay this kindness? With savagery.

"They did right on her when they strung her up and hung her for what she done. That savage got swift justice too. Not more than an hour after she done her deed, she was hanging from a rope," the master said. Charlton stopped crying and stared ahead of him again. He remembered all the master said, but he struggled to process it. Charlton carried on while she lay dead in the ground. He would have given anything to trade places with her.

The master leaned toward Charlton. "Now you listen, boy. I'm the master here. Don't you ever try and cross me like you did. I'm going to keep you here, but I'm going to make your life miserable. You probably noticed that they're giving you a hard time out in the fields. They're under my orders to keep that up for good. You want to stay here? You will suffer for that choice." The master bolted upright. "Paul? Paul, get over here!"

Paul rushed over. "Master?"

"Get this boy back to the fields. His break is over." The master did an about-face and didn't wait around to see if Paul obeyed his order. He walked away with brisk, proud steps.

Paul crept toward Charlton. As the lone witness to this exchange, only he knew about the cruelty that Charlton had faced.

Charlton could see Paul approach out of the corner of his eye, but instead of acknowledging him, Charlton kept his eyes trained on the master. He wanted to keep the torrent of emotions at bay, through sheer willpower, until the evil man could not hear him.

When the master had gone, his will cracked. Charlton folded at the waist and let his face come crashing down onto the ground. Wet, bitter tears splashed out of his eyes and he moaned. The ground around his face began to soften. He could feel the mud cake itself on his face. When it got hard to breathe, he flopped on his side and curled into a ball, trying to give himself comfort.

Not only would he never see his mother again, but he couldn't get the pain, torture, and humiliation she had endured out of his head. Of all the women on the plantation, his mother possessed the most modesty. To have her clothes torn from her, to have her body violated by a sick and disturbed man, transformed her into a violent savage. She had never struck Charlton, not once. Even after his most naughty behavior, she treated him with patience and reverence. Only the worst, most horrible experience could make her do what she did. Yet Charlton knew she acted to bring justice to the man who violated her rights. She gave

Beauregard the punishment he deserved and not just for what happened to her, but what happened to all the people he hurt. What did the white people do in response to this justice? They killed her. They strung her up like a common criminal and hanged her.

His body convulsed with rage and loss. Through his tears, Charlton noticed Paul had backed up as if the enormous man feared a skinny boy. That made Charlton laugh, and the laugh grew and grew into a hysterical howling. He laughed at all of life now; a lonely, disturbing farce that made Charlton long for death. His whole life he waited around for the people he loved to die. His father? He had lost his father to death before he had any awareness of him at all. Then, Ole Joe died. Then, Belle and her childlike innocence died when she married and now his dear mother lay dead in her grave. Charlton had no love, only pain and death.

He heard himself sobbing again. The laughter had died too. Unable to take the soul-crushing pain any more, his breath came to him in gasps, while his heart raced at a speed that could not sustain his life. He needed air to get into his lungs. He clawed at his chest with one hand while pulling at his hair with another.

Without warning, a fist closed around his shirt, lifted him, and a meaty palm swept across his face, fingers spread. The sting of the slap dulled Charlton's senses. His breath came back to him and his heart stopped racing.

Charlton stared into a haze. He allowed the pain of the sting to subside. When it did, he looked at Paul and said, "You hit me!"

"You're acting crazed. You needed me to hit you," Paul said in a measured tone.

The point could not be disputed, but Charlton hated Paul too. "Do you know what I didn't need? I didn't need you to tell the master that my father struck you when all he was doing was defending his son. He thought I was going to be killed you know!" Paul flinched and stared at Charlton with eyes agape.

"I… I…" Paul stammered.

Charlton turned his back on Paul and walked away. If Paul couldn't come up with anything to say, Charlton would not listen to him. He wanted to get back to the field and have the overseer abuse him so he could distract himself from the memories of what he had heard.

He made about twenty paces before Paul overtook him. "You don't knows what happened. Master, he lying. I didn't tell him nothing 'bout it."

"How did he know then? Huh?"

"I don't know. He just knows it. He didn't ask me or nothing, he just sees the mark on me and he sold your pappy the next day. You got to believe me."

"Why do you care if I believe you?"

"Cause Master done you wrong and I ain't done you wrong. I knows they don't like me in the quarters. I'm fine with that. I done some them not so good but I ain't done told Master 'bout your pappy."

Charlton looked into Paul's eyes and saw sincerity. "I don't know what to think. Just leave me alone. I want to get back to work, but I want to go by myself."

"I don't know. Master, he won't like that," Paul said.

"Fine, follow me then, but don't talk to me. I don't want to talk about anything."

Paul nodded and gave Charlton some distance on the way back to the fields. Charlton kept his thoughts with all the strength he could muster. While working, he didn't look up or around. The hired hands had trouble coming up with excuses for hitting him, because he performed so well, but they hit him a couple times anyway.

At dinner, he ate alone and then got into bed. His thoughts rushed at him as soon as his head hit the pillow of lumped straw. Tears flowed down his cheek and wet the straw. He knew he would get little sleep that night. He waited, then snuck out of the cabin and went straight to his book, but his thoughts disturbed him so much the words blurred. He tucked the book back in its hiding spot and stood. He walked down the paths he knew so well under a bright moon.

The walk turned into a run and the run turned into a sprint until he left the plantation altogether. Exhaustion overtook him though, and he realized he would never survive running like this. He had no food or water and all slaves knew about the patrollers that sometimes lurked outside the plantation. He stopped and headed home.

When he got back on the master's property, he dropped to the ground, put his hands behind his head, and stared at the moon and stars. He let his thoughts flood his head and stopped resisting them. Thinking of his mother and his father and all the suffering they endured brought bouts of moaning, crying, and cursing. When it became too much to bear, he resisted the thoughts again.

Instead, he focused on making a plan. How would he live his life without any loved ones? At first, nothing came to him. He stared at the stars and they shone, vanishing from existence for brief moments as he blinked his eyes. In an instant, he had his goal, but not a plan. He had to get revenge on the master for what the man had done to him and his family.

How to do it, though? Slaves had no power, the master had all of it. He needed to get power somehow. Only then could he destroy the master. He set his mind to the task, ignoring the long odds he faced.

Chapter Sixteen

October 1853

Rain poured down over the fields. The hired hands knew they had to stop work that day but waited until after a bolt of lightning struck in the distance to do so. Charlton heard their commands and obeyed.

Charlton had slogged through his life as he did today for the past four years since his mother died. He listened to the whites' commands and he followed them. No more did he let his mind wander during the work. He had endured unyielding punishment from the hired hands for so long that he didn't think before obeying. The slightest hesitation would earn him the whip; and yet now that he set his mind to hear a command and execute it without delay, the hired hands and the overseer had no excuse to hit him. They had not struck him in four months.

Notions like these did not occur to him during the day, though. He learned to put his mind to rest while working. Nights, however, brought him the opportunity to think, explore, read from the book Belle gave him, strengthen his body, and think of ways to get even with the master.

Concluding the end-of-the-workday activities, Charlton followed the command of the overseer and trudged along with the rest of the field hands through the downpour. He spoke to no one on the way, having learned long ago getting close to anyone meant condemning himself to pain when they went away and never came back. He couldn't take the hurt anymore and refused to get close to anyone else. Not that anyone offered.

The group reached the cabins and without a word to anyone, Charlton entered the men's cabin alone. He crawled up into his bunk and shut his eyes, almost wishing the rain hadn't come so he could occupy his mind working the fields. He tried to shut out the memories, but with nothing else to do, they came to him. He reflected on the last four years. Envy filled his heart as he thought about his fellow slaves. The situation on the plantation had changed: on rainy days like this and for supper, most of the slaves gathered in married friends' cabins. They had handmade tables and chairs or benches to sit on and talk. Their laughter and chattering made him long for Ole Joe, his mother, and Belle. He sat alone much of the time for his supper. Sometimes good weather had made eating outside popular, yet no one approached Charlton, and he couldn't bring himself to approach them. He thought about Paul too, but he had built a cabin for himself closer to the Big House and took his food there. The unstated rule around the plantation forbade all but Paul and the house slaves from getting that close to the Big House after work.

Charlton passed the time until dinner by talking to himself. He didn't like the sound of just talking without addressing anyone, so in moments like these, he addressed his mother.

"Mama, I'm so lonely. I don't know what to do. I don't want to be here. I don't want to be by myself. I want to know people. I want them to care about me. No, no, not as much as you did, but a little bit. How do I make friends when the master will have them killed as soon as he finds out?" Charlton stopped talking for a minute and stared at the ceiling.

"Mama? I think the hired hands and the overseer have stopped paying attention to me. Isn't that good? I do the right thing every time. I don't talk, but I always join the songs when they want us to sing. They don't even think to whip me about that because I always do what they tell me. I don't have to worry about that any more. Isn't that good?" The rain pattering on the roof gave him his only answer.

Tears flowed down Charlton's cheek. His mother would never respond to him again. He wanted to believe she heard him and though Belle told him about God and heaven, he believed in them no more than the fairy tales Belle read aloud.

His mind turned away from the spiritual, and he thought instead about his nights. Once he felt bold enough to venture outside after dark, he took almost every chance he could to escape the cabin while everyone else slept. At first, he took to reading the book Belle gave him. After reading it three times and memorizing parts of it, he turned to strengthening his body instead of his mind. He sprinted up and down paths. He climbed trees and hung off branches to pull himself back up. He did all this far from the slave quarters and the big house so no would hear him. Paul had the strongest body on the plantation, and although Charlton knew he would never get as strong as Paul, he felt fit and capable.

He worked his body with one goal in mind; he wanted to fight back against the master. Although no idea for revenge seemed all that feasible, he kept coming back to trying to take over the plantation. One day, he would tear the whip from the white hands, turn it around, and see how they liked it. He would use his strength to choke the hired hands one by one until he beat every one of them, including the overseer. He grinned thinking about how the master would look when he saw Charlton striding into his home with no one to help him.

***

The tobacco harvest season drew closer to the end, which meant less work around the plantation. As much as the hired hands looked for odd jobs for the slaves to do, the slaves tried to avoid them. After harvesting, the curing process occupied some of their time while tending to the subsistence crops took on new vigor. The slaves who came out later than the others after the cowbell rang could find themselves with little to do. Charlton knew the hired hands would notice his absence, so he didn't try to avoid the work.

On one of the final days of the harvest season, Charlton heard a buzz rising up from the other field workers. He took his mind off his work for a moment and looked over to where black and white heads stared. He spotted the master and then saw two men in tan suits, all walking toward the field work. They wore hats that matched the master's Sunday best. Both looked sturdy and tall, but one had a white beard and white hair while the other was clean-shaven and younger. The older man leaned back, his rounded midsection protruding from his waistband, and surveyed the men in the field, seeming to avoid looking at the women. His eyes darted from one black man to the next.

The younger man had a spring in his step that reminded Charlton of himself when Belle came calling. His hat covered long, black hair and his eyes scanned over the field as he spoke out of the side of his mouth to the master. His dark eyes found Charlton. He squinted for a moment, pointed at him, and mouthed the word, "There!"

A rising excitement came up from Charlton's heart, rose through his throat, and exploded out of the top of his head. Though somewhat fearful, Charlton thought that these men might save him from his cursed existence. The questions piled up in his head. *Who are these* men? Am I about to leave this place? Is the master going to sell me to them?*

The master shook his head in response. The older man peered at Charlton and nodded. The younger man and the master bantered with one another. The older man took his place in the conversation too, siding with the younger man.

Charlton's resentment of the master grew. *Why does he have to keep me here? If he let me leave with these men, I wouldn't tell them that I can read. He's got to know I only meant that for Mr. Beauregard. He'd be safe and he'd get rid of me.* He turned back to his work.

The buzz died down a little, then grew again. The men approached. Charlton heard an unfamiliar voice say, "Call him out, Mr. Armand, sir. I see no reason why you object so."

"Oh very well, sir. Overseer, fetch Charlton so these gentlemen can see him," the master said. Pretending not to hear him, Charlton kept to his work.

"Come on, boy" the overseer said yanking Charlton from the plant he tended and pushing him to the three men.

Given the master relented on calling him over, it didn't appear he worried about the chance that Charlton would carry out the threat of telling the men he could read.

Charlton stopped a respectful distance in front of the men. Chest out, he leveled his chin, kept himself stiff as a board, and stared forward with his gaze below their sight line. He knew this pose set off his strength.

Charlton could tell he had impressed both men. The older man nodded. The young man looked Charlton up and down and then circled around him, checking him from all angles.

"Yes, sir, this one will do. What do you think, Father?"

"We want this one, Mr. Armand. This one and another," said the older man.

"I don't know if we want to part with him. I just don't know," said the master.

The father shuffled his feet. "We'll give you fifteen percent more for him. What do you say?"

The master glared at Charlton, his eyes contemptuous. Charlton understood the master wanted to keep him to have control over him. He figured the master did not realize the hired hands and overseer had stopped whipping Charlton. The master continued to stare into the distance, not answering the question.

"Come on William, we have some other plantations to see," the father said. He turned to go and walked back in the direction of the master's house. The master hesitated and looked reluctant to leave.

At long last, he spoke. "Now hold on there, Mr. Zutter. You have yourself a deal. The harvest will be over in a week. You may have Charlton then."

Charlton's heart soared though he forced himself not to reveal it. He figured the slightest trace of happiness from him could make the master reconsider. He would spend one more week with the master, then he could leave behind the place that gave him all his painful memories. He corrected himself right after the thought occurred to him. All his memories formed on this plantation. He had never gone too far from it.

Their business with him concluded, Charlton went back to the field, consumed the rest of the day with thoughts of his improved position. After four years of misery and failing to find a way to get revenge, he could leave behind his suffering and let go of the need for revenge.

Despite his happiness, he still wondered why the master insisted on making the men wait a week and why the men accepted this condition too. If they had bought Charlton, they should get to take him right away. What if he injured himself? The harvest could make any slaves' fingers and hands hurt and grow inflexible by the time it ended. His new masters shouldn't have risked such a fate.

***

At the end of the day, the other field hands asked Charlton what happened. He welcomed their questions and told his story as men and women gathered around him. A lighthearted ease took hold as he spoke with them. With only a week left, he didn't worry about getting too close to any of them.

In the course of the conversation, Charlton learned the men had also bought Phillip, the boy who delivered the water. Philip would not answer anyone though. His parents had taken him inside their cabin, refusing everyone's questions. Charlton kept his distance, respecting their loss.

Chapter Seventeen

The cowbell rang through the quarters, waking Charlton to the day he would leave the plantation behind. He packed his possessions, which consisted of the clothes he had accumulated and his utensils, plates, bowls, and cup. He looked at his meager pile of belongings and laughed at the pathetic nature of his life. He figured Belle had returned to the plantation on visits, but he never saw her as he had not approached the Big House in all that time. With nothing left to keep him here, he longed to leave with the Zutters.

Breakfast went as it always did with Charlton sitting alone. He couldn't help looking over at Phillip and his family. His mother and father huddled over him. None of them had a bite of breakfast. Phillip's father used hushed tones but spoke throughout as if trying to impart a lifetime's worth of wisdom on his son. His mother didn't speak. She cried from time to time, letting out a wail, and then clutched Phillip to her. His father would pause, wait for her to release her son, and then continue speaking.

Before long, the hired hands yelled to the slaves to move into the fields. Two of them went to Charlton and Phillip and told them they had to stay. Charlton nodded and kept eating while Phillip ignored the man who approached him. Phillip's father hugged his son and got up to leave, but his mother pulled Phillip to her and pleaded with the hired hand. "Please, sir, let me stay with my boy, I'll go with him. Those kindly Zutters, they be glad to buy me too. I work real hard for them. Real hard."

The hired hand shook his head. "That's not part of the deal, Bess. Your master tell us your boy going with them Zutters and that all we know we got to do. Now, you best be moving out to the fields. You don't want to catch no whipping, do you?"

She looked from her son to his father to the hired hand. Tears coursed down her face. Instead of heeding the hired hand's advice, Bess seized her son and held him close. "You can't take him! You just can't! A boy belong with his mama."

The hired hand looked around and caught sight of two more hired hands approaching. "Now, Bess, you know that ain't going to work. Look, these men and me, if we got to tear him away from you, well, that's just what we're going to do. Why don't you be a nice girl and let him go and we forget about this whole nasty business?"

Philip's father sided with the hired hand. "Bess, we get along to the fields now."

Bess shook her head and tried to stifle her sobs. She clutched Phillip tighter.

A moment passed with no change. The hired hand turned to the other white men and nodded. Philip's father got out of their way to give them clear access to his wife and son. All three white men headed for Bess. She looked up at them, then buried her eyes in Phillip's shirt.

Despite the odds against her, Bess held on to Phillip for much longer than Charlton imagined possible. Yet in the end, the men had pried her arms off her son and pulled her back. She screamed and fought, kicking one of them between the legs. He staggered out of the scuffle howling in pain, while the other two pinned Bess to the ground. Charlton couldn't take the scene anymore and stood, half ready to intervene on Bess's behalf. Instead, he looked at Phillip's father and saw the man crouched on the ground and running his hands through his hair.

All at once, Bess stopped wailing as if exhausted. The two men got off her, but each kept grip of an arm and yanked her up to stand. She did not look at her son, but kept her eyes down. Phillip continued to call to his mother until the man who got kicked rushed him and said, "Shut your mouth!"

Phillip stifled his crying.

"Take the bitch down to Paul for a whipping and don't let him out of your sight while he's doing it. I know he goes easy on them when our backs are turned," the hired hand said. The man walked over to Phillip's father. "Off to the fields." The slave hesitated. "Now!" Phillip's father took off running in the direction of the fields.

Charlton shifted his gaze over to Bess and her captors. They walked along at a slow pace. He wondered whether either of them could have expected no less than what Bess did when a loving mother faced losing her child. Charlton said under his breath, "It's the master that deserves the whipping."

The man who got kicked stayed behind with Charlton and Phillip. He didn't pay much attention to them, though. He paced back and forth, letting out deep, loud breaths.

Phillip cried by himself, sitting on the ground with his arms resting on his knees and his face stuck between his arms. Charlton didn't know the first thing about comforting someone, but he tried. He put his hand on Phillip's back and said, "It'll be all right. You'll see." Phillip nodded, but kept crying. Charlton withdrew his hand and sat on the ground near Phillip with his eye toward the path from the fields.

At last he saw William Zutter stride toward the quarters on the path. Charlton smiled. The white man had a casual and carefree bounce in his step. He trusted his new master.

Charlton turned to Philip, who had stopped crying, but kept the same position. Charlton tapped him on the shoulder and said, "He's coming."

Phillip raised his head and showed Charlton his bloodshot eyes. He had brought his second pair of overalls out of his parents' cabin and scooped it up as a sort of pocket for his other possessions. Charlton did the same.

When the younger Zutter reached them, he said, "Hello." Charlton and Phillip looked at one another, unsure of how to respond to a white man who greeted them. Charlton nodded and Phillip copied his gesture.

"All right, ready to go?" William asked.

Philip nodded and Charlton said, "Yes, Master, we're ready."

William Zutter eyed their possessions. "I'm sure you don't need those. Why don't you leave them here? You'll use ours." Charlton hesitated, then put his possessions on the ground. Philip didn't move.

"You, um, might want to put them where you can find them again. We only have you for a couple months," William said.

"Master?" Charlton asked. "Didn't you buy us?"

"Didn't anyone tell you? We're only renting your services. We can't keep you. Your master arranged for us to use your services while there's less to do. He'll need you back."

As Charlton frowned, Phillip beamed. Charlton resigned himself to having no choice. He gathered his belongings and put them back where he stored his things in the cabin. The distance to the cabin felt endless as disappointment twisted his stomach into a knot. The escape from his prison would not last.

By the time he returned to see the smiling face of young master William, the knot in his stomach untied. At least his life would improve for a short while. Perhaps he could convince the Zutters that they should buy him. He would work hard and learn whatever trade they practiced. Once they knew he could do the job, they would have no choice but to try and buy him from the master.

The young man grinned from ear to ear when Charlton emerged. "I have to tell you. I am so excited about this. My father and I run a ship-building shop in Charleston. We have had great success there. Many of the ships around here must be imported. That means they are made in one place and must be brought down to Charleston. So, the customers don't get much say in how they want their ship to look. We knew that and came down from Massachusetts a year ago to start giving the people of Charleston the chance to order their ships, tell us what they want, and even come by the shop and watch them get built. The people there love us." William Zutter gestured for them to follow when Philip emerged. He walked toward the house where Charlton assumed a carriage waited in the driveway.

"Could you remind me of your names?" Master Zutter asked as they walked.

"Yes, Master. I'm Charlton and he's Phillip."

"You speak very well for a slave. Do you have formal education?"

"No, master. Our master let his daughter take care of me when I was a child, and she taught me a lot."

William nodded. "I see. Do you feel like you've had a good master?" the young man asked in a conversational tone.

"Yeah, Master," Phillip said without thinking about the question. Charlton wrinkled his face. He liked William, but didn't like the question. Charlton had asked himself a lot whether any good slave master could exist. He decided not a single good slave master had ever lived who didn't release all their slaves as soon as they bought them.

"Charlton, you didn't answer," William Zutter said.

"Master, can I not answer?" Charlton said.

"Of course," said the young master.

They remained silent until they got into the carriage, which was in slight disrepair. A white driver sat above and in front of a compartment with four seats. The young master seated himself on one side while Charlton and Phillip sat side by side on the other. Both slaves looked around.

Charlton wanted to take in everything from this new experience. He had seen plenty of carriages in his time, but he had never gone in one. The inside had thin-cushioned bench seats that faced one another. Dark brown walls, ceiling, and floorboards surrounded them with glassless windows in the back and sides. William Zutter said, "Go ahead, driver," and the old driver snapped the reigns. The horses picked up speed as they drove down the familiar paths Charlton had seen all his life until they broke free from the plantation.

Phillip pushed himself to the window and peered out at the passing countryside. Charlton caught the young man checking his pocket and pulling out paper. Charlton decided to risk asking him about them. "Master, what are those?"

"These? They're your rental papers. If we get stopped along the way, I'll have to show them to prove that I am legally moving you two. If I don't have these papers, they'll think you've been stolen."

He paused, considered, and then spoke. "Phillip, Charlton, I need to speak with you." Phillip and Charlton snapped their focus to him. "I talked it over with my father, and we do not want you to call us "master." I would like you to call me William and my father you will call Mr. Zutter. I'm a mere apprentice to my father and so my father should have more respect, but neither of us wants to be called master. We come from the state of Massachusetts where we do not have slavery and, to be honest, we do not care for slavery at all. The only reason we're even renting you two is so we can finish some orders we have waiting. All the hired help we could find refused to do temporary work. You will be paid what we can give you. Do you understand?"

"Yes, William," Charlton said. He felt honored by an arrangement where he could enjoy living like any white man for a short time. Instead of getting punished, he would get paid for working hard. "You and your father are very kind," he added. William offered his hand and he shook it.

William turned his attention to Phillip, who had not said anything, but stared wide-eyed at William.

"Phillip, do you understand what I told you?" William said.

"No, Master. My mama say I got to call all white folk Master. She say I get a whipping if I don't."

"We have no whips, so how can we whip you?"

"Master, I don' know. Mayhaps, Master whip me when I'm back."

"Why don't you call us 'sir?' Is that all right with you?"

"Yeah, Master. Uh, sir."

"Then, it's settled," William said.

The long ride passed with heavy conversation between William and Charlton. William spoke about the business and about his family. The youngest of twelve children, William had watched all seven of his sisters and four brothers marry and move out of the home. He asked about Charlton's family, but Charlton skipped the details, only mentioning the sale of his father and his mother and when they happened. William did not press for more information, but kept his eyes downcast as he listened.

Charlton felt a light-hearted admiration for William. He could have had complete power over the slaves in his carriage, yet he treated them as equals.

When they approached the city of Charleston, the conversation died down. The cityscape stood out, distinct from anything Charlton had ever seen. Instead of trees heading into the horizon, building after building filled his sight. One stretch of road presented houses of all different colors, like the rainbow Charlton had seen in the sky.

Charlton and Phillip glued themselves to their windows, but also crossed their gazes over to the other side to see the rest. William leaned back and watched with a big, relaxed grin, seeming to enjoy watching them take in the sights.

Charlton's smile faded when he saw a scene somewhat familiar to him. Dark-skinned people lined a stage in front of a concrete building with the single word "MART" above an archway. He stared and saw the men, women, and children who all wore cuffs around their ankles and wrists with heavy chains linking the cuffs. His eyes drew into sharp focus on the wrists of a little girl. Although she didn't wear them on her ankles, the cuffs on her wrists had dug into her skin and blood crowded the flat edge of the metal. She looked up at a woman next to her. The woman ignored her.

Down the row, a white man shouted out numbers, and two other white men grabbed a black man whom they thrust forward onto the stage. The scene disappeared as they forced the slave to turn around and show his body from every side.

Charlton's eyes sprang back to William who had replaced his grin with a frown. Before Charlton gathered the nerve to ask what he had witnessed, William told him. "That's a slave mart where they're having an auction. The men are making bids on the slaves. The man who gives the largest bid will win the auction, pay his bid, and he will own the slave. Father and I find this distasteful. We've come down here and seen families torn apart. It's very sad."

CHARLTON'S GROUND

Charlton nodded. A giant knot formed in his throat, making speech impossible.

The carriage turned left, revealing the ocean. Charlton stared with wonder, having never seen so much water in all his life. Ahead of them, a tiny fortress stuck out in the middle of the water. Charlton stared at both the building and ocean until they retreated from sight.

"That building is a fort. I think it's Fort Sumner or Fort Sumter. No one's been out there for some time, but if anyone ever attacks Charleston from the sea. They'll be ready for them," William said.

The carriage continued, hugging the coast. Before Charlton rose another structure he had never seen before then. The road turned into an arch connecting two parts of the land over where the ocean came back into view. "What is that, William?" Charlton pointed to the structure.

"You mean the bridge? You've never seen a bridge?" Charlton shook his head. "Of course not, you've always lived on your master's plantation. The city of Charleston is surrounded on three sides by water. The bridge helps people get from the city to the west and the north without going all the way around. We'll go across the bridge tonight. We live in Mount Pleasant. We're renting a house over there." William peered out the window just as the carriage slowed. "And here we are."

The carriage stopped in front of a wide building with big doors and holes between the boards that made up the walls. A sign on the door read in white paint, "Zutter's Shipbuilding."

Chapter Eighteen

William exited the carriage and beckoned for Charlton and Phillip to enter the enormous building. They climbed out and followed him through the door. Mr. Zutter talked with a customer—a gentleman with a goatee and wearing a sharp suit in a makeshift office. The office had a large table stacked with papers and three simple chairs, and a large window allowed a view of the entire office. Mr. Zutter caught his son's eye and held up his hand to keep William out.

Charlton and Phillip took the opportunity to look around. Aside from the walls that made up the office, the shop had no other dividers. It looked smaller on the inside, but the massive, unfinished ship hull in the middle of the room made it look smaller. Throughout the building, hooks and shelves took random places on the walls.

Some of Belle's books had pictures with ships, but Charlton had never seen one in person. He walked around the ship hull to study it from all angles trying to memorize the shape of the boards and the equipment used to construct the ship. He wanted to do well in the job, not only because he would earn his own money, but also because he wanted to impress the Zutters in the hopes they would offer the master a lot of money to buy him.

William's father had moved since Charlton last looked over at him. Now Mr. Zutter and the gentleman kept their eyes focused on the table. Mr. Zutter held a pencil over a paper as the gentleman peered at the drawing. Charlton had never seen a man of advanced age move with such grace and skill. The customer spoke and pointed as Mr. Zutter guided his hand over the indicated space. The gentleman studied the change and nodded.

Charlton sized up Mr. Zutter as sharp and skilled. The gentleman had looked skeptical when they first saw him. Toward the end of the exchange, the gentleman and Mr. Zutter both stepped back from the paper and looked it over. A grin spread across the customer's face. He clapped Mr. Zutter on the back. They talked some more and then shook hands.

They left the office chatting about their new deal. This time Mr. Zutter called his son over. The father introduced his son and they greeted one another. Following more chattering, before the gentleman left without paying Phillip or Charlton any heed.

Father and son strode over to Phillip and Charlton, who snapped to attention. "At ease," Mr. Zutter said when he saw them. The slaves looked at each other, then back at Mr. Zutter.

"You two look frightened, but I suppose I can understand why," Mr. Zutter said. He offered his hand to Charlton, who hesitated, and then shook it. Phillip looked unsure of what to do, but followed Charlton's lead with less certainty.

"I trust my son has explained the arrangements to you," Mr. Zutter said, but continued to explain them anyway. "You will refer to me as Mr. Zutter. I don't go in for the master title. We will pay you for your work, but only what we can afford, and since we are already paying your master, we will unfortunately have to take that into account when figuring out your rate. William and I run our shipbuilding operation like we run our lives: in a scheduled and orderly manner. You will find us fair and just. The harder you work, the more you get paid. I'm sure you've experienced the lash. We do not use it here. You may search and look all you want, but you will not find a whip in this building or our home. If the pay is not enough to make you work hard, then I'm afraid I will have to send you back to your master early, but there will be no punishment beyond that.

"Ah, yes, I must discuss the living arrangements. We have a room for you in our house. Every day we take a carriage home for the night. You will be on that carriage and you will ride that same carriage coming back in the morning. We do not work Sunday. Sunday is a time for worship. We insist you attend church service, though our church keeps the white folk separate from the negro folk. You will find the negro preacher to be both enlightening and comforting."

Mr. Zutter reached into his waistcoat pocket and pulled out a silver pocket watch. "It's three o'clock. We have two hours and a half of work left. William, you will show them the rudiments of our art. Our new deal is good news, but puts all the more pressure on us. We have not a moment to lose."

"Yes, father, of course," William said.

Mr. Zutter nodded at Charlton and Phillip and then went back into his office. William showed Charlton and Phillip around the building, indicating supply stocks, tools, and applications. Before he could talk about techniques, Charlton interrupted him.

"Can I write down what you're telling us?" Charlton said.

"Ah, yes, good idea. Wait, hold on, you can read and write?"

Charlton cursed himself for asking the question. "Uh… Please, sir, don't tell anyone. The law says we're not supposed to read and, I…"

William laughed. "Don't worry about me telling anyone. I think it's admirable you learned to read under your circumstances. Your secret's safe with me—and it's William, please."

Charlton's heart calmed. "Thank you, William."

William shrugged. "Unfortunately, I can't let you write down anything in the shop. That door can open at any time. If you're seen writing, well, there could be trouble, but when we go home tonight, you will be free to write whatever you like. I'll help you. Is that agreeable to you?"

"Yes, thank you."

William explained and showed them what to do. Charlton would do the tasks requiring more strength and skill, while they would use Phillip and his small size to do the jobs which required little hands in tight places. Despite the large number of instructions to remember, Charlton absorbed it with such little effort he wondered if he even needed to write it down.

When the end of the day arrived, Mr. Zutter emerged from the office and interrupted the two while Charlton planed wood planks and Phillip sanded them. "Come along everyone. We must retire for the evening." William instructed them to put the tools next to the planks so they could pick up on the work again the next morning.

Though the same carriage came to pick them up, a different, younger man sat in the driver's seat. Everyone went in and to Charlton's surprise, Mr. Zutter and William thought nothing of sitting next to Phillip and Charlton.

William and Charlton talked all the way back to the house in an easy and natural way. William talked about the ride arrangements and about his family and his ambition to inherit the shipbuilding operation when his father retired. His father smiled at William, then returned his gaze to the passing scenery. Charlton asked questions about William, which he answered without hesitation. Phillip said nothing.

The carriage stopped in front of a faded blue house less than half the size of the master's house. It had a covered porch, two levels, and windows all around it. A yard of patchwork grass surrounded the house and, although small by plantation's standard, it extended far more than the houses in the city of Charleston, which Charlton thought stood almost on top of one another.

They stepped off of the carriage and William invited them into the house while Mr. Zutter took his time. Once inside, Charlton heard two women chatting and laughing in the back of the house. "That would be Mother and one of the neighbors, probably Mrs. Herndon. My mother is a delightful woman, always full of joy and very good with others. Come on, let me show you around the house."

He showed them all around except for the kitchen, where he decided not to interrupt his mother's social call. Off the foyer to the left, they entered the study, which had books lining several shelves, end tables, chairs, and a couch. Behind that, they went through an archway into the dining room. A fine, polished table with six cushioned chairs surrounding it struck Charlton as beautiful. The door to the right would have led them to the kitchen and pantry. Instead, they backtracked to the foyer and went through the door on the right, which led to a sitting room with sofas, chairs, and a fireplace.

The staircase led to the second floor hallway and three bedrooms. William only showed Charlton and Phillip their room. Charlton could not believe his eyes when he saw it. It had two beds with mattresses, pillows, sheets, and blankets. Curtains hung in each of the two windows. After sleeping in bunk beds all his life, when he didn't sleep on the floor of the toolshed, Charlton felt honored by the Zutters' kindness. Even Phillip beamed at the new accommodations. Earlier, Charlton had thought Phillip might do a bad job on purpose so he could get sent back to his mother, but he didn't think it would happen now.

Charlton felt a longing to crawl into the bed, get under the blanket, and rest his head on the pillow. He wanted to experience the feeling more than he wanted to sleep in it. He couldn't wait for nighttime to come, so he could sleep in a bed like Belle, the master, and every other white person did each night.

Yet, he thought about the other firsts coming to him, including eating at a table on a real chair. He would also read and write with William. This time, he wouldn't have to disguise that he knew how to do it or need to see by the light of the moon. William had acted surprised, but not upset when he discovered Charlton could read. In all respects, except for the different church service, Charlton had escaped into a white person's world. He only had two months, but he knew he would make the best of his time.

William spoke, taking Charlton out of his thoughts. "I think it's time to introduce you to Mother."

By the time they arrived downstairs, the guest had left. William's mother wore a plain dress and wore her gray hair in a bun on the top of her head. She had her back turned to them, chopping vegetables. William stepped through the doorway with heavy footfalls to announce his presence. Charlton and Phillip stayed back and waited.

"Hello, Mother," William said.

"Why hello, my son!" She came over to the doorway and gave him a hug, then peeked over his shoulder at Charlton and Phillip. "And who do we have here?"

William gave way to her so she could step into the sitting room. "This is Charlton and this is Phillip," he said, gesturing to them.

Charlton bowed when he heard his name and Phillip did the same.

"Welcome to our home," Mrs. Zutter said. "Please make yourself comfortable, while I finish dinner."

"You are very kind ma'am," Charlton said.

"It's a pleasure. It won't be long now. I'll be right out." She smiled and returned to the kitchen.

Charlton's shoulder flinched when Mr. Zutter spoke behind him, "Excuse me," he said and scooted around Charlton and William in through the open kitchen door. He dropped the formality when speaking with his wife, his voice sounding eager to get her approval on his new customer and to tell her about the design of the ship. Charlton peeked inside and saw he had picked up a knife to help with chopping. Charlton felt a pang of longing in his stomach when he remembered he wanted to have this with Belle.

After a moment of observation, William asked Charlton, "How about we go to the study and get started on that writing?"

"Shouldn't we help?" Charlton asked.

"With dinner? No. My parents do this much of the time and never accept my help. Besides there's no room to help. Come on." William gestured toward the foyer and they entered the study where they pulled two wooden chairs over to a desk with a quill, ink well, and paper.

William wrote down much of what he knew about ship building. Not just in words, but also in pictures. He had a graceful drawing style just like his father's and it helped ease Charlton's learning. William moved to the side and let Charlton take the notes as he talked. A pang of embarrassment hit Charlton as he tried to manipulate the quill. He kept feeling the urge to press too hard as he would write with a stick in the dirt. The technique of acquiring ink in the dry pen also puzzled him. Yet with practice, Charlton figured out how to use the pen and his muscles unclenched.

William had patience when Charlton asked him to repeat information. Charlton thought back to his days of first learning how to work the fields. No one, not white or black, showed the level of patience William practiced. When Charlton asked William to repeat himself, he would say something like, "Yes, this is quite complicated."

Charlton relished having dinner in a way he had never before experienced. Instead of eating outside or on the cabin floor with his plate propped on his lap, Charlton sat a table with his utensils, plate, and cup at a place setting. He felt so much freer. Although the enormity of the change caused apprehension, he soon relaxed. Phillip remained wide eyed and stared at the Zutters, trying to mimic their actions.

Not long into the meal, Mrs. Zutter asked, "Charlton, I'm very interested to hear about your life. Do you mind sharing? Forgive me, but I have never had the opportunity to speak to a slave so extensively before."

"I can tell you, but I don't want to upset anyone," Charlton said.

"I assure you it's quite all right with us. We are a family of what are called 'abolitionists.' We have great sympathy for your people. We would be honored to hear what you have to say."

Charlton's eyes turned misty, then he told his story. He told of his relationship with Belle, backtracked to how he lost his father, and continued on to Ole Joe, including how he died. He left out a description of Ole Joe's body, but spoke about the master's lecture to the slaves.

The family continued to eat throughout the story, but each of them looked disturbed. He looked up at Mrs. Zutter and saw watery eyes. She dried them with her napkin when she caught him looking and gave him an embarrassed smile. "You poor dear," she said, breaking the silence following the end of this story. She looked above Charlton's head. "Oh my, will you just look at the time!" Everyone turned to the clock, though neither Charlton nor Phillip could read the time off it. "Charlton, dear, you have a knack for storytelling."

"Thank you, ma'am," Charlton said.

"But, we've been talking these past two hours. It's time for us to retire."

"Mother, Charlton and I must continue our instruction," William said.

"That's simply out of the question. I will not abide by my son and our guests missing the rest they so dearly need. You have a long day ahead of you."

William did not protest further. They dismissed themselves from the table.

"Thank you for dinner," Charlton said.

"Think nothing of it. Now off to bed with the lot of you," she said.

William bid the pair good night. Charlton spoke to Phillip before either of them crawled into bed. "Phillip, did you know I could read and write?"

"No."

"Did you know I'm not supposed to know how?"

"No."

"Well, I'm not. Could you make sure you don't tell anyone?"

"All right, Charlton."

With that, Phillip and Charlton went straight away to sleep in their warm, comfortable beds. Charlton thought he would savor the comfort and the sense of belonging he hadn't had since his mother was alive, but he could not resist the lull of his heavy eyelids. He dozed off to sleep thinking about how much he would miss this new life when it ended.

Chapter Nineteen

The four of them piled out of the carriage and headed into the house. After five days with the Zutters, Charlton found himself in a routine. After tireless work, he returned to the house and proceed to the study where he would engage with William in conversation. Phillip would follow them inside and listen from a chair or from the couch. If Mrs. Zutter had a guest, Mr. Zutter would sit in a chair in the study and listen to Charlton and William or go straight to his wife, if she didn't have one someone to entertain.

Today, William and Charlton spoke without Mr. Zutter present. When they had settled in the room, Charlton spoke first, "So, what are abolitionists?"

William's eyes brightened. "A very good question. An abolitionist wants to abolish or get rid of slavery. We're not interested in discussing it with people who want to change our minds. We hate slavery and don't think your people should be held in bondage. Do you remember when I told you that we took you and Phillip because the hired hands were so expensive?"

"Yeah."

"Well, that was only part of the reason. We wanted you here to get to know you. That's why we ask you about your lives so much. The more we can understand your perspective, the more we can write to our fellow abolitionists up North to figure out how to stop slavery. Your story will help us plead your case."

"Plead our case? What do you mean?"

"To use your story of loss to get the people in the North to understand why slavery is so bad, so they'll fight to end it. We asked them not to reveal our names or yours. If you must go back to your master, you could get into a lot of trouble if we didn't do that.

"Charlton, you don't know what it's like in the North. Don't believe that whites in the North like your people. Many of them hate you just as much as the slave masters in the South. My family sees all people as equals under the eyes of God, but most do not, even in the North. Time and again we've heard in our old hometown slavery must not end because your people would head north and take away 'our jobs' and marry 'our women.' Don't think for one minute they would accept you unless they have a change of heart. That's why your story is so important to us. My parents and I feel that you have not told us your whole story. You've held back, have you not?"

Shame crept into Charlton's heart. He had meant to spare their feelings, but had he known that they needed his story to help end slavery he would have shared it without hesitation. "Yes," he said, "but only to keep from upsetting your family."

"Your story is yours to tell or not. I'm not commanding you to share it as I never command you to do anything, but I ask that you consider it. Will you?"

"I'll tell it."

The topic of conversation turned to the work in the shop. Mrs. Zutter interrupted them by calling them to dinner. After a moment of silent eating, William spoke. "Charlton, can we hear your story?"

All eyes turned to Charlton. He nodded and began with his birth, the story of the small baby, and how Belle had saved him. He struggled to keep his emotions at bay throughout the story of his father's sale, Belle's scheme, and how the master had forbade her from speaking with him. After years of deadening his heart to the grim reality of his past, he even spoke about Belle's marriage, his confinement, the conversation with the master about his mother's ordeal, and the brutal treatment that followed without a single tear.

The Zutters and Phillip listened in silence. Mrs. Zutter's tears flowed and William put down his fork. Charlton spared the details on his mother's rape to protect Phillip, but the boy sat open-mouthed at the rest of Charlton's mother's story, no doubt thinking of his own mother. The Zutters all began with expressions of solemn pity for Charlton, but as he continued the father and son turned angry.

"That scoundrel!" Mr. Zutter said. Charlton flinched at the words. Mr. Zutter turned to his wife, "I told you that man was a no account lout! I have a good mind to throttle him!" Mrs. Zutter picked up her napkin, dabbed at her eyes, and said nothing.

Charlton hesitated, unsure of what to say.

William broke the silence. "Father, are we well enough off to purchase Charlton?"

Mr. Zutter turned to his son and let the rage drip from his face. "Purchase him? Do you think that devil would sell his prize? He clearly wants Charlton in his hold so he can torture him. That man takes an ill pleasure in that sort of business. Do you think he would give that up?"

William paused for a moment. "I think he would for the right price. Men like him can always be bought off."

William's father leaned back in his chair, and stroked his beard. "Yes, they can, can't they?" He stared off into space for a long while. Mr. Zutter brought the legs of his chair back to the floor and then turned to Charlton. "Charlton?"

"Yes, Mr. Zutter?" Charlton said.

"I must ask you. I know you will likely provide a most obvious answer; but I must ask you anyway. Would you like us to purchase you? All your stories point to yes, but if you have any ties to that place which would keep you there, I must know."

An old exhilaration rose in Charlton's chest that he had only felt when Belle would kiss his cheek or his mama would hold him in her arms. He had hope again; a hope that he would have meaning in his life and maybe even find happiness. He tried to speak, but couldn't utter a word through his tightening throat. At long last he spoke at the cost of tears from his eyes. "I don't want to go back. I want to stay with you."

"Then, it's settled. I will try to purchase you. You are the hardest worker I've ever seen and I include myself and my son in that." Charlton glanced at William to note any disappointment that his father has said this, but William only nodded and smiled. Mr. Zutter turned to Phillip, "Would you like us to try and purchase you too, my boy?"

Phillip stared wide eyed at Mr. Zutter. "Please, sir, I want to stay with my mama."

Mr. Zutter's eyes softened. "Very well. I understand." He turned back to Charlton. "The progress you've made and the techniques you've learned are truly astonishing. I would pry you from that scoundrel no matter how you worked, but you must never feel you have wronged us in the price I will pay because I swear under the watch of the Almighty that no price is too great for the justice that will be delivered when I give you your freedom."

Tears welled up in Charlton's eyes, and he let them flow. He wanted to thank the whole Zutter family, but speech would not come to him. Longing for this day and appreciation for the Zutters' sacrifice kept him from forming the words. He could only nod.

Mrs. Zutter rose from her seat and strode over to Charlton. He managed a weak, grateful smile as she approached him. She took her napkin, dried his tears, and said, "Deary, don't worry. If we have anything to say about it, your torment is over." Charlton held back no more. He wept for their kindness and the chance to release himself from the master.

***

As Charlton drifted off to sleep that night, he went over in his mind all that had taken place during dinner. He loved the Zutters, maybe even the siblings he hadn't met because William's mother and father had raised them too. His nagging mind kept returning to the master, but he kept pushing away the obvious: the master's need to punish Charlton would keep him from accepting any price the Zutters offered.

Chapter Twenty

Charlton awoke on his first Sunday with the Zutters ready to experience church. He and Phillip wore the new clothing the Zutters had bought for them. After breakfast, they all headed out of the house, walking to the center of town. Soon enough, they approached the church. It stood tall and white with ornate doors, a steeple with a cross mounted on top, and paneled windows all around.

Two buildings stood near the church. Several yards from the door, the Zutters faced Charlton and Phillip. Mr. and Mrs. Zutter stayed silent while William spoke. "The church won't let you in here. You two will have to go to the smaller building over there." William pointed to the most run-down and distant building. "It's just past the preacher's family home. Do you see it? I'm sorry that…"

Charlton stopped him. "It's all right, we'll go there. Come on Phillip." Charlton eyed a young white couple who watched the exchange with a look of disgust. He cast his eyes down to appear subservient and nudged Phillip in the direction of the other church.

Phillip and Charlton walked the rest of the way to the rundown building. The door squeaked when Charlton pulled it open. Even with windows lining the walls, their grimy and cobwebbed state kept the inside of the building dark and unsettling. Dirt and grime covered the floor as well. Plain, untreated boards with multiple legs formed extended benches. Several slaves sat at these benches and stared at Charlton and Phillip, making Charlton feel cold and judged. He took Phillip by the wrist and tugged him over to an empty bench. Charlton sat and put his head down in supplication, waiting for the eyes to peel off him before he looked up again.

"What we suppose to do, Charlton?" Phillip said in a raspy whisper.

"Sit here, I guess. I've never been to church before."

Phillip shrugged and stared forward. Charlton noticed two boards that crossed each other nailed to the front wall. He searched his memory for anything Belle had said about church service, but realized she had not said much.

He let his mind drift, thinking about the cross. He decided that the up-and-down board meant white people who ended up in a higher position than the other board which symbolized black people. He shook his head at the odd thought while an older black man rose from the bench in the first row and stood in front of the cross.

The man looked older than Ole Joe when he died, but not so grizzled, perhaps not knowing a hard day of work in all his days. When he spoke, his voice rang clear, deep, and commanding. His eyes darted back and forth over the crowd and he looked down on them as if his presence offered more than they deserved.

"Blessed is the Negro!" the preacher said with a sweep of his hands over the crowd. "Blessed is the Negro! God has sent down onto the Negro, two blessings. One is the most glorious Jesus Christ, may his name be sacred in the hearts of all men. God did not stop with one gift though. No! To the Negro he has sent us the white man to protect us and provide for us. We are forever indebted to God's grace. We pay back our debt to God by obeying the word and commandment of the white man. This is His will and His wish for us."

Charlton's body trembled while thoughts flooded him. *How can this black man speak these evil words? Does he know that the white man's no better than any of us and he's lying? Or does he actually believe this? He talks like the master.*

The preacher went on with little variation in his tone or message. With intolerable repetitions, he spoke of the Negro inferiority to the white man, how they must always listen to and obey the white man, and how God gave the black man to the white man to watch over him and care for him. Charlton looked at the faces around him and found encouragement. The men and women stared up at the preacher with blank expressions on their faces. No one nodded their heads, but some slept.

Charlton decided to stop listening altogether and instead he thought about what freedom would mean to him. Maybe he would find Belle and take her away from the South. He decided running away with her would offer him the perfect revenge against the master. Then, the preacher said something that snapped Charlton's attention back onto him. "Many of you know that I am a free Negro, but I envy your place under the rule of a white man. I will walk in the footsteps that my Lord has picked for me, but I do wish that I could take my place beside you. I would not have to find the sustenance of life, it would be provided for me. I would not have to find myself shelter, my master would provide the roof. I would not have to find a job, my master would give me work. You are all truly blessed."

Charlton felt the words forming in his throat and although he tried to choke them back, they came forth all the same. "I'll trade you!"

The preacher who had tilted his head to the roof snapped it back down again at Charlton's words. "Who said that? Stand up. Tell me your name and your master's name!"

Charlton felt like doing just that. He would stare down this fraud and tell him his name, but he worried about what this would do to the Zutters' reputation. He couldn't betray them by giving them away. Instead, with the whole congregation looking around puzzled, he pretended to do the same. He exhaled as he saw Phillip also look around.

The preacher scanned the room. His mouth twitched and his hands shook. "You must tell me! Tell me! I need to know!" the preacher said. He repeated the lines over and over until the congregation started to snicker among themselves. After a while, the preacher demanded silence and continued his rant. Charlton pledged to himself that he would keep quiet in the future.

***

"Now go in peace and seek out your masters," the preacher said.

The Zutters and the white congregants had not yet left their building, so Charlton and Phillip followed the other slaves who sat in the shade of trees while they waited. Charlton and Phillip found a tree apart from the rest and leaned up against the trunk.

After a couple of minutes, Phillip said, "Charlton? Why you say that?"

"I couldn't help it. It just came out. Did you believe that man's words in there?"

"I don't know."

"Don't believe them."

"Why not, Charlton?"

"Because the white man is no better than us. I don't know if there's a god or not, but I do know that if there is a god and he's good, then he would never have put us below the white man. We're just as good as any white man. What do you think of the master?"

"I don't know. He seem fine to me, then you tell us that story and he seem like a bad man. He shouldn't've killed your mama like that."

"He killed my father too, Phillip, and he almost killed my spirit."

"What a spirit?"

"A spirit is what makes us get up in the morning. It's what makes us sing out in the fields. It's what makes us love our mamas and you know, without it we would be no better than one of them animals the master keeps, with no joy or love. That's how I've been living because of the master."

"Was that church man lying, Charlton?"

"No. No, he wasn't lying. He believes what he says. He was telling you the truth that he saw. He ain't lying, but he's wrong. Don't you ever forget that, Phillip."

"I won't," Phillip said as the white congregation left their church. The other slaves lined up at a respectful distance. Charlton and Phillip did the same as the others.

Mr. Zutter nodded his head to Charlton and Phillip and they followed the family. When they had put distance between the other white families, William hung back to walk with Charlton. "What did you think, Charlton?"

"It was fine. Just fine," Charlton said. He didn't want to lie to William, but he didn't want William to think him ungrateful. William nodded and they walked in silence the rest of the way home.

At the start of the path to the front door, Mr. and Mrs. Zutter stopped. "William?" Mr. Zutter said.

"Yes, Father?"

"Please see Charlton and Phillip inside, your mother and I will be calling on the Andersons now to lunch with them. I'm sorry, but this was just an invitation for us."

"Very well, Father. We understand, please give my best to the Andersons."

Mr. Zutter nodded, offered Mrs. Zutter his arm, and they continued down the street. William hurried for the door, opened it, and held it wide for Charlton and Phillip. "Come on in, you two!" Charlton laughed and dashed inside.

William dove into the overstuffed chair, draped his long legs over an arm, and buried the back of his head in the other, staring up at the ceiling. Charlton sat on another chair. Phillip chose to sit on the floor with his back against a wall.

"Oh, I was ever so glad to get out of there!" William said.

Charlton marveled at the young man. He looked more relaxed than he had ever seen anyone. Even Ole Joe himself couldn't have taken relaxation to this level. William seemed to ooze into the chair.

"You don't like Church?" Charlton said.

"Oh, I believe in God and all that, but I don't like sitting there, that's all and don't act like you liked it, Charlton. I bet you hated every minute of it."

"That's not true!" Charlton said. William shot his head up, giving Charlton a puzzled look. "I hated every second of it!"

William laughed and said, "You can't fool me, you rascal!" Charlton burst out laughing and William did the same. Charlton glanced over at Phillip and noticed he hadn't even cracked a smile.

When the laughter subsided, William said, "I'm hungry. How about you two?"

Charlton and Phillip agreed.

William put together a spread of vegetables, fruits, and bread, which refreshed Charlton after his time in the dirty slave church. Charlton felt like the grime and dust in his lungs cleared out of him.

After lunch William asked, "So, what's it like in there?"

"In where?" Charlton asked.

"In your church. I've never been there."

Charlton explained all that had happened. William reacted as Charlton expected. He frowned when he heard about the state of the building and the emotional state of the congregation, furled his brow when he heard of the ranting of the preacher, laughed when he heard of Charlton's comment, and kept a straight face when Charlton described how he kept his identity concealed.

When Charlton finished, William said, "Charlton, I consider you a friend and I am very glad that you have come to stay with us, but aside from all that, you have done me a great service."

"*I* did *you* a service?" Charlton said.

William raised his hand to interject. "I know what you're going to say, but please, just hear me out. You've opened my eyes. You came here and showed me that a man of dark skin color is no different than a white man. Then you showed me what it's like to live in slavery. You moved everyone to tears with your story. How many more are like you? All those people in that church who barely care whether they live or die. How many of them got that way by having their parents torn from them as children? How many felt the sting of the whip for the smallest mistake? How many lose their lives and the law does nothing to save them?

"One of the best abolitionists in the North is a man named William Lloyd Garrison. He and his followers want to put an end to slavery and they will not stand down until it's completely abolished. My family has always been abolitionist, but we never joined them at their meetings because, well, we didn't want to upset our neighbors or our customers. If I ever get back to the North, though, I'm going to join their organization. You've given me the courage to do that."

Tears formed in Charlton's eyes, perplexed how this young man could live in the land of white hatred and come out more pure on the other side.

At the end of lunch, Charlton didn't know what to do with the rest of the day off. William had an idea though. "Would you two like to try swimming?"

"Is that trying to float in the water?" Charlton asked.

"There's more to it than that."

"We can do that?" Charlton gestured between himself and Phillip.

"I don't see why not." William said.

"Then, yes, let's go swimming."

William looked over at Phillip and forced Charlton's glance that way too. Phillip looked frightened. "Phillip, do you not want to try swimming?"

"No, sir, I'm scared to go out there."

"Well, I can't leave you here alone. Come out with us and stay on the beach, all right?"

"Yes, sir."

William produced strange, tight outfits that covered their trunks, half of their arms, and half of their legs. They put their other clothes over them for the walk to the beach. After seeing the sandy shore, William kept walking wherever they found white people. Charlton looked across the water and saw the outlines of ships stationed by the city of Charleston. The sun shone off the white sand, which forced him to squint his eyes whenever he looked down at the ground.

When they found a deserted spot, Phillip sat down in the grass behind the line of sand and stared at Charlton and William. Charlton followed William's lead and stripped off his outer clothes. William ran into the sea, splashing as he went and dove into the water. When he came back up again, he said, "Come on in, Charlton!"

Charlton laughed and went to the edge of the water, allowing it to lap onto his toes. The water felt cold, but not unpleasant. After he got used to the temperature, he crept forward, getting his feet wet. William grinned watching Charlton slink in further until he stood waist-high in the water. The current tugged at his legs. He decided to face the beach to see if his balance would improve. Without warning William said, "Hold your breath." Charlton just managed to hold his next breath when he felt an unexpected force push him down in the water. The world disappeared and garbled noise replaced the sounds of the sea. All at once, the force fell off him and he rose out of the water.

William had scooted back and deeper in the water, laughing at Charlton. "You think that was funny?" Charlton asked with a grin.

"Oh yes, that was *really* funny," William said.

"Just wait 'til I do that to you."

"Go ahead, but you're going to have to come get me."

"Oh, I will. Just hold still."

"Holding steady!"

Already soaked and shivering, Charlton didn't mind sinking into the water more to get William, but as he got closer, he felt himself losing the ground. When the water reached his chin and still William bobbed far from him, he backed up a bit and said, "Now I *know* you're not that much taller than me. How you doing that?"

"I'm swimming."

Charlton focused on William and saw him moving his arms in a sweeping motion.

"You *got* to teach me that."

"I will, but you have to promise not to dunk me in the water. Well, not this time at least."

Charlton laughed. "If you teach me that, I won't dunk you ever."

"It's a deal."

William taught Charlton how to tread water, float on his back, and even how to "swim like a dog" Charlton felt at home in the water. He peered out to the shore and saw Phillip playing with the sand. Charlton wished he would come out to join them and experience something new.

When the sun began to set, the two friends came out of the water. Charlton's fingers felt spongy. William shook the water off himself and put on his outer clothing. Charlton did the same. Phillip followed the two of them, and they went back to the house.

Charlton couldn't stop smiling. He liked swimming. When he thought about it, he realized the ocean disguised his race. Even with his head above water, he could swim far enough from shore that a white passerby might not notice the color of his skin.

"William?" Charlton said as they took the road to the house.

"Yes?"

"Can we go back next Sunday?"

"Of course," William said with a smile.

Chapter Twenty-One

December 1853

On the last Sunday before the rental time expired, Charlton woke in his soft bed and looked over at Phillip who still slept. "I don't want to leave," he said aloud.

Fearing he would wake Phillip, used his inner voice.

If the master still hates me, he'd want to be rid of me. So, he'd sell me to the Zutters, but he might hate me so much that he won't let them buy me. How can the master hurt me if I'm with them? Is money more important to him than his hate?

After church and lunch, Charlton moved to put on the swimming suit he had worn every Sunday; even as the days got colder and the times they had for swimming got shorter. "Charlton, I have to talk to you first." William said. "Phillip, will you excuse us?"

"Yes, sir." Phillip went to the study and sat crossed legged in the corner.

William shut the door for privacy and turned to face Charlton, a serious look on his face. "Charlton, I know Phillip has a mother at home and he probably longs to see her. He shouldn't know what I have to tell you."

"What is it?"

"Do you remember what I told you about William Lloyd Garrison, the abolitionist?"

"Yes. You said he lived in the North and he's on our side."

"He is. He's a very good man and I wrote him."

"You did? What about?"

"Well, I wrote about you, Charlton. He wants to help you escape."

"But, you and Mr. Zutter...aren't you going to buy me from the master?"

"Charlton, you and I both know that man won't sell you for any price. We're still going to try, but we need a backup plan. Wait right here." William pushed through the door into the study. Charlton heard a drawer open and close and when William came back he had an envelope, two sheets of paper, and a small, metal disc.

"What's this?" Charlton asked. A lump the size of an egg formed in his throat.

"These are all yours." He slid the papers and object over to Charlton. The envelope read, "Mr. Mortimer Zutter," with their address in Mount Pleasant, but the return address read, "Mr. Lawrence Simon."

Charlton looked up at William. "That doesn't look like 'Garrison.'"

"Yes, that's my father's friend. We couldn't write to Mr. Garrison directly. The authorities would've been suspicious and opened it. Mr. Simon is our middle man."

Charlton nodded. He had trouble reading the penmanship, having only learned to read cursive when he arrived at the Zutters.

Dear Master William,

I was grateful to receive your touching letter about your friend, Charlton. Unfortunately, cases like Charlton's are all too common. I can barely imagine the fortitude and strength that could have carried him through the tragedies that have befallen him. The evils of slavery will create many more orphans, widows, widowers, and childless mothers, until our country is forever rid of this scourge.

I shared Charlton's story with the Society and we are very interested in seeing him delivered to freedom. Unfortunately, Charlton is so deep inside the South; this journey to freedom will be fraught with danger and insecurity. We would encourage you to deliver him yourself, but the rental agreement you described will not allow you to get past the first patroller. You must encourage Charlton to escape using the Underground Railroad.

The Underground Railroad is a series of stations that stretch across the slave states and beyond, until we can deliver an escaped slave to one of our own member's houses in the North. Enclosed is a map. Based on the location of the Armand plantation in eastern South Carolina, we have the good fortune of locating a station only a mere two and a half miles from his plantation.

You have said patrollers are not allowed on the Armand plantation. While this is good, they will have free rein much of the way. Be sure to tell Charlton to avoid being seen by any white people as he journeys to the station. If they find him, he will be severely punished, if not killed.

If he reaches the station, he will need to stay there and take care of himself until a conductor finds him, which unfortunately may be weeks or even months. I have been informed that the station is an abandoned barn. He may feed himself on errant crop, but water will be more difficult to come by.

I also suggest you give Charlton a compass. If he gets lost or separated from the conductor, he will need it to find his own way. I must also ask that Charlton not bring this letter or map back to the plantation. I am taking a large risk in sending you this, so I ask that you destroy both the map and letter as soon as Charlton has the map committed to memory. If either is found, the station will be burned to the ground by sunset of that day and patrollers will keep watch of it at all times.

I am afraid that this is as much as I can do for your friend. This is a dangerous business, but one I hope you will continue to pursue in as safe a manner as possible. Please take care of yourself and give Charlton my best.

Respectfully yours,

William Lloyd Garrison

A tear trickled down Charlton's cheek and onto the letter.

"How did this world make this man?" Charlton said.

William looked at him with watery eyes. "I don't know, Charlton. He doesn't even know you, like I do, but yet, I don't know. It's like he was there with you every step of the way."

Charlton feared he would weep with gratitude for both Mr. Garrison and William unless he distracted himself. He picked up the disc. "Is this the compass?"

"Oh, yes. Let me show you how it works." Charlton handed the compass over to William, who clicked it open. "You press the latch up here and pull it open at the seam. The arrow points north all the time. Look, I can turn the compass any which way, and it always points north." William demonstrated and although the arrow fidgeted somewhat, it always pointed in the same direction.

"You'll have to use it if you get separated on the Underground Railroad from the conductor."

"But, I'll just stay with them."

"No, Charlton. You must not think that way. If patrollers come, everyone will have to scatter and remain hidden until the patrollers go away. It will be easy to get lost. This is very, very dangerous. If you get caught trying to escape, your master will have the law on his side and can kill you. You need this compass and you're going to take it. Understand?" William stared him down, daring Charlton to deny him.

"Yes," Charlton said.

"Excellent, now pay close attention. This may save your life. You will want the arrow to point to 'N' and to travel that way as much as you can. 'N' is for 'North' and that's the opposite of what?"

"South," Charlton said.

"Yes, where slavery is allowed and where you will never be free as long as your master elects to keep you a slave. If the arrow points north with the compass in front of you, then you are headed to freedom. Now, I want you to try it."

"I know how to use it."

"Then, it won't hurt to show me. Where is North?"

Charlton took the compass and saw it pointing in front of him. HH He pointed forward.

"Good now, turn a little," William said.

Charlton turned to another wall and pointed to his left.

"One more time."

Charlton faced another wall and pointed behind him.

"Good." William sat with a thump into the chair. "You're headstrong, Charlton, and I admire you for it, but I just have to know you'll get to safety."

Charlton saw the pleading in William eyes. Filled with deep affection for his friend, a young, white man, Charlton walked around the table and embraced William. William returned the embrace and held it up for some time before William clapped Charlton on the back, pulled away, and said, "What are we waiting for? There's an ocean to swim in and we're wasting time."

Charlton and William changed into their swimming suits and took Phillip with them to the beach. With the air colder than the water, it felt more welcoming than ever. Charlton ran into the water, dived under the surface, and only came up for air when his lungs burned. Treading water, he looked toward the shore and marveled at how far he had swum. In the short time since he started swimming, he felt powerful and full of life. He wouldn't miss swimming as much as he would miss

William and his family, but swimming in the ocean brought him more enjoyment than anything else he had ever done, and he would miss it. *But if the master sells me to the Zutters, then…*

He shook his head and his hair sprayed water around him. He would not ruin this last time in the water with thoughts about how he might never get back into it.

***

Two days later, Charlton stood next to the carriage in the Zutter's yard. Mrs. Zutter kissed both Charlton and Phillip on their foreheads and embraced them. Mr. Zutter planned to negotiate with the master for Charlton, so he prepared to go along with them.

Charlton looked at is fellow travelers and saw a mix of emotions. Phillip smiled with excitement at returning to his mother. Mr. Zutter took on a serious, confident expression. William's eyes moved from side to side and he twisted his head to peer out the four windows: every odd sound, from the carriage wheel or rock kicked up by horse hooves, startled him. Charlton's muscles tightened throughout the trip, causing him to ache all over his body. William and Charlton tried to converse, but they couldn't keep it up for long.

When they arrived at the plantation, a sense of foreboding kept Charlton's heart in a vice. He would never leave here. He knew the master would not sell him for any price, and the escape would never work. He would belong to the master forever.

The plantation greeted him with sickening familiarity. As Charlton looked at all the old sites, he felt the urge to jump out of the carriage and run, but he couldn't do it. The sight of the Big House burned at his eyes, a house he had never entered, but which held his enemy. The wind blew in his ears as it kicked up dust from the trackway where he had stared down death and woke up alive with a broken body. The smell of the tobacco crops tickled his nose and made him queasy. Would he ever smell cedar wood shavings again?

The carriage pulled up at the end of the trackway. Phillip got out first, then Charlton. The driver helped Mr. Zutter exit the coach.

At first, the door to the house remained closed. Charlton hoped the master had died as they approached. All hope was dashed when the door opened and the master came out. He looked older than Charlton remembered. "You're late, Mr. Zutter," the master said when he made eye contact with William's father. He ignored the rest of the party. "I thought I might have to report you to the constable for running off with my negroes."

Charlton looked at Mr. Zutter, who glared at the master. He almost hoped Mr. Zutter's rage would make him run over to the master and begin throttling him, but that would get him arrested. Instead, Mr. Zutter said, "If I could have a word with you, Mr. Armand."

The master seemed somewhat surprised by this request, but granted it. The master turned around and spoke to one of the house slaves, no doubt requesting that he retrieve Paul to lead Charlton and Phillip back to where they needed to go. Mr. Zutter nodded his goodbye to Charlton and Phillip and followed the master into the house. He motioned for William to stay back, so he could negotiate alone.

When the master and Mr. Zutter disappeared into the house, William looked around and rested his eyes on the driver who had wandered down the trackway, then he turned to Charlton and said, "I hate your master." He pushed his thumb in the direction of the house. "I'm sorry Charlton, but I don't see a deal. You must escape. Wait as long as you think you need, but you must escape. There is no way you can stay here with that man."

"I know, William. In case I never see you again, I wanted to tell you that you've been a true friend. I can't tell you how much I 'preciate all you've done. There's just no way to repay you. You're a good man, William, the best I've ever met."

They stood in silence for a moment and looked up as they heard footsteps approaching on the trackway. Paul's robust body ambled up to where the three of them stood.

"That's Paul. He's going to take me away. Goodbye, William. I won't forget you," Charlton said.

"Be strong, Charlton."

Paul approached without a greeting, and with his hand beckoned the two slaves. Charlton paused, then strode over to Paul and Phillip. Charlton looked back one last time to see William staring back at him.

Chapter Twenty-Two

Paul didn't bother bringing Charlton back to the fields: the carriage ride had taken long enough that the workday neared its end. Charlton almost wished he could have worked. He entered the cabin, put his compass and money in the folds of his extra set of clothes, and went back outside with his possessions to wait for notice that the master had sold him. Sitting and waiting gnawed at him. With each passing moment, he lost more hope. He knew a miracle could happen and William could come into view to tell him that the master sold him and ended his torture. But as time passed and the sun set, Charlton knew that the parties had reached no deal. He would remain the master's slave with escape as the only option.

Almost worse, he would never see the Zutters again. He had never experienced such kindness and his friendship with William meant so much to him. It gave him hope and strength. He reflected on how he went to the Zutters with a mind clouded in despair, but they reached in, cleared away the darkness and renewed him. Even if he never saw them again, he vowed not to return to the despair in which they found him.

He waited some more with his possessions by his side, refusing to move from the spot where he could see William walking down the path. Phillip had already stashed his things in his family's cabin and had raced off to hand out water to the slaves in the field.

When he heard the voices coming down the path and he recognized his fellow slaves returning from the fields, he gave up his last bit of hope and returned his possessions to his bunk. A new overseer tagged along behind them and Charlton's eyes focused on him. He looked just as cruel as the last one. The overseer made sure the slaves settled down with their meals, then wandered off to his own supper. The overseer remained the only white man that Charlton saw that evening. He had no doubt that after a short and frustrating attempt at negotiation with the master, the master had booted both Mr. Zutter and William off his property and told them never to return.

Charlton received a few nods of acknowledgment when some of

his fellow slaves saw him. A terrible loneliness crept over him. After his friendship with William, how could he bear not having a friend on the plantation? Charlton regretted never putting himself forward to develop new bonds in the slave camp. As he got up for the supper line he thought about the Underground Railroad station.

Escape to freedom would mean finding the abolitionists. They would accept him without question and get him started in the North as a free man. He felt certain he would get back into shipbuilding. It would be the answer to many of his dreams, if he made it there. If he didn't, he would get caught and killed. *How different would getting killed be from being here? I could live as old as Ole Joe and still end up no more than another dead slave. I want to get even with the master, but what if I never can?*

***

The days passed and Charlton fell back into his old work. He spent his evenings dining alone and the mid-day break by himself. He listened to the talk around him though, and found out that disease had struck the plantation.

Though Charlton thought the master lacked any tenderness, he understood that he did what he could to keep his slaves healthy. He made his slaves bathe with soap in the creek every Sunday when they only worked a half day and he made them wipe their teeth every night to avoid tooth rot. If a slave got sick, he would order Peter, who had some healing skills, out of the fields to care for the sick slave with his herbs. If that didn't work and some hope remained, the master would bring in a white doctor.

The sickness started with Ben. He came down with a coughing jag and a few days later, the cough turned into a fit. When blood started flying out of his mouth one day in the field, the hired hands ordered Peter out of the field to take care of Ben. Ben's pregnant wife Betty soon joined her husband in Peter's care. She started coughing soon after Ben and then coughed up blood too. The rumors indicated that no matter what Peter tried, it didn't work. Ben died in his sleep one day and four days later Betty died.

The news of Betty's death intensified everyone's fear in the camp. Every cough meant a quick retreat from whoever coughed. Even the overseer's whip couldn't convince them to tend parts of the field where someone coughed.

Between the disease and loneliness, Charlton knew he had only one recourse. One afternoon when the day's sky showed a crisp blue without a trace of clouds Charlton resolved to go to the Railroad station in the light of the night's moon.

***

Charlton crawled into bed that night and waited until the other men slept, then slipped out of the cabin with his possessions held tight in his extra clothes. The map he had studied at the Zutters house lay clear in his mind, so well memorized that he could close his eyes and see every feature of the map including the wrinkles in the paper. He stared forward outside the door and made out, though overgrown with weeds, the path he needed to take between two of the thickest trees on the plantation.

In the bright moonlight, Charlton could see the compass needle and it drove his legs forward. When the compass needle fell under shadow, he followed the path under his feet. His whole body leaned forward and he let the rhythm of his driving muscles propel him. In what seemed like no time, he noticed the barn looming before him.

Painted a now-faded red, the barn stood out in the moonlight. The roof had caved in on one side, but it looked sturdy on the other. Garrison had also written true about the crops. Charlton found stalks of corn, wheat, and, closer to the ground, beans scattered near the barn.

Charlton got to the barn and walked through a door under the caved portion. He stayed under the open portion so he could avoid places in shadow to keep from stepping on something dangerous and sat in a grassy spot away from the rotting roof boards. Leaning his back against the wall, he wrapped his arms around his knees and began waiting.

Charlton would not get any sleep and he knew it. He tried to settle himself by lying down on the grass to at least rest. Instead, his heart beat too fast to make any sleep possible. Fear of getting caught and the reaction to his absence in the morning kept him from relaxing.

The thoughts moving through his head kept pulling at him, and he decided to stop fighting them. He thought first of William Lloyd Garrison and then his friend William. His thoughts wandered to Belle, and his mother, and then his father. He couldn't help thinking about his parents. Their spirits wouldn't let him go. He couldn't avenge their suffering by running away from the plantation.

The master's actions killed them both and Charlton needed to pay him back. He needed the master to suffer, to feel the pain of losing something or someone important to him. The master needed the lesson that evil will get repaid. Charlton couldn't rely on God or one of his fellow slaves to teach that lesson. He had to do it.

Charlton searched his memories of the master to find his greatest love that he could destroy. *The mistress? No, Ole Joe told me they didn't love each other. Belle? I could never harm her and even if I could, nothing's worse for her than her marriage and the master likes that. Robert? I'll never get near him.*

A jolt shot up Charlton's spine when he realized the answer. The master loved nothing more than his plantation. He could find a way to destroy it. Maybe he could set it on fire and burn it to the ground. Perhaps he could find a way to stop the ground from growing crops.

Though he knew he had no plan, he got up, gathered his possessions and headed back to the plantation. He needed to go back right away, before the sun rose, so he sprinted, keeping his possessions tight in the sack so they wouldn't jangle and alert patrollers. The landscape rushed past him. Despite the precautions, the utensils clanked against themselves. If patrollers lurked, they would catch him.

Charlton's luck held out. As the trees by the men's cabin came into view, he slowed and looked up to the sky, which had brightened somewhat. He exhaled in a sigh of relief. If his idea had come to him a little latter, he would have gotten caught out of the cabin after hours or had to stay at the station with his parents forever unavenged.

He spotted a shape weaving in and out of shadows, but approaching him. He squinted and made out the hulking shape of Paul. The man strode the rest of the way to him.

"Paul, what are you doing here?" Charlton said.

Paul shook off his question. "I don't know what you doing out here, but you best go back to your bunk now."

With a nod of appreciation, Charlton went back into the cabin and into his bed. Exhaustion drove him into a short sleep before the cowbell rang echoes in his head. He rose to face a hard day of work on his mind and body, but after that, he would have the thrill of a plot to consider.

Chapter Twenty-Three

May 1854

Charlton stood in line for his supper and heard the cough as soon as everyone else did. The slaves surrounding the one who coughed all pushed their way backward or forward to give the cougher room. Charlton kept his eye on the poor man who looked sheepish as his eyes darted from the man behind him and the woman in front of him. The damage had already happened though. Charlton recognized the cougher as Jacob and he decided to avoid him for a few days.

Charlton sat by himself and ate as he thought about the time that passed since he got back. He feared the disease, called the consumption, as much as all the others. Disease had killed several more slaves and even Charlton worried about his life. Five months had passed since he returned to the plantation from the Underground Railroad station, and he had not yet figured out how to destroy the plantation, but he wanted to live to enact his plan.

With no one to speak to as he ate, Charlton looked over the clearing to study the way people acted with each other. Jacob sat alone, abandoned by his friends. The groups of slaves that stuck together kept more distance between each other than usual. Charlton stared back down at his food and thought about the events of the past few months.

Next, Phillip's mother came down with a cough. The hired hands took nothing for granted and ordered her to see Peter. Despite not caring for anyone else after Betty died, Peter had not returned to the fields. Soon after Bess went to see him, everyone knew for sure that Peter had the disease too. Peter died two weeks later and two weeks after that, Phillip's mother died. Phillip's father tried to take care of his son, but the coughing had started with the father already and he died three weeks later.

Charlton's heart grew heavy thinking about the events. He counted Phillip as dead already. He hadn't seen him in a while. Hester, a young slave, had carried the water to the fields since Charlton last saw him. She couldn't perform the job and the field hands suffered for it, but still

Phillip did not come back.

***

Charlton gasped when he saw Phillip hauling the water buckets down the slope to the tobacco fields again. He kept his gaze on the crops while his ears listened for Phillip's breathing as he approached. Charlton heard no coughing, only sniffling.

"Want water?" Phillip asked in an almost inaudible voice.

Charlton looked up from his work and tried to make eye contact with Phillip, but he wouldn't look at Charlton. "Phillip, I'm so glad to see you. I thought you got sick." He dipped the ladle into the bucket and drank the water.

Phillip shook his head, "Master say I get y'all sick if I come with the water, but I never coughed. Mama and Pappy..." Phillip's voice trailed off into crying. He picked up the buckets and hurried off before Charlton could say another word.

***

Charlton lay awake in his bunk on a cloudy night. He couldn't keep Phillip off his mind. For days Phillip had stuck to his job delivering water to the fields, but he walked with a slump and a vacant expression. Even the men who joked about him went easy on him as he went through the motions of his job. He refused to speak to Charlton or anyone else.

Once again, Charlton tried to think of what he could say to bring comfort to Phillip, but even though they shared losing both their parents, Phillip had lost both of his at once and couldn't blame anyone for their loss. Charlton never knew his father and he could blame the master for the deaths of his parents and drive himself forward through the pull of revenge.

Charlton had another reason why he knew he could not allow himself to speak to Phillip. The lure of Phillip's cabin kept him restless. *Phillip's cabin would make my life so much better. I could get out at night easy and I could hide my compass, money, and my book. But is it right to want to talk to him so I can move into his cabin?*

***

Charlton worked in the fields and heard the sounds of Phillip dragging himself toward him. A compelling thought entered Charlton's awareness. He could teach children like Phillip what he knew about rights, the world outside the plantation, and most of all, reading. He realized the reason why the law said slaves could not learn to read. They wanted to keep slaves ignorant and stupid, so they wouldn't rebel against slavery. Everything made sense, then. Why had the master gotten so angry about the words in the trackway? He didn't want his slaves to rise up against him. If the master didn't want that, then Charlton had to make it happen. He could lead them on the path of reading and of knowledge, to the point where they couldn't tolerate obeying any more.

With that, Charlton had absolved himself of the guilt he felt that prevented him from trying to move into Phillip's cabin. He had enjoyed learning from Belle and from William and so Phillip would enjoy learning from him. Besides, Charlton wanted so much to become the teacher that his breath came in stronger and his hands worked quicker from thinking about it. He couldn't take the role while living with little privacy out of the men's quarters. He needed a house and Phillip had one.

The more Charlton thought about it, the more he decided to talk to Phillip that night. The other slaves kept themselves from claiming the cabin: afraid of the sickness that came to the house. When that fear stopped, they would question why the water boy would need a cabin all to himself. To save Phillip's house for Phillip, Charlton decided that he would need to move into it.

As soon as he made the decision, Charlton felt the sting of the whip on the end of his elbow. He snapped his attention to the source and saw the overseer bending down over his horse and peering at Charlton. "What you think this is? Break time? Get back to work!"

Charlton snapped back to the tobacco. The overseer bounded off to another corner of the field.

***

In the supper line, Charlton looked for Phillip and found him as he got his portion and headed toward his house. Charlton followed him once he scooped out his dinner. It didn't take long before he caught up to Phillip, who strolled more than walked.

Charlton didn't know what to say, so he followed Phillip at the same pace for a while. Right before Phillip got to his door, he stopped and spoke toward the door, "Why you following me, Charlton?"

The shock that Phillip had noticed him took a moment to fade away before he could speak. "I'm sorry, Phillip. You just seem so sad and I'm not sure what to say."

"You don't have to say nothing. I'm fine."

"Phillip, I know you're not fine. Let me come in. Let's talk. I know kind of what it's like for you. It'll help to talk to me."

Phillip turned toward Charlton. His eyes had turned red as tears trickled down his cheeks. He said nothing, but motioned with his arm to welcome Charlton inside.

Charlton tried to give Phillip a reassuring smile, but he had already turned around and headed through the door. Charlton followed. He took the two steps in through the front door and looked around the simple cabin. Wood planks made up the floor and roof, which formed an angled high point to let rain course off. The log walls had square spaces sawed out to make room for four windows with wooden, hinged shutters. The furniture consisted of two larger beds pushed together in the far right corner, a smaller bed in the near left corner, and a table and chairs in the middle of the floor. Two plates, cups, and utensils set two of the spots at the table. Folded clothes, which Charlton recognized as belonging to Phillip and his parents rested under the larger beds.

Phillip placed his plate and cup in one of the spots between place settings to his right and left. He pulled out his chair and slumped down at the table. Charlton looked around the table, unsure what to do. Would Phillip mind if he sat down in one of his parent's chairs? Did he want to keep the house just like his parents left it? Phillip made no move to help Charlton decide.

"You 'fraid of the sickness, aren't you?" Phillip asked.

"No, I'm not. I just don't know what to do."

Phillip gestured to the chair opposite him, unoccupied by a place setting. Charlton guessed that Phillip would never move his parents' place settings to keep their memories alive. Charlton decided not to disturb them.

Phillip stared at Charlton for a bit, but Charlton couldn't speak. He had convinced himself at the end of the work day that he could speak to Phillip with ease. Instead, he felt a lump in his throat that prevented any words from coming. Phillip gave up and started to dig into his food.

Charlton sat motionless. He had to begin, but hadn't bothered to figure out how. His thoughts screamed at him to start.

Phillip broke the silence. "You just going to sit there? Cause then I'd just like to eat by myself."

Charlton forced himself to talk. "Phillip, I don't know exactly what you're going through. I never knew my father, but I knew my mother and when she was taken from me, well, I just didn't know what to do." As Charlton spoke, the lump disappeared and the words began to flow. "Do you know what I did?"

"Nope," Phillip said, his eyes trained on Charlton, no longer looking down.

"I decided to stop talking to everyone. I got so lonely. My mama was my only friend here and I know the others, they felt bad for me, but I didn't want to talk to them. When the people who care about you the most go away, there's a hole in your heart and you know that no one can fill it no matter how hard they try. I think you're feeling the same way. Is that right?"

"Yeah," Phillip said. A glistening tear raced down his cheek. Charlton understood that Phillip did much better with the loss of his parents, than Charlton did when the master sold his mother. He wouldn't have let anyone into the house as Phillip had. The offer was Phillip's concession and his strength.

"I'll tell you right now," said Charlton, "that I hurt myself even more when I did that. I got real lonely, but you should get someone's help."

"Are you going to help me, Charlton?"

"I will, if you'll let me. I want to help you, Phillip. I don't want you to go through the same thing I did. Let me take care of you, Phillip. We can get through this together. Will you let me?"

"You can't be Mama and Pappy," Phillip said.

Charlton winced. "Of course not, I can't be them and I'm not going to try. I'm not going to do as good a job as them. But I'll do my best."

"Why you do this?"

"You'll be my friend, Phillip. I also want to teach you, if you want."

"What you going to teach me?"

"I'll start with reading and writing, and then I'll teach you what I know about life. Do you remember living with the Zutters?"

"Uh huh."

"I saw you there watching me and William and I thought that maybe you'd want to learn the same things we knew. Am I wrong?"

"No. I wanted to learn, but I didn't say nothing."

By the end of that evening, Charlton and Phillip decided that Charlton would live in the cabin with Phillip. Phillip would keep his old bed with Charlton in Phillip's father's bed, relocated to another corner. The next night Charlton moved into the cabin taking his book, compass, and money from their hiding spot. He found a loose floorboard in the cabin and hid everything underneath it. He would have everything ready for Phillip's lessons beginning after dinner the next night.

As Charlton lay in his new bed gazing at the ceiling that night, he thought of all the freedom he would have from this new arrangement. He escaped from the men's cabin and he'd learn the pleasures of teaching. Most of all, he improved his chances of getting revenge on the master.

***

Charlton pulled up the floorboard, and took the school book and the slate off the platform he constructed to keep his possessions off the ground. He placed the floorboard back as Phillip finished his supper. He smiled looking at the makeshift slate. He had found the broken shovel lying in the grass on one of his walks at night and thought that it would serve well as a tool to teach Phillip to read. They spread loose dirt on it and traced letters in the dirt, just like he had done with Belle. When the lesson concluded, they tilted the dirt into the catch at the top of the shovel and no one could see what they had done. The system worked well.

"Phillip, are you almost done?" Charlton said.

"Yeah, I'm done."

Charlton sat back in his chair by the table. "We're going to try our letters again. I'll write one and you tell me the sound it makes." He spread the dirt over the slate and went through letter after letter. Phillip repeated back the sounds without flaw, even giving each sound the vowels made without prompting.

"You're doing good, Phillip," Charlton said when the light receded too far to continue. "I wanted to read more of the book to you tonight, but I can't see well enough. Maybe tomorrow."

"Why you read to me, Charlton? I don't learn nothing when you read."

Charlton looked in Phillip's direction, unsure how to respond. "What do you mean?"

"I'm not learning to read. You do it all."

"We have to start somewhere, Phillip. We'll go on to words tomorrow. It's just that there's more to learn than how to read. You need to know about the world out there and you need to learn about rights."

"What are 'rights'?"

Charlton smiled. "Good question! Rights are something we get when we're born. They say that it's good for us to live the way we want to and work and protect ourselves from harm. You know, Phillip, I thought I knew about rights, but then we went to the Zutters and William taught me so much more about them and now I know that they're more important than anything else."

"We don't have no rights," Phillip said. He stared back at Charlton with defiance.

"What do you mean?"

"The white people, they got rights. We don't have none of them. We slaves."

Charlton's hands tightened into fists and he pounded the table with them. Phillip flinched. "No!" Charlton said. "That's the white people talking. We have rights as sure as they do, but they don't let us use them. I've known that for a long time. It's their laws that say they can do this to us. We got all the rights they do!" He threw the words out of his mouth, tasting the acid they left behind.

"I'm sorry, Charlton. I didn't mean to make you mad." Phillip got up from his chair and crawled into bed. Charlton stared in Phillip's direction and heard him crying.

Remorse tugged at Charlton's heart. He knelt by Phillip's bed and put his hand on his back. "No, I'm the one who's sorry. I'm not mad at you. I just have to be a better teacher. It's been a long day. You get your rest. I'll try again tomorrow."

Charlton got up and sat on his own bed, counting the moments before Phillip stopped crying.

Chapter Twenty-Four

September 1854

After the half work day on a bright Sunday, Charlton and Phillip met at the cabin. As Phillip reached for the door handle, Charlton said, "Let's stay outside."

They walked along in silence as they passed men and women relaxing and the plantation's children playing. They turned down a path away from the others.

"This is the path I took to get to my book when I snuck out of the men's cabin. Do you know why I had to hide the book?"

"Cause us slaves ain't s'posed to read."

"Yeah, but do you know *why* we're not s'posed to read?"

"Cause the Master say so."

Charlton let out a gentle laugh. Phillip stared back at him with a degree of hurt in his eyes.

"I'm sorry," Charlton said. "I'm not laughing at you. I'm laughing because the master's tricked us and he's not really that smart." Phillip gazed up at Charlton with a wrinkled brow.

"I've been teaching you for a long time now, Phillip. You're doing good and I've got so much more to teach you. Today, I want to tell you what I learned about white people and slaves. When we talked about rights before, I knew you needed to know about this. We're supposed to think that they're better than us, but they're not. It's the law that makes them think they are. We can make fun of them when they're not around, but if they're around we can't because they can hit us with the whip, but one day we can stop listening to them. It's us who work the fields. We grow the crops and the white people take what we did and they use it to help themselves. Someday, we'll be free and won't have to do what they tell us to do."

Charlton decided to tell Phillip about his life. He repeated much of what he said at the Zutters because now that he felt like a father to Phillip, he knew the story would take on a whole new meaning. When he told of Ole Joe, Phillip looked up at him smiling. Charlton guessed

Phillip thought of him as a kind of Ole Joe. Phillip stopped walking and gaped at Charlton when he heard of the first time Charlton had written the words and how Belle could never speak to him again. He yelped when Charlton explained how the master had nearly killed him with a sword. He gasped when Charlton explained how the master gloated about sending his father to certain death.

The stories continued, but Charlton refused to bring up rights again. He had mentioned them too early that one night, so he wanted to break down the image of the master in Phillip's mind before he got into rights again.

When the sun began to set, Charlton stopped Phillip and said, "Before we go back to the quarters, I need to tell you something. You understand why I hate the master, don't you?"

"Yeah."

"I need your help, Phillip. Will you help me?"

Before hearing what he had to do, Phillip said, "Yeah, I'll help you. What you want me to do?"

"Thanks, Phillip" Charlton said with a smile. "Before I tell you, you need to promise me that you'll keep it secret."

"I promise."

"I need to get revenge on the master."

"What revenge?"

"It's when you give back to someone the pain they gave to you. I'll never get my mama or papa back. The master took them from me. I want him to feel the pain of losing something that belongs to him. I want to take his land from him by poisoning it."

"What that mean, Charlton?" Phillip said.

"It's from this old fairy tale that Belle read me. A wicked queen gave a lady a poisoned apple and when she ate it, it made her die. I was thinking maybe if that happened to a person, it could happen to the master's land."

"The master's land going to die?"

"Well, not die, but make it so it can't grow nothing no more." Phillip stared at him, looking puzzled. "Do you know why the master grows tobacco?"

"No."

"No one eats tobacco, but he can sell it to people who want to have it. The master gets money. You've seen money, Phillip. That's what the Zutters gave us. He uses the money to get other things he wants. If we stop him from growing tobacco, he won't have any more money and then I'll get revenge on him."

"What happen to us if you do that?"

Charlton paused thinking about the question. Phillip didn't speak well, but Charlton knew he had smarts. "Well, the master needs money, so he'll have to sell us."

"Charlton?"

"Yes?"

"When we sold, are we going back to Mr. Zutter?"

Charlton put his hand on Phillip's shoulder. "I think so. The master will get more money from them than anyone else." Charlton kept back part of what he thought from Phillip. He didn't want to poison the field and leave it a mystery how it happened. Instead, he would tell the master that he did it to him and then laugh at him. The master wouldn't sell him, he would kill Charlton out of anger and then, after all these years, make Belle run away from Robert.

"What'll I do?" Phillip asked

"You're going to spy for me." Phillip looked up at him and scratched his head.

***

Charlton walked back to the quarters with the other field hands. For four weeks, no news came from Phillip's spying. He would often tell Charlton about how the master would come out on his porch, perhaps chatting with his wife about topics like the weather or who they would visit next. Phillip reported everything to Charlton that he saw.

While they sat at the table, eating their supper, Charlton asked, "Find out anything today?"

"I don't know if this help, but Master, he got into a fix today. He out there ranting 'bout someone call the plantation manager."

"I saw the plantation manager years ago when I used to carry the water," Charlton said. "He's the one who tells the master what to plant and how to run his fields. He comes out here now and then and talks to the master and the overseer. What did the plantation manager do?"

"He die," said Phillip.

"The plantation manager's dead?" Charlton could feel his heart pounding beneath his ribs. He didn't quite have the idea in place yet, but he figured this news held a lot of importance. He bolted out of his seat and paced back and forth in front of the table and around his chair.

The excitement rose in Phillip's voice too. "Yeah and Master, he not know 'bout who do the job."

Charlton stopped pacing and stared at Phillip. "Say that again."

"Master, he not sure who'll do it. He don't know no one who do the job."

Charlton stood and gaped. He had mixed feelings about this. His chance had come. He'd need to become the plantation manager. With that job, he wouldn't need to mix and spread the poison himself. He'd write out a plan and get the field hands to do the work for him. Yet, he puzzled over how he could get the job.

"What you thinking of doing, Charlton?" Phillip said.

"It may not work, but if I can, I'm going to be the plantation manager."

***

That night Charlton stayed up thinking as Phillip snored in his corner. He kept himself awake planning how to get what he wanted and by the time his eyes closed, he had a strategy.

He awoke to the sound of the cowbell. Though fainter than when he slept in the men's cabin, it could still pull him out of sound sleep. Today, he woke excited and ready to take his first step in destroying the master.

He gobbled down his breakfast and rushed to get to the start of the line. The overseer as usual led the line to the fields. Charlton got to where the line started well before any others. He heard a click and the sound of splintering wood to his right and he glanced in that direction to see the overseer. The overseer lounged against a big tree stump with his back while he pushed out his legs, crossed at the ankles, in front of him. In his right hand he held a beat-up knife and in the left a whittled stick. "Ain't you the eager beaver?" he said to Charlton with undisguised derision.

"Yes, sir," said Charlton. He let no time elapse before he put in his request. "I know about Master's problem with the plantation manager and I can help."

The relaxed stance of the overseer vanished and he bolted upright. He tossed his knife and stick to the side and strode up in a menacing way to stare down Charlton. "I dare you to repeat that to my face."

Charlton looked the overseer in the eyes and said, "I want you to tell the master that I know about his problem with the plantation manager and that I can help." The overseer's eyes got wide. Charlton was glad that the overseer had dropped the knife and branch. He belted Charlton across the face with the back of his hand. Pain shot through his jaw and cheek. Charlton's head snapped in the same direction as the overseer's hand. Despite the urge to crumble to the ground and clutch his face, Charlton willed himself upright and stared back into the overseer's face.

The overseer paused looking at Charlton dumbfounded. In a moment, he shoved Charlton. This time, Charlton fell to the ground and stayed down. The overseer pointed his finger at Charlton and opened his mouth wide. "You think I'm your damned messenger boy? I ain't going to tell your master nothing. You best watch yourself boy, 'cause if you *ever* speak to me like that again, you're going to get a lot worse. Now you stand up in that line and you keep your damned mouth shut. I'll beat the respect into you, if I see it again. I swear to God Almighty on that." The overseer huffed and resumed his spot at the tree stump.

Charlton did as instructed. He felt a rising heat inside his chest urging him on to challenge his attacker, but it would serve no purpose. He had relayed his message and no matter what the overseer said about keeping the message to himself, Charlton knew he wouldn't. The man couldn't stop talking. He would tell someone about the proper-speaking slave's insolence.

The next day, Charlton came to the line later than any of the others and began his work like always. About two hours after the start, Paul came down to the fields.

Charlton saw Paul out of the corner of his eye and grinned. Paul stood towering above Charlton as he tended to a tobacco plant. After several moments, Charlton spoke. "Paul? What can I do for you?" Charlton didn't bother to look up as he spoke.

"Master want to see you," Paul said.

"When?"

"Now."

Charlton stood. "Lead the way," he said.

Paul and Charlton got on the path to the where the master summoned Charlton. The master sat on the ground against his favorite tree stump gazing up at the sky with his arms crossed behind his head. Charlton's stomach turned when he saw the master. He felt anger rise up from his stomach to his head and heat his flushed face. The master couldn't see him like this. He took a couple of deep breaths and strode into the master's view.

Chapter Twenty-Five

The master spotted Charlton and smirked. Charlton wanted to attack the master. Instead, he bowed his head. The master began with less hostility than Charlton expected. "Well, well, well, look who came crawling out of the woodwork. I heard you wanted to talk to me and when I heard that, I thought, 'well this ought to be rich.' I haven't had a good laugh in a while. Why don't you tell me what you want?"

"Master, sir, I need to tell you that I'm sorry," Charlton said.

"Hah! Go on…" the master said, his grin growing.

"I know that I done you wrong. You're trying to run a business, Master, and I only thought of myself."

"Well, ain't this a change of pace, boy? But, I don't give a damn that you're sorry. You told my man that you were going to help me out of my fix. So, you either tell me what you're going to do or get the hell back to your work."

"Master, sir, I…" Charlton said, but the master interrupted him.

"I *own* you, you know. You're mine. You should've never done what you did. You had no reason to do it."

"Yes, Master. You're right, but I want to do the right thing now. You need a new plantation manager. I can do it."

"You want to be my plantation manager?" The master cut the last word short as laughter intruded on his speech. He slapped his knee and produced a belly laugh as strong as Charlton had ever heard. Charlton kept his eyes downcast and waited for the master to regain control of himself. "You're as crazy as you are dark, boy. What makes you think I'd *ever* let you do that?" The master leaned back on his stump again looking at the sky.

Since the master didn't call Paul's name ordering him to remove Charlton from his sight, Charlton's confidence grew. "Master, you own me. You won't pay me, but you did pay your plantation manager and you would pay another one too. Why pay someone when you can have me do it?"

"You don't know nothing about managing a plantation," the master said looking at Charlton with a faint hint of interest.

"No, Master, but I can learn. The Zutters told me all the time that I learned the ship building faster than they had thought possible. I can learn this too."

"Hah! The Zutters! Those idiots fell in love with you. I never seen grown men so confused. Besides, how will you learn? The manager's dead. You can't learn from no one." At that moment, Charlton knew the master had no better option.

"Maybe he left something behind that explains farming, Master. Did he have a book?"

Instead of answering, the master stared down Charlton. "Why should I trust you, boy? I sold your parents to their death."

Charlton felt anger rising from his chest that the master would dare bring up his parents. He suppressed the feeling. "Master, you didn't kill my parents. I hate Mr. Beauregard, but he's dead. You had every right to do what you did."

The master shot up and Charlton flinched despite himself. The master began pacing around Charlton. "So, you changed your tune, huh? That's right. I'm not the man who killed either of your parents. Are you ready to accept that you're my property? I could make you manage the plantation if I wanted to."

"Yes, Master, I'll do whatever you say." Charlton thought it pointless to argue that he came up with the idea. If the master wanted to claim it, he refused to correct him.

"Paul!" the master said.

Paul rushed over to the two men. "Master?"

"Go back to the house and fetch the plantation manager's book. It's the only book on my desk. Make it quick."

"Yeah, Master." Paul hurried off toward the house. Hope rose from Charlton's chest into his throat.

"Boy, I don't know if you're up to something, but I do know that I need a plantation manager. I'm not averse to getting one for free. You need to prove to me that you can do it though, boy. I'm giving you *one* field," the master said as he stuck his index finger in Charlton's face. "If you can't grow anything on that field in a month, I'm going to make life hell for you again. If you can, then I'll let you manage more."

"Can I have help, master?" Charlton said.

The master laughed at him. "You think I'm going to let someone do this with you? Boy, you sure are dull. Nobody's helping you. You do it on your own or not at all. I'll choose the field and you'll make it work." The master paused. "I was just about to give you the chance to back out of this, but you're not backing out of nothing. You shot your mouth off, now you live with it."

A dark thought came to Charlton and he darted his eyes from side to side. With Paul gone, the master spoke to him with no protection. Charlton's tall lean frame with muscles he worked so hard to achieve could beat the short, overweight, old master with little to stop him. He could end this all here. Throw the master to the ground and before he had the chance to yell for help, Charlton would have his hands around the master's throat and squeeze out any chance of another word escaping the master's foul lips. He'd squeeze until the master stopped moving and then he'd keep it up until Paul returned with the book. Any let up in the force of his hands until Paul pried them off the master would give the master the slightest chance of breathing again. Charlton banished the thoughts instead. Ending the master's life without taking away something he loved? He couldn't think of it again.

The master and Charlton stayed silent while waiting for Paul to come back with the book. The master didn't bother looking at Charlton. He resumed his seat on the ground by the stump and gazed back up at the sky. Every part of the master's stance dismissed the danger that Charlton posed to him.

In what seemed like forever, Paul came up the path from the house carrying a well-used book with a frayed cloth-bound cover. His breath came heavy and his eyes opened wide. "Master, I'm sorry. It just, they was two books on that desk, but I not know which one so, I would've asked Mistress, but she not around so I had to wait and…"

The master raised his right hand still staring up at the sky. He darted his gaze back at Paul. "I ain't interested in your excuses, Paul. Just hand the book over to the boy."

"Yes, Master," Paul said. He handed the book to Charlton and backed away. Paul made it clear he wanted to fade into the background. Charlton sympathized with Paul. This giant of a man felt intimidated by a middle-aged, out-of-shape man. Not only that, but Paul didn't make a mistake. The master told him the wrong thing and Paul couldn't read to make the right choice. Yet, Paul had to give the excuses.

The master got up again and sauntered over to Charlton. "Boy," the master said, "you best keep that book to yourself. I don't want *anyone* seeing you read that. You keep to yourself and Paul will tell the overseer that I told him to leave you alone. Got it?"

"Yes, Master."

"Good. Tomorrow, the overseer will lead you to your new field." The master paused. "You know what, go see him now. Paul, tell him that the boy is to work in the new field. He'll know the one." The master turned back to Charlton. "Now get out of my sight." Paul cuffed Charlton around the shoulder and led him away as Charlton stuffed the book into his waistband and under his shirt.

On the walk back to the fields, Paul fell silent while Charlton reflected on the conversation. He couldn't believe that the master gave him a chance, but didn't like the sound of the "new field." A new field must mean one that they had never tried to use and he worried about why.

Paul and Charlton arrived at the fields without seeing the overseer. They rotated in and around the fields and caught sight of the horse among the subsistence crops. They hid next to the corn and some distance over while the overseer picked beans, pushing off the dirt, and popping them into his mouth. Paul gave Charlton a telling glance. He never knew that the overseer did this and now Paul seemed content to wait him out.

"Paul?" Charlton said.

"Yeah?"

"We can't let him know we know he's stealing."

"Nope."

"Then, let's sit by that tree 'til he stops." Charlton gestured to a tree near them, which would provide cover from the overseer.

"Yeah."

They sat down in silence and as time passed and it got too uncomfortable, Charlton said, "Did you know the overseer did that?"

"Yeah, I seen him done it."

"He's just always there, in the fields, I mean, but he's been down there for a while now. How does he always seem to catch me doing something wrong?"

"I don't know," Paul said.

Charlton let some time go by, but his nerves got to him and he wanted to talk. "What if you tell the master? He'll listen to you and the overseer will get punished."

Paul turned to Charlton and said in a firm voice, "I ain't no telltale."

"The master said you told on my father." The words came out of Charlton before he had a chance to stop them. He felt bitter about Paul's part in that and some part of him still wanted resolution.

Anger filled Paul's face. To Charlton's relief it went away fast, but he continued to look Charlton in the eye. "I told you once and I tell you 'gain. I didn't tell Master. He guess it."

"But, then why'd the master say…?"

Paul raised his index finger and shook it in the air, "Master's a liar. If you ain't figured that yet, you ain't never going to."

Charlton sat staring into Paul's face and saw hurt in his eyes. Paul turned his head to resume staring at the overseer through the tall grass. Charlton decided to let his distrust of Paul go. He knew the master lied, better than anyone else, but he didn't realize that Paul knew it.

"I'm sorry," Charlton said. Paul nodded continuing to stare at the overseer

"Paul?"

"Yeah?"

"Do you like the master?"

Paul chuckled. "Course, I don't like Master. No one like him."

"The master knew he told you there was only one book on the desk, but you told him it was your fault. Why?"

"Cause I ain't dumb. Master, he ain't no good, but this the life I live. I can't have it no other way. So, I makes the best of it. Mayhaps when I get old and run down, Master, he let me retire. That mean I sits 'round and do nothing and that sound just right to me."

"You knew Ole Joe right?"

"Course I did."

"The master never let him retire."

"Cause Master never like Ole Joe, but he like me and mayhaps I gets to retire."

Charlton thought about that and let Paul go back to staring at the overseer. He realized that Paul thought no different than any other slave. They all wanted to escape their state. Maybe they could run away and not get caught. They could also get sold to someone better, like when Charlton lived with the Zutters. Most accepted that they would never escape and they worked hard to avoid the whip knowing they would die working for their master.

Paul chose another path; one Charlton never considered. Didn't Paul realize that the master would never let him retire? How old would he get before he realized that retirement would never happen? How would Paul feel when he lay dying and never got to taste retirement?

The overseer snapped Charlton out of his trance when he groaned, stretched, and got up. He yawned and scratched himself. Paul rolled his eyes. When the overseer started on his way, Paul gestured for Charlton to stand.

They made a straight line for where the overseer headed and intersected him. "Yeah? What?" the overseer asked, sneering at Paul and spitting to his side when he saw Charlton.

"Master sent us, sir. He want you to show us the new field. He say you know the one. He going to work it to grow some crop," Paul said hooking his thumb at Charlton.

The overseer leered at them in a dumb way. He made it obvious he didn't know what Paul meant. Then, he shook his head. "Ah, yeah. I know it." His malicious grin put a hard lump in Charlton's throat. He suspected the master had set him up to fail.

"You best pay attention. I ain't going to show you again. I ain't your damn servant boy."

They followed the overseer for a while. Charlton knew the entire plantation, but he couldn't think of where the master had a new field where he could farm that didn't already have crops. When they approached his field, the lump in Charlton's throat grew. He knew where they headed, but not how he could grow anything on it.

The overseer confirmed his suspicion when they crested a hill and pointed to the land below. "There. Down there. Good luck, boy," the overseer said. A mocking laugh burst forth from the overseer's mouth along with some spittle that landed on Charlton's arm. The overseer then turned his heels and headed in the other direction, continuing to laugh as he went back to the real fields.

Paul and Charlton stood on the hill and stared down for a while. Charlton's heart sank. Rock and sand sat scattered all over the craggy ground as if God had vomited up this field during its creation. Charlton shook his head to dispel the image. He realized that water had once coursed through the field, but had long ago thought the field unworthy and took another path instead. The thought of trying to grow anything in this ground made Charlton groan. Paul nodded an unspoken understanding.

Charlton shook his head, letting despair fill him, but only for a moment. The image of his mother holding his head in her lap and stroking his hair played in his mind. A tear escaped his eye. "For you, Mama. I'll make the crops grow for you," he said aloud. Paul clapped him on the back, then turned around to leave Charlton to his task.

Chapter Twenty-Six

October 1854

The pinch in Charlton's back did not soothe itself on his walk to the slave quarters at twilight. He paused and stretched. Nothing. He reached behind him and pushed against the spot, wincing at the tenderness. He continued on his way to the path, quicker now to avoid the fate that awaited him three days ago when the cook had removed the cauldron before he got any food.

When he reached camp, the cauldron had disappeared from its resting place. His eyes searched with the remaining embers of daylight receding from view and found the cook, Lizzie, hauling the cauldron to the edge of camp to dump the remaining contents where the master's dogs could get it. Charlton ran over to her shouting "wait!"

The stocky woman stopped, raising her eyebrows and finding Charlton. She looked halfway between disappointed and disgusted. "Boy, you ain't never going to learn. I told you I ain't waiting for you no more. You best get here when everyone else get here." She proceeded to maneuver the cauldron into position for tipping.

"No, please, Lizzie. I need it. Can't you just wait a bit?"

She let the cauldron come to rest against the ground. "Oh, all right, but if you ain't back soon, she's going over."

"Thank you," Charlton said. He raced off to his cabin and without so much as a word to Phillip who greeted him, he scooped up his plate and spoon and charged back out the door. When he got back to Lizzie, he could only make out the shadows of the cauldron and Lizzie sitting on the ground with her arms wrapped around her knees.

"It's about time," she said.

"I'm sorry," Charlton said. He scooped into the cauldron and pulled out spoonful after spoonful of stew. *The more, the better, I need my strength back after pulling all those rocks.* "Can I help you with that? Since you waited for me and all."

"No, just go back now and eat. I ain't waiting for you again, Charlton."

"I know. Last time," Charlton said. On the way back to the cabin, he shoveled stew into his mouth, savoring the taste. He finished before he got to the cabin. The moon managed to wrestle itself out of the grasp of the clouds, casting light through the window. *That's better. Now I can read tonight.*

Phillip lay in bed staring at the ceiling when he got into the cabin. "You still awake?" Charlton asked.

"Yeah. Charlton?"

"Yeah."

"Do you still like me?"

Charlton's brow crinkled. "Of course I do, Phillip. Why you ask that?"

"'Cause you ain't taught me nothing in a long time and you ain't even talking to me or nothing. You just running 'round all the time."

Charlton rolled his eyes. "I'm sorry, Phillip, but you're just going to have to give me some time. I'm trying to get that field to grow crops. It's really tough. I don't know what I'm going to do. If I don't get it to work, the master's going to do bad things to me. If I get it to work, I might get even with the master for what he did to my parents."

"My mama and pappy died too."

Charlton took in a breath and let it out slow and steady. "Yeah, and that was really bad, but they didn't get killed by the master."

"He didn't kill your mama or paps. Old man Beauregard killed them."

"You know what, Phillip? Why don't you go to sleep? I got work to do."

Phillip didn't respond, but after a pause, Charlton heard him crying. Remorse tugged at the pit of Charlton's stomach. He forced himself to ignore it in favor of doing more work and took out the field manual, positioning himself next to the window to let the moonlight shine on the pages. After a while, Phillip stopped crying and slept.

Charlton found his place in the book and read from start to end. Fatigue from a hard day of work caught up with him soon, and he found his eyelids growing heavy. He straightened up more and shook his head to wake himself out of a tired stupor. It didn't work as intended. He slumped and his eyes grew heavier again. To stay awake, he stopped reading and leafed through the book instead. Each page had a black and white illustration of the discussed plant.

Toward the end of the book, Charlton spotted an odd-looking plant with fuzzy, circular blooms. The book called the plant cotton and it set him to searching his memory. He had seen the plant growing at some point. The book described the plant as "King Cotton" because so many in the South planted and grew cotton, which made them a lot of money. Charlton felt the urge to skip past the section because he didn't want to make more money for the master. Yet he read on, intrigued, awake, and alert because the plantation manager had scribbled notes all over the section.

The notes gushed about the profits that could be dug out of the crop, but the note at the bottom of the page said, "Nothing doing, plantation's too small." Charlton scanned the text of the page and a faded underline caught his eye. Above the underline, the manual said, "Cotton must not be grown on a plantation of small acreage. A cotton grower must expect to lose fields where cotton is grown for long periods of time as cotton savages fields."

The word "savages" caught Charlton's eye. His memory of the master calling his mother a savage raced into his head. He considered the justice she brought to Beauregard by beating him until he had no face anymore. If cotton would savage the fields and the master described Beauregard's death as savagery, then Charlton needed to grow cotton at the plantation. He could kill the master's land.

Clouds moved in to block the moonlight and Charlton put the book back below his bed, keeping the spot opened to the cotton section. He continued to search his memory for where he had seen the plant as he faded into sleep.

***

The memory came back to him the next day as he dug up rocks in the new field. He thought about nothing else but pulling a rock from the field when the impact of the image made him flinch. He had sat leaning against a wall and noticed the stalk silhouetted against the moonlight. The Underground Railroad Station held the key to his revenge.

***

Charlton's heart thumped in his chest as he came in sight of the station. He had to wait two days for the clouds to stop blocking the moonlight, despite his desperation to get here. The barn, left unrepaired, still had the same caved roof, but it looked a bit worse. No cotton plants met his eyes.

He squinted, cursing in his thoughts that he couldn't get out except at night in moonlight. He found the chore more difficult than anything else he had done at night. Roaming the plantation meant following in the dark, paths he knew well in daytime. Reading the schoolbook and writing in the trackway meant positioning himself in a place where the light shone on the words. He couldn't force the cotton plants into the light, though.

Charlton stopped and closed his eyes. He took control of his heartbeat by breathing in and out without thinking of anything else. With his mind off the plight he found himself in, Charlton focused on how to see in the dark. He imagined the moon halfway up the sky and the plants below it. An adjustment in his perspective would give him what he needed. He stood at full height looking down at the plants, yet he needed to crouch low so the moonlight would come down at an angle on his eyes and cross through the plant tops, in the same way he had seen the cotton in the first place.

Charlton did as he visualized. After a bit of maneuvering, he saw fuzzy orbs growing up against the backdrop of the sky. He stayed crouched as he moved forward, focusing on the orbs until they bumped his nose. He took the spade he borrowed from the plantation, guided his hand down the stalk and dug out the plant. Clutching both the plant and the spade, Charlton moved in the same way to the next location and repeated his chore six more times.

Out of exhaustion, the idea crossed his mind that he should take the plants to the cabin and plant them later, but he refused to listen to his aching body. Instead of going back to the cabin, Charlton went straight to his field, where he planted the cotton plants. He would not risk anyone seeing him planting full cotton plants because he needed to pretend that he grew these plants on his own.

Charlton went to the clearest spot in the field and dug into it. He hadn't removed all the stones in this section, but he didn't have a better patch of land to use. When he struck a rock, he worked it out of place and tossed it away. The digging went on for longer than usual because he couldn't leave even half of the stalk exposed to the air. To keep up appearances, he had to bury most of the plant. The master would never believe that he had grown the full stalks in so little time.

As dawn approached, Charlton finished his last planting. As he headed back to the slave quarters, the cow bell rang out. Charlton gave up all pretense of trying to get back in time without notice. He turned around and went back to his field.

***

Charlton pulled a ball of cotton off the plant and worked it with his fingers, feeling for the seeds. The experience over the last few days of working on cotton as the book described made his chest puff up. Only he knew how to work cotton, and if the master let his greed bring Charlton into a position of power, he would teach the rest of them, even the white hired hands, how to do this. Focusing on the seed, he picked at the cotton strands around it, until he exposed the seed and then pulled it free.

Hearing footfalls, Charlton whipped his body around to see Paul's balding head cresting the hill. He closed the cotton and the seed each into one of his fists. "Come on," Paul said when Charlton came into his view.

Paul led Charlton in silence. Moving aside, Paul stood with his arms crossed to reveal the master who stood at attention in front of his usual stump. Charlton saw the impatience and apprehension in the master's eyes.

"How in hell did you manage to grow crop there?" the master said. Charlton realized that he had already won this battle. The master didn't look at him when he spoke, keeping his gaze on nothing in the distance.

"Master, the plantation manager kept the seeds in the book on the cotton page. I found 'em and planted the next day. They grew fast, I guess 'cause nothing grew in that field for a long time, so the soil was nice and fresh. I read the part about cotton, and I..." Charlton said.

The master interrupted him. "Cotton! We ain't equipped to grow cotton!"

"Please, Master, how do you mean?" Charlton hadn't accounted for the master knowing about the problem with cotton.

The master's twisted expression spoke to Charlton about what he didn't know. "Rundy never said, but I know we ain't equipped."

"Master, he wrote all over the book and it said in the cotton part it was too much work to grow cotton. He just didn't want to do it. I can fetch…"

The master interrupted Charlton, "That no good, lazy, lying bastard! I knew I could grow cotton here!" He pointed his finger at Charlton. "Let me see it!"

"Master?"

"The cotton! Let me see it! Show me you grew it. I don't believe you."

Charlton stuck out both fists and unraveled them. The master stared at the puff of cotton, then plucked it out of Charlton's hand. Holding it between his fingers, he lifted the tuft above his eyes, inspecting it against the sun. "Yes, that's it! You grew this in that ragged field, you say?"

"Yes, Master."

"Then, we can grow it. That bastard did lie to me. What do you do with it? Tell me."

"You pull it off the stalk, then push at it with your fingers, until you find a seed. It's got to be taken out, if you do, then you look for another one. Once you got them all, you put the cotton in one bag and the seeds in another. It's easy when you done it a while."

Charlton used great restraint to keep himself from smiling. His bluff had worked.

"I ain't going to lie to you, boy. I want to grow cotton. That's how to be rich. You're going to make that happen. But don't you be getting on no high horse about it. You're still a slave and no white man going to start taking orders from you on my plantation. You got that?"

"Yes, Master, I surely do."

"Paul?"

"Yeah, master?"

"Lead the way back to the tobacco fields. I'm coming with you. We're going to get everyone familiar with the new plan. Boy," the master said turning back to Charlton, "get back to your field and wait for the hired hands to get there. You're going to show them what to do."

Chapter Twenty-Seven

January 1856

A moonless night offered no light, and yet Charlton lay awake, his thoughts racing in his head. *My life has changed so much since Mama died. Now I run this place. Oh sure, the master thinks the hired hands don't have to listen to me, but they do. They hate me for it, but they listen. The fields are growing cotton because I decided they would.*

How long before the cotton starts killing the fields? Not much longer, I don't think. I'm going to get him. The master's going to lose his fields and I did that to him, and he doesn't know it. He wanted to grow cotton so much, he never even bothered to look in the book and check up on me.

I hate when he talks to me though. He's always talking. Thinks he's so important. I don't care about any of it. I hate the man. He don't even know.

Charlton let a grin spread across his face. Sleep didn't take him as his heart beat quicker. *"Why can't I sleep? Is it Phillip? I can't do anything about him. It's so hard to get back into teaching him. I haven't been able to do it and I don't need him to spy for me no more. The master talks to me himself. He tells me too much. I don't even want to know it. When he tells me about Belle and her son, I don't want to know. I want him to shut his mouth, but I can't tell him that. I have to be 'a good boy.' When is he going to stop calling me that? I'm not a boy any more. I'm a man, but no matter how much money the master makes off of me, all he'll see me as is a boy: beneath him in every way, but he should know by now that I'm smarter than him.*

Nobody likes me around here, I'm just like Paul now, not even Phillip, but do I need them? I don't even know half of my own people here. The master's been buying up the new ones and having Paul break them. How am I supposed to keep up with them? What do I do now? Charlton shook his head. *Same thing I've been doing.* With that, he turned on his side and let sleep silence his mind.

***

Charlton worked the fields pulling the cotton, lamenting his need to do this even though he also worked as plantation manager. Yet those duties didn't even come close to taking all his time. The master had decided to keep half of his tobacco crops and converted the other half to cotton, yet kept increasing the cotton as it earned him more money.

Charlton's thoughts shifted to the new slaves the master had bought. The additions seemed to blend together with no one to distinguish from the others, except for one. The others called her Angie, and Charlton thought her beauty outshone all the other women on the plantation. He wanted to speak to her, but couldn't think of what to say.

His thoughts broke off as he glanced up to see Paul walking toward him, leading three children who hurried to keep up behind him. Paul called out from across the field. "Master got a job for you!"

Charlton looked to see three dark-skinned children, two girls and a boy, all with the same thick, curly hair, which the girls wore long and the boy wore short. They looked about eight to twelve years old, not to mention frightened and uncertain. "What is it, Paul?" Charlton asked, keeping his eyes fixed on the children.

"Master want you to stop your doings and take them around. He say you got to keep them nights too." Paul turned around to walk away.

"Wait. Wait!" When Paul turned around, Charlton said, "Where are their things?"

"Don't have none. You got to get them," Paul said.

"What are their jobs?"

"Yeah. The boy going to fetch the water. The big girl going to do laundry. The little one going to the Big House. They show her what to do there."

When Charlton nodded his understanding, Paul turned on his heels and headed back to the Big House. The children watched Paul go, then turned to Charlton. He kneeled to their level, though the older girl now stood over Charlton. "What are your names?" Charlton asked.

The children exchanged glances with each other. The older girl spoke for them, "I'm Joy. My sister's Nellie and my brother's Arnie."

"I'm Charlton." He put his hand out to shake theirs, but they only looked at each other confused. He withdrew his hand "I'm sorry. White people shake hands when they meet, but you don't have to. It's good that you three got to stay together. What happened to your mama and papa?"

The younger children looked up to Joy to answer. "Our pappy sold when we young. Our mama," Joy gulped and her face contorted, but she regained her composure soon afterward. "Our mama got killed when she ran away with us. Master sold us after that."

Charlton wished he hadn't asked as a pained expression crossed his brow. "I'm sorry to hear it." He let some time pass, then started again. "Looks like you're stuck with me now. Come on, I'll show you where you're going to live."

On the way to the cabin, Charlton decided to tell them about the situation. "I'm not what you'd call the most liked slave here. The master made me the plantation manager, which means that I get to tell even the whites who work here what to do. I made the master a lot of money when I got him started on switching from growing tobacco to cotton. So, the others, they see I get treated better than them, and they don't like it. Can't say I blame them. The big man that brought you to me's named Paul, and they hate him too. He's what they call 'the master's right-hand man.' He used to do all the things the master wanted, but the master keeps on buying more slaves and so Paul had less to do. The master likes buying a lot of his new slaves from a place called Cuba, but those ones come from Africa where they don't know how to speak like us. I overheard him say he ain't supposed to do that, but no one stops him. Paul's s'posed to break them."

"What that mean? Break them?" Joy asked.

"It means he keeps them shackled and keeps food from them, and he hits them when they do something he don't like. When they stop fighting him so much, he gives them food and when they're good for a long time, he takes off the shackles. It makes them do what the whites tell them to do. Here we are," Charlton said as they reached the cabin. He pulled open the door and ushered them inside.

"Phillip's not going to like this," Charlton said aloud, too late to stop himself.

Joy looked up at him. "Who Phillip?"

"Uh, he's the boy that lives here. He's about your age. His mama and papa died of some sickness that got around here. He told me he didn't want anyone to move their plates, forks, or spoons, or sleep in his mama's bed, but y'all are going to need them. He's just going to have to let you. Joy and Nellie, you're going to share his mama's bed, and Arnie's going to share with Phillip. We'll build you new ones when we can."

Arnie stared at the ground, while Joy and Nellie nodded.

Charlton led them out of the cabin, bringing Nellie to the Big House to let the house slaves show her the job. He knew how to do the laundry from his mama and how to fetch and carry the water, so he took Joy and Arnie to show them those jobs. Worry tugged at Charlton as he tried to think of how he would tell Phillip the news.

***

By the time Phillip came back to the cabin, the three new residents sat eating at the table in his parent's spots, from his parents' plates, and using their utensils. Charlton ate from his extra plate on his bed, not wanting to take Phillip's spot. Phillip gaped at them a while before speaking. "Who are they? What're they doing?"

Charlton opened his mouth to speak, when Phillip rushed the table, "Get out of those chairs! Get out of here!" The children scampered out of the chairs, dropping their utensils. They gathered around Charlton. Charlton raised his hands palm up as Phillip rushed at him shouting. "Charlton? Why'd you let them do that? Those are Mama's and Pap's."

"Stop, Phillip! Can't you see they're scared?"

"I don't care! They can't do this to Mama or Paps!"

"They're dead, Phillip! Dead!"

Phillip stood trembling with anger. He sank to his knees, peering up at Charlton. "What you saying? What you saying?"

Charlton crouched to his knees and looked Phillip in the eyes. "I'm sorry," he said. "The master said they have to stay with us. He just bought them."

Tears poured from Phillip's eyes, yet he regained some of his anger, "No, no. No, no, no. Nope, they can't. No. They can't live here. It's my house!"

"The master said..." Charlton said.

Phillips eyes grew wide and he sprang back to his feet. "The master! You don't care nothing for the master. You hate him!" The children went from staring at Phillip to staring at Charlton.

Charlton rose to his feet too. "Yeah I do, but what can I do? This is not yours, mine, or even their house," he said gesturing to the children. "This is the master's house just like everything here. Hell, he owns us too. If I tell the master no, he's going to hurt me and he'll still make them stay here. We got nothing to say about it."

Phillip stared at him hard, his trembling growing fiercer with each passing moment of silence. "I won't stay here with them!"

"Phillip, they have to stay here and they're taking your mama's and pappy's things. They don't have anything else."

Phillip stared at Charlton, but seemed not to know what to say. Phillip's eyes darted back and forth, as he said, "I can't stay."

He went to his bed and pulled up the blanket. "What are you doing?" Charlton asked.

"I'll sleep in the men's quarters. I ain't staying here with them."

Charlton stood speechless as Phillip put his blanket on the floor and put his extra clothes, dish, bowl, and utensils it. He scooped up the blanket to make a bag and reached for the door.

"Don't go. You should stay," Charlton said.

Phillip's tear-streaked face turned to Charlton, "I know why you don't like me, Charlton. You wanted me gone from here a long time. It's your house now. I won't stay with them." With that, Phillip yanked the door open, stomped out, and slammed the door shut behind him.

***

Charlton stood facing the door of the master's study inside the Big House, where the master had summoned him. It was too early this month for his report on the cotton harvest, and he wondered what else could have caused the summons, and why Paul hadn't delivered it. He knocked on the door ready to get it over with.

"Yes?" the master said from inside. Charlton opened the door on the master in his chair at his roll-top desk writing with a pen on some parchment. The leather chairs, bookcases and couch sat in their usual places. It reminded Charlton of the Zutters' study.

"Ah, Charlton. You're not here to give your report. I have news to tell you. You're taking over Paul's messenger duties."

"Master?"

"Yes, what is it?"

"Well, Master, did something happen to him?"

"Ain't you the curious one? I don't owe you an answer, but I'll tell you anyway. Paul got beat and the doctor ain't got nothing good to say about it. He's never going to get better. Paul's done being useful around here.

"The savage that Paul was breaking had the devil in him, I tell you. Nothing worked on him, then somehow he got them shackles off when he was alone. He waited for Paul right next to the door and when Paul come in, he hit him over and over with the cuffs, then he kicked him and when Paul lay there as if he was dead, the savage tried running. He didn't get very far. The overseer done shot him dead right down the way. Paul's laid out in his cabin. The doctor said his knee's so broken, he'll never walk without a cane again."

Charlton nodded. A lump formed in his throat thinking about what Paul went through, though he did treat the now-dead slave with cruelty. Even still, the master ordered that cruelty. The master deserved the beating and the bullet, not the two slaves. Charlton had one question he dreaded asking. "Master, will I take over Paul's breaking duties too?"

The master stared at him, stroking his beard. "I could make you. You've developed quite the strength for it, I think, but no, I won't do it. I already lost one useful hand, I'm not losing another. We're out of the business of breaking slaves now. Too much risk in it." Charlton let the breath out of his lungs in a gush. The master grinned at him.

"But, I tell you what you're going to do," the master said. "You'll report here once every morning and once every afternoon break to see if I got anything waiting for you. Some days I will, some days I won't, but I ain't going to come looking for you, so you best be coming here to make sure. Now, go away. That's all."

"All right, Master," Charlton said, bowing his head and backing out of the doorway as he swung the door closed again.

He passed Paul's cabin on the way back to the field, but decided against stopping in to look at him. All Charlton's life, he had known Paul as a tower of strength. He didn't want to see him as anything else now.

***

The master appeared at the slave quarters one Sunday a couple months after the attack on Paul and right before supper. The overseer rang the cowbell to get everyone's attention and they all drifted over to the commotion. Charlton's eyes grew wide when he saw Paul sitting in a chair looking proud and in fancy clothes. He looked healed in all ways, except that an ornate cane leaned between the chair arm and

Paul's leg.

When the slaves had gathered, the master spoke. "So many times I have come before you with bad news, but today I come to you with good. Let what I say be a lesson to all of you. We have before us my loyal servant, Paul. Paul fought for this plantation and he took on much more than any of you have. His last job was to domesticate the savages that came to live with you. He did an admirable job. The last one could not be domesticated, though. When the bullet ended the savage's life, it was well deserved. He nearly killed Paul, for all the good that Paul was trying to do for him. We can rest assured that the savage burns in hell for what he did.

"Paul got beaten so bad that he can no longer work for us anymore. Instead, I gave Paul the chance to recover here and now he is as healed as he can get. Paul will never walk without a cane again, but he will live as a free man. I gave him his freedom. The master flashed a document that reminded Charlton of the ship building contracts in the Zutter's shop.

Everyone's heads turned when the steady beat of walking horse hooves reached the end of the path to the slave quarters. The men, women, and children who blocked the path to Paul cleared out of the way.

"Ah my carriage!" the master said. "Now, I wouldn't be any sort of man if I just gave this crippled man his freedom. He will need more than that to survive. I am not only giving him this fine suit, but I am going to add one hundred dollars to it" The master handed a beaming Paul a wad of money. Paul bowed his head as he accepted the money and shoved it into his pocket.

"Not only that, but on his journey to the North in my carriage, I will send three of my finest men to accompany him. They will settle him in his new home.

"I wanted all of you to see this, so that you can know what it means for you to serve me well. I reward those who show me loyalty."

Charlton stood shocked. The master's words reflected the opposite of every impulse the master had ever shown.

The rest of the ceremony swept past his eyes. Paul staggered up the carriage steps, using his cane, and waved to the gathered slaves who ignored him. Charlton shuddered at their palpable hatred. He raised his hand to say goodbye. Two white men followed Paul into the carriage, and the third hoisted himself in place as the driver and snapped the reigns to drive the horses down the path.

***

As he had done for the past two months, Charlton used the afternoon break to go to the Big House and see if the master had any tasks for him to do. He arrived to see the carriage that had taken Paul away return three days after they had left.

The men came out of the carriage chattering with each other, but Charlton stood too far away to hear the words. One of the men pulled a cane out of the carriage and another pulled out folded clothes of the same color that Paul had on when he left.

The map of the United States he saw at the Zutter's house showed the size of the country. Charlton knew that a carriage ride back and forth from the plantation to the North would have taken more than three days. The white men had not delivered Paul to the North.

***

Charlton got out of the cabin without any notice by the children. He thanked his luck that the moon shone bright that night. He found the clearing where the master spoke, then tracked the carriage wheels. Charlton walked a long while, but knew he could not retreat or give up his pursuit. When weariness set in, he considered turning back, then saw something.

The moon shone on a large lump on the side of the road. He heard labored breathing coming from it, rushed over to the form, crouched down, and rested his hands on Paul.

"Paul?" Charlton said.

The figure roused itself. Paul responded in a weak, raspy voice. "Yeah?"

"It's Charlton."

"Charlton?" Paul shook his head, tried to get up on an elbow, and fell back to earth, too weak to do even that much. "What you doing here? You got to get back."

"I'm not going anywhere. I need to help you."

Paul blew a puff of air out of his mouth. "Help?" Paul tried laughing, but only ended up in a coughing fit. "You can't help me. You got to go back."

Charlton couldn't stand facing the thought of letting Paul lie here to die alone. Yet he had to agree with Paul, he couldn't help him. "What happened?"

"What you think happened?" Paul said. "The men pushed me out the carriage when we got here. I fell right on top of my knee and I scream. Then they stop the horses and come back over here, and took my money, and my cane, and my paper, and my suit. They dumped my old work clothes on me. One them say, 'When they find him, they think he a runaway.' Then, one them, he kick me in the gut so hard, then the rest of them kick me, one time in the knee. I couldn't get up cause no cane. If I had it, I'd fight them, but they too much for me with my knee hurting. When they left, they say, 'now let's have some fun.' Master must've told them not to come back for three days to make it look like they help me."

Charlton wore Paul's story on his face in an expression of pain and guilt. Paul had treated Charlton well for the most part. If he hadn't tried to get even with the master by getting him to grow cotton, the master would have never started making enough money to buy the slave that Paul tried to break, who ended up breaking him.

"Kill me, Charlton," Paul whispered. "Kill me and end all this."

Panic rose in Charlton's chest. Take a life? He couldn't. "No, no. I can't, Paul. I can't do that."

Paul looked up at him with watery eyes, tears he couldn't spare in his condition. Charlton wished that he had brought water with him.

"I'm hurting, Charlton. Real bad. I'm hungry. I'm thirsty. I aches all over. My head hurt. You got to kill me. You got to. You got. You got…"

Paul's unblinking eyes stared into Charlton's as his chest ceased moving. "Paul? Paul!" Charlton said. The relief of not needing to kill a man set in Charlton's mind before he discarded the thought. He scooted up to Paul and cradled his head in his lap. Charlton leaned his head over, but did not feel any breath. He folded over onto Paul and wept.

Thoughts filled Charlton's head as he walked back to the cabin. He reflected on shutting Paul's eyes for him and rolling his body into a ditch. He covered him over with leaves, but he couldn't bury him without a shovel. Charlton considered bringing a shovel to the site the next night for only a brief moment. He faced long odds of finding Paul's body again nor did he think he could get out of the plantation grounds undetected with a shovel for the second sleepless night in a row. The crows and vultures would claim Paul's body.

The guilt of leaving Paul's body for the animals weighed on him less than reflecting on his own attitude. Charlton had begun to take pride in his role on the plantation. He had started to think that if the cotton failed to destroy the master's crops, he might get to retire as Paul thought that he would. Charlton felt superior to other slaves because of that, and yet the master ordered his most loyal slave left for dead with nothing on the side of the road. Charlton pledged to himself that he would never dare think he had it good again.

Chapter Twenty-Eight

May 1857

Charlton lay down in the grass with his hands behind his head, staring at the deep blue sky. He came to this spot to get away from the hired hands. Now that he had become the master's messenger, he could go anywhere he wanted at any time. He could spare some time from work. Now, he had to think.

He smiled. Angie had the darkest skin at the plantation. Charlton thought about how darker meant less desirable among members of both races at the plantation. He cared little for others' opinions though. To Charlton, Angie's beauty shone from her. Her hair wound down her back in tight curls. Like all the other female slaves, she kept it in place with a headscarf in the fields, but she always removed it when she reached the dinner line. Whenever she did, she would shake her head and let her locks twist in the air. Charlton loved to see her do it, swearing to himself that he'd never seen a prettier sight.

***

Angie glanced over as Charlton looked at her and hesitated a moment. Her tall, lanky frame had the rhythm of a gentle breeze through the tree tops as she strode over to him, "Why you stare at me?" she asked, speaking the first words exchanged between them.

"I… I…" Charlton shook his head in disgust as he failed to say anything. He decided to tell her the truth. "I think you're beautiful."

She froze, stared at him for a moment, and allowed a careful smile to form. "Thank you," she said. She giggled, then rejoined the dinner line. She snuck a couple of glances at him as he stayed in the same spot. He met each gaze with a broad smile. She grinned back each time, then turned to keep her place in line.

***

The next night, Charlton spotted Angie approaching the dinner line with her plate and ambled over to meet her. They made eye contact and she stopped to smile at him as he made up the rest of the distance. "I'm…" he said, as more words failed him. *I'm what? Not sure what to say? Not that smart? Embarrassing myself?* "Uh, I'm, um, Charlton."

"Are you sure?" Angie asked still smiling.

Charlton smiled back. "Yeah. I'm just, well…" Charlton couldn't think how to finish the sentence and let it trail off.

"I'm Angie," she said. They walked together to the dinner line and talked about Angie's time at the plantation. She next spoke about her past and how she had already worked cotton fields before her former master died, which forced his widow to sell Angie and many other slaves to pay his debts.

When they had both taken their supper, Charlton said, "Well, I ought to get back to my children."

Angie looked disappointed. "Oh, you've got children."

"Well, they're not mine."

"But, you just said…"

"I know, but I take care of them and they lost their parents and they didn't have no one else and so, they came to live with me, but I kind of think of them as my children because, um…"

"It's all right," Angie said giggling and putting her hand on Charlton's shoulder. The tension Charlton felt as he stumbled over his words changed into excitement at her touch. "I know what you saying and it's kind of you to raise them. Best go back to them. I like talking to you, Charlton."

"Me too," Charlton said, shaking his head at his awkward response. He hurried back to his cabin, but paused to glance behind him and saw Angie still smiling at him. He returned her smile as his heart warmed with the promise of what had happened.

***

Each night thereafter meant greater interaction until Angie joined Charlton and the children in the cabin. At first, Joy volunteered her spot at the table and ate cross-legged on the floor. The next day, Charlton and Angie chose to sit together on the floor, leaving the table to the children.

Apart from her physical beauty, Charlton delighted most in her voice, which he thought sounded like the happy trilling of a bird. She chattered with him about one topic after the next, all of her choosing. Charlton let any hard feelings he had about slavery and the master drip away when he spent time with Angie.

***

A few weeks later, Charlton spied Angie after the work day as she came back from the fields. It looked as if her love of life had drained out of her. Her face sagged and her eyes looked puffy and tired. Charlton rushed over to her.

"What is it, Angie?" he asked.

Her sad expression broke Charlton's heart. She gazed at him, hesitated, then shook her head.

"Please tell me," Charlton said.

Angie swallowed with a loud gulping sound. "I got the lash, Charlton. Out in the field. The wind knocked the cotton cart over. I didn't do nothing, but I was there. They tied me up, pulled down the top of my dress, and hit me. I never been hit so hard." Angie sobbed and fell into Charlton's arms. He held her close as she cried. Anger gripped Charlton as he repeated words of comfort to her. His voice shook and his body trembled.

Angie stopped crying, but Charlton still trembled with anger. "Why you shaking?" she asked in a whisper.

Charlton pulled himself away and cradled her head in his hands. "Can't you tell? I hate what they did to you. I love you."

The pain left Angie's eyes and face. The moment restored her beauty and delight returned to her, though her tears came back. "I love you, too," she said.

He brought his face closer and they kissed for the first time. The sensation pulled Charlton into a reality he did not know existed until now.

When he lay awake in bed that night, recalling the kiss, he thought of his parents. A father he could not remember and a mother who died as punishment for her son's actions. Now he knew a pleasure that his parents experienced together. He wished never to know the pain.

***

As Charlton stared into the blue sky, reality returned to him. He remained a man owned by another man, subject to the whims of that man over his body, his possessions, his choices, and even his life. Angie too. Everything applied to both of them. He wanted to marry her, but he couldn't because marriage meant children and children meant more people for the master to own and worse, more loved ones that the master could sell.

He thought about his important role on the plantation, and how he made himself so useful to the master that maybe the master would give him special treatment and let him keep his children and wife. He shut his eyes to close out the world as the reasons why he couldn't count on favored treatment weighed on his mind. First, he planted cotton because the master's land could not handle it. When the master caught on, he would destroy Charlton's family. Even if the master's land could handle cotton, Charlton knew what happened to Paul. The moment the master thought of Charlton as useless to him, he could expect the worst.

Charlton clenched his eyelids tight together. He might enjoy these moments of solitude and other privileges, but he would never know the joy of having a wife and children of his own. He almost wished to discard all of his smarts and knowhow. If he didn't have either, he would propose marriage, have children, and maybe even keep them until the end of his life. But with the knowledge he had, he knew he couldn't have any of it.

***

The weeks spent with Angie sped past. Every day brought them closer together. Charlton dreaded the moment she would mention marriage. The white world and the slave world shared the same rule that women did not ask men to marry. Angie alluded to marriage quite often, with hypothetical situations. Each time Charlton figured out how to change the subject. Angie's sighs and twisted facial expressions grew in intensity with each dismissal.

Months after their first contact, Charlton and Angie strolled the plantation hand in hand on a Sunday afternoon. Charlton felt Angie's palm grow hotter as they swung their hands. Charlton tried to doubt the evidence, but as her breath grew heavy, he knew what she would say as she slowed them to a stop.

"Charlton," she said as her eyes held tenuous contact with his gaze. Though she opened her mouth to say more, she said nothing.

"Yes?" he said.

"I love you."

"I love you too."

She sighed. "Why haven't you asked to marry me?"

Charlton shook his head. "I can't," he said.

Her eyes flashed and she dropped his hand with a flourish and continued to walk. He rushed forward to catch up with her. "Please Angie. You got to understand."

Angie stopped and whirled on Charlton. "Well, then tell me!" she said.

Charlton sighed. He knew she deserved an explanation. "I never told you about my parents. I need to tell you."

The frustration Angie wore on her face fell away. "You told me the master sold them and left you all alone."

"That's not all. I love you, Angie. I didn't want to tell you the truth. I don't want you to know."

"We slaves, Charlton. Bad things happen all 'round me all the time. Tell me."

"All right." They sat and Charlton threw away his reservations to tell her all about his parents' ordeal. He didn't stop there though. He told her about his past and his plans for the master. Angie listened in silent, troubled attention through every word.

He ended with his discovery of Paul. "Don't you see why I can't marry you?" For the first time to Angie, or even himself, Charlton drew in his breath, ready to state the obvious conclusion.

Angie's eyes grew wide and she began to shake her head, the action gaining vigor as she went. "No. No, don't say it!" she said. She stopped shaking her head and instead put it in her hands to cry.

Charlton scooted around behind her and wrapped his arms around her waist. "Don't touch me. Let me go," she said in a weak voice. Charlton obeyed.

"Angie, I'm really sorry. I have to protect you."

His words stopped her crying. She looked up at him with red, sore eyes. "Protect me? By breaking my heart?"

Charlton moved in front of her. "I don't want to break your heart. The master's cruel. When he finds out I married you, he'll use you against me. He'll hurt you, if he wants me to do something and I don't.

But even if he doesn't, he can't keep growing cotton or his fields will die. When that happens, he's going to do bad things to me, like sell you away. If we had any children, they'd get sold too."

Angie stared into the sky, her eyes moving back and forth. She turned to him after what seemed like forever to Charlton. "What if the cotton don't kill the fields? Then, he won't do nothing."

"Angie, we're slaves. He can do a lot to us. Remember what happened to Paul. He did all the master wanted and he still got killed."

Angie turned her eyes to the sky again, where she kept her gaze as she spoke. "My mama taught me being happy is all that matter in this world. We in love and we should get married. The master sell us apart, but he can't stop our love. If we ain't together, we still love each other."

Charlton thought it over. "Let's stay the way we are and not get married. Then, the master wouldn't ever sell you away to hurt me."

Angie shook her head. "No, Charlton, they all knows 'bout us. The women folk keep asking me when we're getting married. The master could know by now."

She looked at Charlton, hope gleaming out of her bloodshot eyes. Charlton felt caged. He'd cornered himself by getting too close to Angie already. He stuffed his head in his hands. He spoke between them. "We can't be seen together any more, Angie. Please don't come back to me."

He looked up at the sound of her weeping. She lay curled over on the ground. "I can't stay. I'm sorry," Charlton said. He sprinted away toward his cabin. When he had added enough distance, he dropped into the grass and wept.

***

For two weeks, Charlton and Angie kept apart. For the first week, neither acknowledged the presence of the other. By the end of the first week, Angie attempted to catch Charlton's gaze. She kept her eyes fixed on him, but he refused to make eye contact.

Two weeks later, Charlton lay awake in his bed, viewing the moon through his makeshift window. He alternated between thinking of Angie and trying not to think of her when he heard a gentle rapping on the front door. He closed his eyes tight knowing the source of the sound, but he could not keep himself from rolling out of bed and opening the door. Angie stood before him, tears dropping from her eyes. When he opened the door, she threw herself into his arms. The contact forced the air out of his lungs a little too loud. He spun and looked at the children, but they continued to sleep.

Angie cried into his shoulder. His arms folded around her. "It'll be all right," he said again and again.

After a while, Angie took control of herself and pushed away from Charlton to look into his eyes. He couldn't stand to see her cry and appreciated the lack of light to avoid seeing the effects of her crying. "Charlton, please take me back," she said, her voice cracking.

"I want to, but…"

"But, what? We don't have to be married, Charlton. I don't care about that. I just can't stand us being apart no more."

"It's not about marriage, Angie. It's about you being in danger with me. The master will hurt you."

She shook her head as if shaking his words from her memory. "Charlton, I can do things with you. Things that will make you forget about the master. I wanted to wait until marriage, but…"

Charlton backed away as Angie loosened her neckline and pulled her dress over her head. In the moonlight, he could make out only her silhouette, but even still she presented the most beautiful image he had ever seen.

"Angie, please. The children," Charlton said in a whisper.

She shook her head, her locks arcing in the moonlight. "The children sleep like rocks. They won't know." She removed the distance between them and pressed her body and lips against his. He longed to wrap his arms around her and give in to temptation. Instead, he pulled back and said, "No. I want to. How I want to, but I have to protect you."

Shame seemed to grip Angie; she covered herself with her arms and backed away toward the door. She ducked down to the floor. Although Charlton lost sight of her in the moonlight, he could hear her hands brushing the floor. Her head popped back into view, then the bunched up dress came back over her head and arms. In no time, she shot up to full posture and grabbed the door, yanking it open.

"Angie, please," Charlton said.

She responded with a sputtering sound and then resumed crying. She bolted out the door and Charlton followed to the doorway. "Angie, please, come back," he said in a hushed tone. Yet, his feet remained planted to the floorboards. He could not pursue her; he had hurt her enough that she would not return.

He took reluctant, pained solace with the results of the encounter. He reassured himself that even though it would pain him, he hoped Angie would find a man that she could love. He heard a door shut in the distance, knowing Angie made it back to the women's cabin. He headed for his bed to try to get sleep.

Chapter Twenty-Nine

The next day, Charlton talked to himself in the field, trying to stay away from everyone as much as possible so as not to appear crazed as he worked with the subsistence crops. When he returned to the quarters at the end of the day, he could hear a buzzed chatter from the group.

As he approached the camp, Charlton's heart thumped in his chest. All eyes turned toward him, many of them glaring, the others looking shocked. Out of the crowd, Harriet, an outspoken widow, emerged and stepped right up to him.

She waggled her index finger at him. "You filthy boy. You killed her! You killed our angel," she said.

"Killed? Your angel? What are you talking about?" He figured she meant how he broke Angie's heart.

She stared at him, her face twisted with anger. "Don't you play dumb, boy. You know what I say."

Charlton nodded. "Angie? Where is she? I'll talk to her."

Harriett and those around her stared at him. After an awkward moment, Harriett spoke. "She dead. She slit her wrists because you broke her heart." Charlton stood staring at her, unable to process her words.

She got closer to him, screaming in his face. "You beast! You don't even care!" Harriett's face flushed red as she turned her gaze to the ground and spat near Charlton's feet. She spun around and stomped away.

The murmurs continued. Charlton stood still. The sound of a swarm of bees filled his head, trying to drown out the echoes of Harriet's words. He heard and saw nothing after those words. How could someone so full of life die? No. The chattering, Angie's absence, Harriett's anger, and the news all added up to Angie's suicide, yet Charlton could no more accept the news than that he himself had died. His feet remained fixed to the ground while he shut out the world.

***

Night began to fall and Charlton remained in the spot where Harriet told him the news, except sitting now. The children came to him. Joy's cheeks stood out red with dried tears. Archie and Nellie looked shaken. They surrounded him, but Charlton only glanced up, then resumed staring at the ground in front of him.

After glances between each other, Archie and Nellie fixed their eyes on Joy to prompt her to speak.

"Charlton?" Joy said.

Charlton looked up at Joy, confused. "Yeah?" he asked.

"We, uh, we want you to come back to the cabin. You can't be out here past sundown."

"I want to see Angie," Charlton said. "Is she there?"

Joy exchanged glances with Archie and Nellie. Tears found their way to Joy's cheeks again. "Yeah," she said.

Charlton rose to his feet. "All right, let's go."

The younger children scolded their older sister on the way back, but Charlton didn't listen to what they said.

When he got to the door, Charlton yanked it open. "Angie, I'm here!" he said.

He squinted at their spot and saw the wall. "She's not here," he said. "Why'd you say she was here?" Charlton asked Joy.

"Charlton, please don't be angry. I needed you to come back and mama always say the dead don't leave us. They're always with us. So, so, I knew when we got here she'd be here too. Oh please don't be angry. We loved her too. Oh please don't be mad." Joy's eyes met Charlton's and Charlton could see tears.

In a rush, the reality of what he heard flooded Charlton. He sank to his knees, then onto his back drowning in the news. He gasped for breath as tears splashed out of his eyes. He screamed out his hatred for the master and for himself. In his hope of protecting Angie, he had crushed the flower in his hand. The master had done nothing to Angie. Charlton did it to her. He killed her. Harriett spoke the truth.

He stopped screaming and opened his eyes to see the children backing away from him; their fear made him realize that he needed to compose himself for their sake. He sat on the floor, trying to get his breathing back under control, but an image of Angie's smiling face came into his mind, which folded him over at the hips with his hands covering his head. He wept longer than he had since learning of his mother's death. The guilt tripled his pain. Harriett's words that he had killed Angie echoed true in his head. All the words from the previous night gave him pause as he considered all that he had done wrong.

The thought of killing himself to join Angie crossed his mind until little hands pressed on his back. The children kneeled around him. Joy repeated the words he spoke to Angie when she came to him, "It'll be all right," she said.

Anger at himself coursed through his veins. He told Angie the same thing Joy said to him now as this sweet, caring child tried to console him. He had experienced profound loss with Ole Joe, Belle, and his mother. How could he not see how Angie felt when he took his love away?

As Joy kept repeating herself, Charlton's heart softened. He tried to regain control of himself. He thought of the children, all now placing their hands on his back, trying to coax him out of his position. They hurt too. They too would never see Angie again, a woman they had loved.

With all the effort he could muster, Charlton ceased weeping and straightened himself up to sitting. He tried to speak, but choked on his words. He cleared his throat and tried again. "I'm sorry. You loved her too. I need to be strong for you," he said in a rasp.

One by one Charlton hugged the children. He wanted to show them that they didn't need to avoid talking about Angie. He brought up the first story about her and when he finished, the children joined him by telling their own stories.

When the hour got too late, they went to bed. Charlton thought they all seemed better. As he struggled with another night of pain, Charlton kept his bouts of sobbing as quiet as possible.

***

The days and weeks after Angie's suicide dripped by at an excruciating pace. He lay awake at night hating himself, the depression that drove Angie to kill herself, and most of all slavery. He could not deny that he hurt her, but he would never have caused her pain if not for slavery.

Charlton wanted to stop hating himself, but he knew his fellow slaves hated him, which made forgiving himself harder. Harriett continued to spit at his feet when he passed. She even took the lash once when the overseer saw her do it. The others didn't spit, but they eyed him when he approached. Everyone knew that he broke Angie's heart and that led her to take her life. Parents warned their daughters against talking to Charlton and wondered aloud when the master would order Charlton's children out of his cabin. In his bed staring at the ceiling, he scoffed at their feelings, which had grown from mere jealousy at his favored position with the master. They despised the wrong person.

***

Charlton persevered only by refusing to think about the suicide. He could do nothing else. The desire to seek revenge on the master grew in his heart as he thought of what it made Angie do. Charlton found a renewed focus on savaging the master's fields.

One cool November day, the master ordered one of his house slaves to fetch Charlton to the big house. The skinny older boy approached Charlton in the field. "Charlton?"

Charlton looked up from his work inspecting a cotton plant that was beginning to show signs of wilting. Annoyance crept into Charlton's muscles at the interruption. He wanted to further investigate this sign of his coming revenge. "Yeah? What?" Charlton said seeing the shy face.

"Master, he want to see you," the house slave said.

"Can't it wait?" Charlton said.

The boy's eyes grew wild darting back and forth. "Uh, I don't," the boy said, but he couldn't finish.

"I guess not. Where at?"

"The big house."

Charlton nodded and got up. The boy waited for him, but Charlton dismissed him. "I don't need you to go with me," Charlton said.

The house slave turned around and jogged back toward the house. Charlton marched along, not the least bit curious what the master wanted. The master had called for him plenty of times with no real point.

When Charlton approached the house, a carriage and horses stood visible in the trackway. The master had never called him to the house when he had visitors. Charlton's pace quickened as he made his way to the kitchen door that the master ordered all the slaves to use. The idea that the Zutters had purchased him crossed his mind, but he doubted it. After all these years when Charlton took on such importance to the master, he knew the sale couldn't have happened now.

He entered the house when the cook failed to show up to answer the door. As he opened the door, he saw the master's graying beard and then his beady eyes staring at him. The master's expression projected a sort of forced calm, but with a degree of mirth. "You sent for me, Master?" Charlton said. Charlton's mind raced as he tried to put together what the master had planned. Did the guest have something to do with it?

"Yes. Yes, I did," the master said. "I see the way you conduct yourself around here, Charlton."

"Master?" Charlton said.

"Oh, don't pretend that you don't believe you have top billing around here. I know you even think you're better than me. I am the master of this place, not you."

"Master, I promise you, I don't think that. You are the master and I'm your slave."

"You lie!" the master said, getting animated and sticking his finger out at Charlton. "Not another word! You listen to me. I've been too kind to you. It all started when you were just born and I made you the plaything for my very own daughter. Then, I let you go off on a vacation with those dastardly Zutters. Then, I made you the plantation manager and bestowed favor on you that you didn't deserve. I have done far more since then and I think you know of what I speak." The master's tone remained even and steady, but his eyes betrayed his feelings as they darted around the room, never falling on Charlton.

Charlton wanted to argue with him. Belle took care of Charlton only because the master didn't want to kill a slave. He would have mentioned that the Zutters had to drive a hard bargain to take Charlton into their business or that he had made more money for the master than the master had ever dreamed. But Charlton held his tongue as ordered.

The master continued his speech. "I have to bring you back to earth. You have to find out who you really are. Follow me." The master did not wait for assent. He turned out of the kitchen and down the hall. Charlton obeyed.

The master led Charlton to his study and behind the door; Belle gazed out the window with her back to the door. Charlton's heart pounded in his chest.

Chapter Thirty

The scent of Belle's perfume struck Charlton first: a strong aroma of flowers, but something she had never worn when he knew her. Charlton flinched as he tried to reconcile the sweet, innocent girl he loved with the slave mistress who stood too disinterested to look at the man she had promised to marry.

"Belle, my dear," the master said.

"Yes, Father?" Belle said in a voice deeper and colder than Charlton recalled. She turned with her gaze crossing over Charlton as if he didn't exist and meeting her father's eyes. Charlton realized he hadn't given the master enough credit. He thought that he had sunk to the bottom over Angie's suicide, but to have his childhood memories of his first love crushed might just break him for good.

"I need you to speak to him, like we discussed. I'll go for a walk with my grandson while you take care of this. Tell him what you told me," the master said.

Belle nodded. "Father?"

"Yes?" he said.

"Could you please shut the door on your way out? I don't want anyone hearing what I have to say to this slave."

"Yes, of course." As the master shut the door, a lump formed in Charlton's throat at the way Belle referred to him in such a cold manner. He detested her mannerisms. She had changed and aged too. Charlton pictured her as older when he still thought of her. She would have creases of a smile pressed into her skin at the mouth and eyes. She would be relaxed and maybe a little overweight, not rigid and tight as she stood in the master's study, looking like her mother.

She didn't speak, but seemed to evaluate him. Charlton had half hoped she would soften with the door closed, but her eyes still appeared detached. Already though, strength built in Charlton's core. The master planned to hurt him, but he stood resolute facing the new Belle and deciding that the girl he loved had died and another cold Southern slave mistress lived in her place. He had no reason to mourn the death of his memories, which would remain unchanged for a girl who had passed away.

At last, Belle spoke. "My father tells me that his kindness to you has made you forget your place. He was convinced that the time I spent with you when we were both children were making you forget who you really are. He wanted me to strike down any memories that you might have. I think this meeting is a waste of time. He should be whipping the pride out of you. I promise you that my husband would not hesitate to do so.

"It is a troubling sign of my father's weakness that he would call me in to address you directly. How can I, a lady of a vaster plantation than my father's, be expected to lower myself in such a manner as to address a common slave?" The anger rose in Charlton's chest. His neck muscles tightened and his blood vessels outlined the fight that built inside him. He hated Belle less than the South, the depraved and sick South. It took an innocent girl and twisted her into a monster. He wished to torch all the Southern plantations to the ground and take out white and black alike.

"But, this is the task that my father set before me, and I will honor his wishes," she said. "I was a naïve girl. I knew not the way the world worked, nor did I accept my place as a part of the better race. The Negro race is low, where mine is high. The members of your race have neither grace nor intelligence, whereas the members of my race are blessed with both. In short, we are God's chosen people to care for the lower race. Had I realized this, you would have never experienced a moment of my companionship. I am sorry for it." She gazed at Charlton, at last meeting his eyes.

Charlton met her gaze and Belle flinched. The flinch carried her gaze and her whole posture back to looking out the window. Charlton cursed himself as a fool. Her reaction told him the girl inside Belle still lurked behind her mask. Her act had tricked him.

"Are you not going to speak?" Belle said still gazing out the window.

"If you wish it, I'll speak." Charlton said.

Belle gasped. Charlton knew the sound of his voice caused the crack in her composure. He relished the moment, letting silence penetrate the gulf between them.

At last Charlton spoke again. "I don't believe anything you've said."

"How dare…" Belle said in a weak voice.

"You will let me speak," Charlton said. He said it less as a command and more as a statement of truth.

"When I was born, your father thought about having me killed because I was small and thought killing a child would make it easier to make his slaves fear him." Belle, who had begun slumping, stiffened her back. "You heard about it and made him promise to take care of me. So, he sold my father. Your father told me my father tried to escape and was beaten to death by slave catchers. I never knew him, but I miss him.

"I learned to read, write, and speak like a gentleman because you were kind to me. I learned to love because of you. I learned to hate because of him. He sold my parents and they both got killed."

"Both?" Belle asked in a soft tone, still staring out the window.

"You should've let him kill me the day you got married. Instead, he sold my mama to the same man who killed my father. He beat her and took her and then she killed him. When she defended herself, she was hanged." Charlton kept his eyes trained on Belle. She trembled. Still, she refused to look at him.

"Then, I fell in love with a slave woman. Angie. She set my heart afire," Charlton said. He paused to study Belle's reflection in the window as she closed her eyes and her chest went up and down in a sigh. "She killed herself when I told her I couldn't marry her and we couldn't be together anymore."

Belle spun around on him, looking deep into his eyes. "She took her life?" Belle asked, eyes wide in a perfect impression of the girl he knew. Charlton nodded. "Why did you break her heart?"

"Belle, we loved each other. I wanted to marry her and have children, but I couldn't do it. How would you feel if your son could be sold away from you and all you could do was lay back and let it happen or you'd get the skin whipped off you? I couldn't have children and do that to them, but even if we didn't have a child, she'd be in danger cause your father would know that he could punish me by taking Angie away. I fell in love and I hate myself for it because I couldn't live with her and promise that she not get harmed, so I broke her heart and she slashed her wrists open and bled to death."

"Oh, no!" Belle said as her face contorted in shock and sorrow.

"And now I'm hearing from the one that cared about me as a child that your people take care of mine. If that's how your people take care of mine, then all I want is for your people to stop caring for mine. Your people beat and kill mine. Your father took away everyone who cared about me, except Angie. I did that myself. I have nothing left to give because of slavery. How would you feel if…"

"Stop! Please stop!" Belle said. She threw her arms up, then dropped to her knees, clasping her hands together. "I'm sorry, Charlton! Oh, I hope you'll forgive me. I didn't mean a word of it. My father put me up to it. He told me that if you didn't stop and learn your place that he would be forced to sell you and I wanted to know you were here."

Charlton wanted to believe her, but he had to know something first, "What about your promise, Belle? You would leave your husband if I was ever sold."

"But, Charlton, I can't leave Robert. If I did, I would have to leave my son. He needs me!"

"And your father knows that…"

Charlton walked around Belle to take his turn staring out the window. He kept his eyes trained on an old tree. Memories of his childhood flashed into his thoughts until the curtain in front of the window closed. He saw Belle's arm withdrawing from the sash. Then, he felt a gentle hand on his shoulder. Belle's hand rested there for a moment and then pulled at him, easing him into turning around.

Charlton fixed his gaze on Belle's face, where tears streamed. She opened her mouth to speak, but no words came out. She tried again and managed to speak, "Charlton, I need you to forgive me. Forgive me for what I said. I always felt secure having you on my father's land and I didn't want you to be sold even if I couldn't see you. But Father knows I can't leave my son and now he can sell you at will. He knows I don't feel about you the way I spoke. He promised that if I spoke to you today, he would keep treating you well. Oh, you do forgive me, don't you?"

Charlton's heart warmed and beat stronger. The girl who the master had stolen from him years ago stood before him and he had brought her back. "I forgive you," he said. He smiled as he wiped the tears from her cheeks with the thumb of each hand as he cupped her face with his palms. He gazed at the contrast of his dark hands on her pale face and lingered as Belle smiled and let a nervous laugh escape her throat.

Charlton half expected Belle to tear away from him and escape the room, but she didn't. Instead, she reached with her own hand to his face to wipe a tear that he had shed without realizing it. She used the back of her hand to caress his cheek, neck, and then his chest.

After Angie had offered herself to him and he refused against all of his urges, the touch of any woman may have aroused Charlton. He couldn't resist it now with his first love before him. He looked down at Belle's hand, then their eyes met. The smiles faded and their faces took on expressions of grave seriousness. Charlton guided Belle's face to his and their lips met. Her lips felt moist as they parted. The first kiss felt restrained, the second lingered, but the third consumed him.

Chapter Thirty-One

Charlton's and Belle's bodies came together in a tight embrace. Lips still locked, Charlton's hands explored Belle's back and sides and passed lower. Belle's hands worked over Charlton's body, lingering over his chest and shoulders. Belle sighed and moaned. She pawed at his shirt and managed to pull it off his body. She took a step back to admire him. "Oh, Charlton, you're a vision!" she said.

Charlton didn't want to talk though. He came to her again. Locking her lips with his and her body with his arms. He tried to undo her blue Southern society dress, but he fumbled with the rigging and Belle did not seem at all interested in helping him. He gave up to grope at her breasts through the dress. Belle groaned in pleasure. Her hands worked at his pants as he kicked off his boots and before long his pants fell down. Charlton stepped out of them, now exposed from head to feet.

Belle came at him again, running her hands all over his body and not showing an ounce of care that she stood on the threshold of making love to her father's slave while in his house and married to another man, the father of her child. Charlton let go of the thought as the lust he felt for her pushed him forward.

He worked his hands under her dress, but he only met more and stiffer fabric. He had always wondered how women's dresses had retained their bell-like shape. Charlton grew frustrated, but Belle nudged him back to her father's sofa where she prodded him into sitting. She grabbed the back of the sofa and hoisted herself up to a standing position and thrust her hips out. The dress pushed forward and allowed Charlton to get his hands under all the layers of fabric. He touched one more layer of soft cotton. As Belle moaned, he explored all around her hips, until he moved up and found a knot in some string. He had undone knots plenty of times at the Zutters' business and pulled this knot free. He tugged at the strings and loosened the fabric, which clung to Belle's hips. It came free and then dropped. Belle balanced from one leg to the other and flicked off the flimsy pants.

Belle's body felt soft to Charlton's touch. He worked with his hands as he had done all his life to get material to bend to his will. Belle quivered and shook more when his hands reached a region with moist skin below and a mound of hair above. He found a rhythmic pattern to his stroking that made Belle's moans reach a frantic, yet quiet pace.

When it seemed she could take no more and Charlton became a bit nervous, Belle guided Charlton to lay down on the sofa and crouched on top of him. She wiggled and Charlton found himself in his new concept of heaven. He groped her breasts and Belle accelerated her breathing. Her hands found his chest and she gripped on tight. It hurt Charlton, but he kept moving, guided by his instincts alone. She reached her peak first and plopped down onto Charlton's body, but his body continued to thrust with a will of its own. Utter bliss surrounded him.

After his peak, they laid with her body folded over his while he remained inside her. Their breathing remained heavy, then slowed to normal. "I never... I never felt anything like that," Belle said, still somewhat breathless.

"Me neither," Charlton said.

"I love you," Belle said.

"I love you, too," Charlton said. He looked Belle straight in the eyes, but something bothered him about the way she looked back at him. She said she loved him, but he couldn't tell whether she meant it or not.

"Belle, run away with me," Charlton said.

"Charlton, put on your clothes. Quickly!" Belle said.

She pulled herself off him. Charlton rolled off the sofa and put on his clothes. From the floor, he snuck a glance at Belle's naked lower half as she maneuvered her undergarment back on. He relished the view while believing that he would have many chances to see it again.

Belle stood up, smoothed out her dress, and took out a compact mirror to fix her hair and check her face. "Why do you want to run away with me, Charlton?" she asked as she went through the motions of putting herself back together.

"Why wouldn't I, Belle? What we just had together! We love each other. I can't stay here. I'm raising three children, but they're not mine and they'll be fine. I'm tired of living to make money for your father. He made you try to break me. I have to go from here...with you."

"No, Charlton, you don't. You need to stay here so I know you're safe."

"But, I'm saying you would go with me. We could work our way up North and I would pretend to be your slave. We could escape together."

"You know what would happen, Charlton. You know my father would disown me and he would have slave catchers chase and kill you."

"I'll take the chance, Belle. It's better to die in freedom than live as a slave."

"Maybe so, maybe so. Charlton, I can't leave with you."

"Why not?"

"Because of my son! I can't leave my son. He needs me. He's a good boy, he's not like his father. If I leave him, he'll be exactly like Robert. I can't let that happen!" Belle said. She pleaded with her eyes for him to understand, to give his consent, but he didn't offer it.

"Your promise, Belle. You promised to do this with me."

"I know, Charlton, and I want to, but things have changed. I'm a mother. I have responsibility to my son."

"We'll take him with us," Charlton said. He didn't want to take Robert's son with him, but he'd do it if he had to.

"I can't do that. Even if we made it to the North, they'll hate you up there more than you think my father hates you. They'll say you have me under a spell and are corrupting my morals. You think your people are loved up there while they hate you here, but they hate you just as much in the North. You don't want to live there and I am not bringing my son into all that."

"But, Belle, what about what we just had? That was wonderful."

"Oh, Charlton! I dreamed of that moment and thought for so long of what it might be like. It was all that I dreamed and more. When Robert takes me, he doesn't care what I feel. He mounts me like he would mount a horse when he needs to go into town." Belle made a face to show her distaste for her husband and Charlton mirrored it.

He wanted to think less of her for the remark, but he couldn't because what Robert did to her sounded like what Mr. Beauregard did to his mother. He realized Belle got nothing out of it, but gave up her body to a man she detested to fulfill a duty. Yet, after experiencing what she did with Charlton, she would go back to the man she hated and let him use her? How could she not choose to run away with him?

And with sudden conviction, Charlton understood. He hadn't brought the old Belle back into this world from the dead. She looked down at him with pity as he sat crouched on the floor with his arms hugging his legs tight. He could feel himself withdrawing from the world. The master had accomplished his purpose because after this encounter, he left Charlton's childhood memories torn and scarred. Belle would never regain her innocence. She had grown up from a sweet girl into a disenchanted, unhappy woman. Her moment of passion with Charlton meant no more than pleasure seeking and she had used him to satisfy her desires as much as her husband used her to satisfy his.

The words started escaping Charlton lips without thinking. Belle faded from his view. "I can't do this anymore. I can't be here. I need to escape. I need to fly. Why can't I fly? Grow wings from my body like the ground grows crops. I could look back down on the ground and never have to talk to another person as long as I live..."

"Charlton? Charlton, what are you talking about?" Belle crouched down and tried to pull Charlton's arms off his knees, but the power of his body left no room for getting overtaken by Belle's feeble strength. He took little notice of her efforts.

"I can't stay here. I can't stay here. I can't..." Charlton repeated the sentence. All the years of trying to get his revenge on the master when all he had ever wanted to do, escape with Belle as his wife, had come so close only to slip from his grasp. The moment had passed though and she would never fulfill her promise. He loved the children, but not enough to give him hope. One wilted cotton plant after so much time had passed stood as the only sign of Charlton's plan working. Any number of causes could have made the plant wilt, least of which that the master's land had failed him. How would he get his revenge if that didn't work? He only ended up giving his enemy more money, so he could hurt more people.

Charlton realized that he had stopped even mumbling to himself, he only sobbed. Over the noise he could barely make out Belle's voice as she said, "It's Father!"

He didn't care if the master saw his display. Despair filled his mind as he accepted that every fantasy he had about Belle lay destroyed before him, as did his hopes for revenge on the master.

"Belle? What's happening in there?" The master burst through the door before Belle could answer.

"Belle, what did you say to him?" the master said in a tone of bemusement.

Belle gained her composure and lied. "I only did what you told me, Father. You wanted to take the pride out of him didn't you?"

"Yes, of course."

"Well, I did it. Father?"

"Yes?"

"Please don't ask me to do that ever again."

"No, of course not. You did well."

"Where is Samuel?"

"With your mother."

"I need to go to him."

"Of course."

Belle left, but Charlton took little notice. His sobbing echoed in his head, while the salty tears poured into his mouth.

The master cleared his throat. Charlton's sobs faltered. The master gave Charlton time to collect himself, but his patience wouldn't last forever. Charlton didn't care about the master's patience, but didn't want the master to see him acting weak any more. First, Charlton stopped his tears, then waited while his breathing got back under control.

Before Charlton had stopped panting, the master spoke. "Well, well, well. That worked better than I hoped. Seeing you on the floor like that at my feet; it's where you ought to be. You reeked of pride and now, just like that, it's all gone. You needed to be grounded, boy."

By now Charlton's breathing returned to normal except for a desperate intake of breath every once in a while. The word "boy" grated at him. Despite Charlton's obvious adult age and the fact, hidden from the master, that he had just made love to a woman, Charlton felt like a boy. Not any boy, but the boy who heard from his master that a mob had killed his dear mother after she defended herself. He felt the same crushing humiliation of wearing his emotions in front of the man who wronged him.

The master continued. "This was done for your own good. You might have thought that I favored you from the start by offering you the friendship of my daughter when you were a child. Yet, we all need to see our place in the world. You are favored, but by virtue of your skill and what you can offer me. I wanted my daughter to show that the childhood favor you received had passed. She is a different person now. She is someone who does not care for you as you may have thought she would always do. You are favored because of what you offer, not because of who you are."

Charlton braced himself up to a sitting position and gazed at the master, his panicked breathing gone. A sense of calm swept out the tension that had consumed his body and he saw the master not only as an evil man, but also a confused one. He had thought it an act of caring to sweep Charlton's fond childhood memories into the dustbin. The master thought of himself as kind to rid Charlton of his illusions, but this speech revealed the master for who he accused Charlton of being, a man filled with delusion.

Charlton knew that this day had changed everything for him, but could not label what it meant. He looked up at the master who flicked his eyebrows upward as if expecting something. "Well?" the master said.

"Master?" Charlton asked, his voice cracking.

"When do you plan on thanking me? I have done you a favor. A master doing his slave a favor and he gets no gratitude?"

Charlton forced all his willpower into suppressing the urge to grin, snicker, or burst out laughing. He looked the master in the eye and said, "Thank you, Master."

"Ah, good. You may now continue your work." The master gestured to the door to allow Charlton to see himself out. As Charlton left with a steadiness that surprised him, the master clapped him on the shoulder. Charlton recoiled.

He made his way out the door and back to the fields, crested the hills to look out, and headed for the land where he could check on his revenge. The field he sought grew cotton that the field hands had packed too close together. If cotton savaged the field as the manual said, then it should have started there. He walked among the rows, sinking to his knees for closer inspection. Not a sign of weakness appeared in a single plant he checked. Desperation weakened his muscles. His hands moved and his eyes followed from plant to plant. All the plants grew solid, healthy, and strong. His plan had failed.

Charlton had cried himself out in the master's house. He had no more tears left inside of him. Instead he sat on the ground and stared at the landscape.

The germ of an idea had always fascinated Charlton. This idea began with a little spark of hope straight from where his heart beat. The spark began to warm his chest and spread outward. Next his arms felt a surge of power and his legs tingled. Then the breath caught in his throat and the idea popped into his head with one name, "Belle."

The master loved his land; of that Charlton had no doubt. Yet, the master had credited a slave with improving the crops that came from his land. Charlton knew from the master's past rants that he considered his race superior to Charlton's people. Still, he gave favor to a slave for what he could do with the land without hesitation. The master insisted on taking away Charlton's connection to his daughter though.

The master did not know that Charlton had made love to Belle. Charlton managed to compromise the master's daughter in a way that would cause horror and disgrace to settle into the master's mind for the rest of his days. All this time, Charlton had tried to poison the master's land, but the land took second place in the master's mind. He loved his daughter far more than the land. Had the master not given a slave the chance to have his way with the land? How would he feel to know that a slave had his way with his daughter?

Charlton stood tall and proud now, unaware of the action that got him to stand. He considered what had happened in the master's study. The master's land couldn't offer or take away consent for actions done to it while the master's daughter chose to give herself to Charlton. The land sat idle while others took action on it, while Belle had stripped Charlton bare and thrust her body onto him. The ground had given no resistance as shovels and spades penetrated it, Belle put Charlton inside of her. The fields had submitted to Charlton's will, the master's real pride and joy had given herself to a slave. The land had to accept seed that got tossed into it, Belle thrusted herself on Charlton and moved until he planted his seed inside of her.

Charlton froze as he considered the actual act and what it meant. He had released his seed in Belle and she had done nothing to stop it and everything to encourage it. Even now it raced inside of her seeking the ground that would plant and grow it. If the master knew, he would see Charlton's seed in his daughter's womb as the greater poison than cottonseed in his land's womb.

He jolted upright casting his hands into the air, reaching for the sun. With eyes shut, he tilted his head to the sky and saw nothing but red emblazoned through his eyelids. The master's crop could wilt and fray and he would care a fraction for that compared to welcoming his dark-skinned grandchild into the world. Charlton couldn't wait to explain to the master how Belle came to be with child.

Chapter Thirty-Two

October 1858

Charlton awoke early in the morning before the sun rose. He lay in his bed thinking about time. For everyone, time kept passing until death. Everyone would end up dead, no matter their skin color. Then what happened?

The master believed heaven awaited whites and hell awaited blacks. In the Charleston church services, some of Charlton's fellow slaves believed they would go to heaven along with the whites. Charlton didn't know what to think, except that slave masters wouldn't go anywhere but hell if life continued after death. As Charlton waited for a death he thought would happen soon, he hoped he would get to heaven where his parents and Angie waited for him. He knew the first thing he would do is beg Angie for her forgiveness. Of all his hopes, he wanted that chance more than anything else, even more than telling the master what happened with Belle.

As he lay in bed, he listened to the children breathing. When he died, they would become orphans yet again. Charlton had mixed feelings about this. In truth, Charlton welcomed his imminent death. He had almost nothing left to achieve now that the news had made it around the plantation that the master's daughter would bring another child into the world. Belle, his childhood love, had fulfilled her fantasy with him and he knew, whether or not he told the master about how he fathered the child, the pieces would fit together and he would get killed anyway. Charlton could still escape on the Underground Railroad, but he wanted to leave that to the children. If he tried to escape with them, the master would spare no expense to find him and put the children in far more danger than if they went alone.

No, Charlton knew he had no desire to accomplish any other goal, save one. He did want to see the children grow and prosper. He had failed with Phillip, but these children loved him and maybe they still needed him.

A sudden realization struck Charlton and made him flinch. What would the master do to the children after he died? Would he take vengeance on them as punishment for what Charlton did? He thought about maybe setting them off on their escape before confronting the master.

Peace once again settled over Charlton's mind. Not once did the master discuss the children with Charlton in all their meetings and with that Charlton convinced himself that the master didn't remember that he ordered them to live with Charlton. They would remain just as safe until they decided to escape and they couldn't do that before he died because they wouldn't leave without him. Charlton decided that future events had to unfold like he planned or not at all.

As Charlton listened to them breathe, he allowed his mind to picture their future of working for money in the north, maybe with ship builders like the Zutters. He would tell them to take the Underground Railroad and see to it that they live free of slavery. What better way to take care of them than to send them away from the hell of the master's plantation?

***

Despite the warm fall season in the Deep South, Charlton found the steady breeze and cloud cover relaxing, so he indulged himself with lazing back in a field no one worked that day. He let the plan take form. That night, he would sit around the dinner table with the children and tell them what they would do. They would use all the assets that Charlton collected to find their way to freedom including his knowledge of the way to the station, his compass, his schoolbook, and his money. They would probably take their cups and utensils as well, but not the plates. They would need to travel as light as possible.

***

Charlton smiled as he watched the children eat their breakfast. His thoughts turned to his plan to sacrifice himself and he wondered why it didn't disturb him more. Knowing he would die soon should have brought fear and reluctance, yet he felt none of it. He beamed at his children as they ate, and each of them seemed to notice as they grinned at him.

"What is it, Charlton?" Joy asked.

"What you mean?"

"You seem awful happy. Something good happen?"

"Sort of. I need to tell you some things, but first I have to ask each of you something. Did you have a good day today?" All three children agreed that they had good days.

"You're all wrong. None of you had a good day. You're all slaves working for someone else without getting anything for it. What keeps us working hard here if we don't get any of the money we make for the master? It's what we get when we don't work hard. They hit us and hurt us. None of you have ever had a good day and you won't while you live here."

The children stopped eating to stare at Charlton. He had never spoken like this to them before then. He told Phillip about how bad he had it as a slave and it did no good, but he couldn't expect them to want to leave unless he told them the truth. Charlton had more to say too. He gestured to their plates and they went back to eating.

"Do you know why I taught you to read?" Charlton asked. He answered before any of them could try. "Because you're not going to stay here. You're going to leave."

The children exchanged glances with one another, but they heeded Charlton's directions and kept eating. "The whites shouldn't hit you. They don't even have the right to make you work for them for free. Think about it. What makes them different from us? The only thing I can see is the color of our skin, but what makes white better than black? Nothing. All we do is good things for them. Our work gives them crops and their crops are sold to get money and that money gives them nice houses and clothes, but it's *our* work that gives them these things, and we get nothing but hurt for helping them."

Archie looked confused. "Archie? You got a question?" Charlton asked.

"What's money?"

"It's paper, like the pages from our school book and whites want it. They can use the money to get other things. Here, I'll show you." Charlton got up and lifted the loose floorboard and pulled out the leather pouch the Zutter's had given him. He put it on the table and fished out his pay, showing it to the children. The bills had frayed and faded a bit, but looked good enough to use. The children stopped eating again to gaze at the money.

"When you use it, you have to look at the number on it. The higher numbers get you more than the lower ones. That's why I taught you about numbers. If you buy something and the number of dollars you give is higher, the seller has to give you money back."

The children had finished eating and stared at Charlton confused. Joy spoke up first, "Charlton, why you telling us this?"

Charlton felt a lump rising in his throat. The confidence drained out of him as he wondered how to tell them what would happen.

The children exchanged glances with each other. Charlton couldn't keep them from the truth any longer. How would they feel when he told them they would try to escape again as they did with their mother, this time without anyone to help them until they got picked up at the station?

"When you leave here, I won't go with you." The children stared at Charlton with eyes wide. He didn't know how to comfort them and ease their minds. Children shouldn't have to do anything so dangerous on their own. Yet, before any other family took them in after his death, they needed to go out on their own when they had no one else to look after them. If they didn't, they would get tied down to a new family, which would keep them from leaving.

As Joy cried, Charlton decided he must press forward. "I wanted to help you all your lives. Believe me. When the master said I had to take care of you, I didn't know what to think, but I took you here to live with me and I taught you how to read, but you taught me instead. You taught me how to care for others. I didn't know how before, I loved people in my life, but they always took care of me. My life is so much better 'cause of you. I'd go with you, but there's something I got to do and then I won't get to go with you."

"What, Charlton? What you got to do?" Joy asked.

He wanted to tell them everything; how he sought revenge and that he already did what the master would kill him for doing. All the stories he had kept from them about his life stood at the end of his lips; how his mother had endured humiliation and rape by the evil Beauregard only to get hanged by a mob, about his father getting beaten to death, and the murder of Paul. He wanted to tell them this, but he would not because these stories belonged in the grave with him.

"When the time's right, I have to tell the master about something I did, which will make him angry. He'll sell me away from you when I tell him and I'll have to live somewhere else."

Joy wiped away her tears. "Charlton, just don't tell him. You can leave with us. You don't have to tell him nothing." Archie and Nellie nodded with enthusiastic agreement.

Charlton chose his words to avoid giving away too much. "Joy, I'd do that, but what I did, the master will find out and he'll get so mad he'd give someone a lot of money to find me. All the slave catchers around here will try to get me back. That'd put you in danger. Oh, he'll try to find you too. But he'd want me back more. You got to run on your own and I got to tell the master what I did. It's the best way to help you."

The children cast their eyes down at their plates. Finally, Archie said, "What you do?"

Charlton knew he couldn't say what he did with Belle, but he did something else and he planned to tell the master about that too, so he didn't have to lie to them. "I got to be manager 'round here by telling the master I could make him more money. Then, I found out that the master couldn't grow cotton here too or his land wouldn't grow nothing no more. I wanted to hurt his fields 'cause he deserved it. When the master finds out what I did, and he'll know soon, I'm done for.

"That's why you got to run. The master'll sell his slaves when his crops die 'cause he'll have to make more money to keep on. When the master sells you, he'll be sure to sell you separate 'cause that's what happens. You got lucky to get sold here together, but it won't last. You need each other. How would you feel if you never saw each other again? You got to stay together. I know you're afraid 'cause your mama ran with you, but she didn't know about what I know. I know how to get you up North safe. You got to go to a place called the Underground Railroad station. You'll wait there, then someone'll come along to help you out, and they'll get you the rest of the way. I'm going to write out just what you need to do and leave it under the floorboard. You'll do just what it says and you'll be all right. Do you understand?"

The children's nodding faces exposed deep sorrow. "I got more to show you," Charlton said. He took out the compass from the pouch and showed them how to use it. When the light faded away, Charlton told them about William Lloyd Garrison and the Zutters. The children sat still, eyes wide.

***

When sleep overtook the children, Charlton lay for a long while in his bed thinking about what would happen. As much as he didn't want to have a child with Angie so he could keep the master from having new slaves, he smiled thinking about Belle having his child. With the child coming from a white woman, he had no worries about anyone owning his son or daughter. His child would grow up free. He refused to let any doubt change his mind about that. A tear came down his cheek. He wanted to see his baby, but he knew it wouldn't happen.

A snorting sound came from Nellie and he went silent listening, but she went back to sleep. He decided that he wouldn't wait another day before telling the master what he had done. He had concluded the conversation with the children intent on not giving them a final goodbye, so he could keep them from begging him to stay with them. They needed him to disappear without any more warning.

**

Charlton ate breakfast with the children the next morning, then took his usual path to the Big House. The hired hands expected him to have his morning meeting with the master, so they had no reason to stop him. He knocked on the kitchen door. The cook ushered him inside. "Thanks," Charlton said and headed to the master's study.

Chapter Thirty-Three

Charlton walked forward, glancing at the walls. His confidence made him feel like he owned the home. He reached the study door and knocked. "Come in," the master said.

Charlton nudged the door open. The master sat in his study chair. He didn't wait before saying, "Nothing for you this morning, Charlton." When Charlton didn't leave, he said, "Yes? What is it?"

"Master, I wanted to say congratulations," Charlton said with his arms out.

"What? Oh yes, Belle is expecting a child. You must have heard from the hired hands. Yes, we are all very proud around here." The master's face contorted into his usual sneer. "Well, well, well... You know, I didn't expect this out of you, Charlton. Didn't think you would even speak of my daughter again."

Charlton matched the master's grin and moved inside the room, closing the door behind him. The master's grin vanished and his face looked a little concerned. Charlton knew he didn't have permission to close the door.

"What the hell are you doing?" the master said.

"Closing the door. I don't expect that you want others to hear what I'm about to say," Charlton said.

The master looked worried. A surge of power coursed through Charlton's muscles. "Do you know what revenge is?"

The master gripped his hands around the edge of his chair arms. "What is this? What you getting at, boy?"

"When someone does you a favor, you got to do something good for them. Well, revenge is when someone does something bad to you and you do something bad to them."

"I know what revenge is! What you getting at boy? You're about out of rope."

"Well, John," Charlton said, then paused to watch the master's face contort in anger. He gritted his teeth and shot a death stare at Charlton, but he said nothing. "You sold my papa when I was born. Then, he ran and white people found him and beat him 'til they killed him.

Then, you let Belle take care of me and I loved her. She taught me how to read and write and speak like a white man. She loved me back and told me if I wrote some words into the ground so you would see them, you'd let me go free, but you wouldn't let her see me no more. When I found out she was getting married, I wrote the words again, so I could stop it."

The master gripped the arms of his chair tighter and made as if to get up, stopping midway. "How dare you?" Charlton shot his hand up, and half to his surprise, the master closed his mouth and sunk back in his chair to let Charlton continue.

"You locked me up in the toolshed. While I rotted in there, you sold my mama away and then laughed at me when you told me she got killed. I swore I'd get back at you for it, but I didn't know how." Charlton glanced at the master who sat fuming. His eyes stared at Charlton in wonder. He sat powerless as Charlton appeared to have nothing to lose with the master. After years of allowing Charlton to have access to him alone in his house, he had little protection from him.

"When I heard your plantation manager died, I thought, I'd try to take the job. I found those cotton plants somewhere else and moved them to that field, and acted like I grew them. You know why I picked cotton? I read that your land couldn't grow it for long, but it worked and there's no reason to think it'll stop." The master released a little tension from his arms at these words. Charlton smirked.

"I thought I'd lost, but then you made a mistake. You made me talk to Belle. You told me you wanted the pride out of me. But you don't know what happened here." The master's arms tightened again on the arms of his chair as he sat with jaw clenched.

"She did what you wanted and told me how I had to get put in my place. She told me how kind you were to me and how bad I was, but I knew she didn't mean any of it. She loved me, you know, and she still loves me. It didn't take much to get her to tell me what you put her up to. She begged me to forgive her and I did."

The master stood at that point and approached Charlton, "So, this is what you wanted to tell me. You're lying, boy. When I came in this room, you was lying on the floor crying your eyes out. You said I made a mistake. You made the mistake, boy. You think you got it all figured out. This lie is going to cost you. I swear it on my father's grave, God rest his soul."

Charlton put his hand up and took a step toward the master, "Sit down, you old fool! You think I can't beat you with my bare hands? You got no one here to protect you. Now sit down or I'll make you sit down." The master's eyes grew wide and he stumbled backward into the chair.

"You'll pay for this. I swear it," the master said in a hushed tone.

"I know I will. I'm ready to die. You know I been since I was a boy. You'll want to hear the rest of this." Charlton took in a deep breath. "We stood there looking each other in the eyes. When I saw tears roll down, I wiped them off her face and she started to touch mine. Then, we kissed and we kept doing it." The master craned his neck forward and tightened his back into a distinctive hump.

"She touched me all over. She took off my clothes. We went over to your couch. I never made love to a woman before that, John."

Charlton looked over at the master and studied him, surprised to see that he had lost some of his tension. The master stood up, but got no closer to Charlton. "You're one sick boy. I know you lie. You lie and there's nothing more to it. I saw you here on this floor crying like a child. I never seen such a pathetic person in all my life. Of course, you're going to get punished for this story and your insolence, but your lies have only revealed who you are."

Charlton laughed and after carrying on for a while with the master froze in confusion, he spoke. "You saw the end of it. Before you came back, I asked Belle to run away with me, but she said no. She hates her husband, but she wouldn't leave her son. I told her we'd take him with us, but she didn't want him to grow up on the run. Can't say I blame her. I cried 'cause she wouldn't go with me and that's all." Charlton did not allow a pause. "And that's the truth and you'll know it 'cause it's my child."

The master reeled back as if struck. He stumbled, tripped, and fell in his chair. "No. No. No..." the master said.

Charlton took the chance to drive the truth deeper, wanting to keep the master from denying the truth. "Yes!" Charlton said, leaning toward the chair. "Doesn't Belle seem worried now? Does she speak faster? Is she staring at nothing at all? I wonder what my child will look like. What color will the skin be? How about the hair? I fell in love with a slave woman, but I turned her away 'cause I didn't want to give you any more slaves, but I found a way to have a child that won't be a slave. You know who that child is? Your grandchild."

Charlton relished the expressions on the master's face. A moment ago, he knew Charlton lied. Now he moved his eyes from side to side, as if searching for excuses to keep denying the truth. He could see the master scanning his recent memories of Belle's face and actions. The master's chest heaved from the effort.

As the master confirmed the truth that Charlton spoke, he moved from confusion to anger. He bolted upright and approached Charlton, pointing his finger at his face. "You! You bastard! You devil!" the master said, making the last word into a roar.

Charlton stood strong, pushing his chest out and speaking in a commanding voice. "Yes! Yes, do it! Kill me! Strangle me! Get out your sword and hit me with it! I got you. I won, you lost. I've got nothing else to live for."

The master lunged at Charlton and grabbed his neck, as he pushed Charlton against the wall. Charlton's instincts told him to fight back and take out the master first, but he wanted the master to continue. The master would witness the birth of Charlton's child, knowing that his bloodline had become tainted. He would hope that his son-in-law had fathered his new grandchild only to have those hopes dashed. Charlton's revenge would become all the more difficult for the master to endure. Charlton could use his strong body to break this old man in two, but he allowed the chokehold to remain, feeling that same desperate need for air he had as a boy standing in the master's trackway.

"You're the devil! You're the devil! I'll kill you!" the master said.

As a panicked need for air gripped Charlton, he almost couldn't help using his arms to push the master away from him. Instead his body got a sense of relief. Little wisps of air passed through his throat. The master's grip relaxed. Charlton raspy voice came forth. "No!"

The master released Charlton altogether. "You want to be killed, you son of a bitch. You want me to kill you. I won't. I won't give you what you want," the master said.

"You, you son of a bitch! Finish what you started!" Charlton said in a rasp. Anger built inside of Charlton. Everything had worked out like he wanted until now. He needed the master to kill him so that he could find out what happened when he died. He wanted Belle to know that her father had killed her baby's father. His death could save Belle from her father, but only if she found out that he murdered Charlton.

"No, I won't. You think I'm cruel. Just wait until you go to another master. The suffering you will receive under a new master will be too much for you to bear. I'm going to make you hate yourself for ever doubting my generosity," the master said. The master took on an eerie calm tone, speaking to Charlton as if in a dream. Charlton decided he needed to bring the master back to his anger.

"John, Belle told me after we were done that she had always wanted to do it with me. She told me Robert mounts her like a horse, but she never felt as good as she did with me. You know, she said that she loved me too."

The master said nothing, but picked up a cane from behind his desk, an object that Charlton had never noticed. A shiny, metal ball sat perched on the top of the cane and glimmered from the sunlight that shot through the window.

Charlton stopped speaking and smiled at the master as he approached him raising the cane above his head. Charlton leaned his head forward to give the master a clean shot. The master raised the cane, and let it fall.

Chapter Thirty-Four

When he awoke, Charlton couldn't remember feeling worse, except when he found himself in the tool shed. His throat felt like he had swallowed sand and it had gotten stuck halfway down. His head felt like it had split open. He groaned and tried to keep himself calm. Yet again the master had struck him hard enough to make him lose himself, but not kill him. *Why can't I just die?*

Charlton opened his eyes, but no light reached them. He wished he had some idea where the master had put him. He felt his back pressing against something long, flat, and a little damp. His legs extended along the same surface with his arms stretched above his head and also wet. He tried to pull his arms apart, but heavy shackles at the wrist held them together. His legs wouldn't come apart either, bound by the same heavy restraint as his arms.

He tried to bring his arms toward the rest of his body, but he at once heard the clink of metal against metal and felt resistance, then rested for a moment to assess his situation. He lay outside on the ground with shackles around his ankles and wrists on a cloudy, moonless night. The wrist shackles held fast to the ground by a spike through a loop in the chains and as he thought about it, he realized it must be a rather humid night because his breath ran stuffy and warm.

Charlton lifted his legs and bumped up against something. It surprised him and made him raise his head to investigate. In an instant his head filled with an even more intense, crippling pain as he bumped his forehead against something and then the back of his slammed into the ground where the master had hit him. Charlton screamed in pain, but through his damaged throat it came out as a squeak.

The pain took a long time to subside. When it did, Charlton faced a rising panic. *Where am I?* His breathing became more rapid, which only filled the space with ever more damp air and made him more panicked.

It took great will to overcome his fear. Charlton focused on controlling his breathing, and when it had returned to normal, he took stock of what had happened to him, trying not to move. He had no light and no space to move. The evidence indicated that the master had ordered his hired hands to put Charlton under the Big House. With everything all closed around him and a spike keeping his wrists in place, he couldn't escape. He couldn't move in any direction and he had no space to attempt to get out. Only his hands reached outside, but the space above him left no room to pull out the spike.

Exhausted from his effort, Charlton closed his eyes. It didn't take long for sleep to find him.

***

Charlton awoke to the clatter of steel against steel. He heard someone speaking, "Come on you bastard, give!" He felt his hands pulled up and heard the thud of the spike dropping to the ground. Without warning, Hands gripped his wrists and dragged him free from under the house. He flattened himself and relaxed to make sure he wouldn't get bumped on the way out. His headache remained as he blinked his eyes in the sunlight. He could make out the silhouette of a burly white field hand. "Well, well, well, look what we got here. How'd you sleep, Sleeping Beauty?" the hired hand said.

"Pretty good," Charlton said, his voice improved somewhat from the choking.

"Blast it! Shut your mouth. I don't care how you slept. All I cares about is that I'm going to have a good couple nights. You and I, we going for a ride and then I get to hole myself up in one of them fancy hotels and wait to collect the money. Boy, you about to get yourself sold at auction. You must've done something big and bad, your master said he ain't going to be happy 'til you gone. I even gets to keep some of that money."

Charlton thought that if he got up behind the man, he could wrap his shackle chain around his neck and choke the life out of him. The field hand would struggle, but Charlton had a weapon. The thought crossed his mind, but he decided against it. He knew about the Charleston slave auction and where this white man could find a fancy hotel. Charlton thought he would enjoy going back to Charleston. He wanted to see the city one last time before he died and maybe even hurt the master more than he already had.

"Look, boy, I don't want no trouble from you. If you try anything, I'll squash you flat. Your master, he made no bones about it: I can do anything I want to you, short of killing you. He say he get a good price for you and well," the man said as he sized up Charlton with his eyes. "I think he's right. Now get up, let's go."

The white man reached out his hand, but Charlton didn't take it. He rose to his feet in his own good time as he heard the shackles around his legs jangle against his boots. Walking with shackles presented some difficulty for Charlton. The chains only let him lift his feet a little. He almost tripped on the way to the master's spare carriage, but faced no more trouble as he learned to shuffle his feet forward.

The spare carriage had a seat in front allowing the driver to grab the reins and steer the horse. The seat in the back held one or two passengers. The leather seat had torn, the stuffing long gone. Only a sheath of cloth covered the wood. The hood that used to cover the passenger seat lay tattered and useless in the back.

"Don't you feel like royalty or nothing sitting back there and just so you don't try nothing..." said the field hand as he undid one of shackles around Charlton's wrist and latched it to the wrist again, this time behind Charlton's back.

***

The ride bumped and shook Charlton with his hands behind his back. He recognized the route to Charleston. The visions of the slave auction in Charleston rolled through Charlton's mind. He had no doubt he would end up there. Charlton looked at the driver and thought about killing him, decoupling the wagon, and riding the horse to freedom. Confidence that he could bring his feet up and step over the chain held the fantasy. The driver would have the key to unlock his chains.

Two thoughts prevented him from doing it. First, he couldn't ride a horse, so slave catchers stood a good chance of capturing him. Second, he relished the idea of getting into a slave auction in Charleston. He longed to see the city again, but more than that he wanted the crowd to appear before him on auction day.

The master had pulled a dirty trick on him, not killing him as Charlton had planned. He intended to make the master pay for it.

***

The driver and Charlton took the hours-long ride in complete silence. When they approached the city, Charlton heard voices again and marveled at the return of the buzz of city life and the odor of the sea, that he knew in his time with the Zutter family. He wanted to jump out of the carriage and get lost among the crowd, but knew he wouldn't get far.

The driver stopped in front of a large, white building with an enormous archway. The word "MART" stood out above the arch. A large iron fence lay open into the building.

The driver spoke again after securing the horse. "You're coming with me. I'll leave you here and come back tomorrow to collect the fare, but you'll be gone by then, won't you?" The driver laughed.

The driver undid the wrist chains, then locked Charlton's wrists in front of him again. He yanked on the chain holding Charlton, but not too hard.

After Charlton jumped down from the carriage, almost falling in the process, the driver pulled Charlton into the building through the archway. A large table stood to the side. A young man with a stubble beard leaned back in a chair, reading a newspaper. A book stood open before him at the back end of the table. A feather quill and ink-well lay near the book.

The driver approached the clerk. He cleared his throat to announce himself when the man failed to acknowledge him. "Yes?" the clerk said, annoyed.

The young man put down the paper and looked up, first at the driver, then Charlton. "Please tell me you're dropping that off for the auction tomorrow." He pointing at Charlton, his gaze bouncing all over Charlton's body. Charlton averted his eyes from the worker.

"Yeah. You going to get a lot for him then?"

The clerk looked at the driver with a grin. "Let's just put it this way. Whoever owns him, I assume not you, is going to get his reward."

Charlton smirked at the words. He would see to it the master got his real reward. The man at the desk caught Charlton's smirk and looked at him with eyes squinting, eyebrows flickering. Charlton wiped the expression off his face and resumed staring at the wall.

"Master's name?" the clerk asked, ready to get down to business.

"Mr. John Armand," the driver said.

"Spelling?"

"Uh."

The worker laughed. "Never you mind. I got it." He wrote the name in the book and made a mark in front of the entry.

"Slave name?"

"Does it matter?" the driver asked, chuckling.

With his head still pointing toward the book, the clerk lifted his eyebrows and looked up at the driver. "The auctioneer uses it at auction. Just tell me." He sighed.

"It's Charlton."

The clerk straightened up and attended to the driver again. "Does he have a connection to the city?"

"What city?"

"What city? This city, Charleston. His name sounds like it. Are you…? No, it's not worth it." The clerk returned his gaze to the book. "I assume Mr. Armand sent you. Your name?"

"Clancy Sherman."

"You know our policies?"

The driver opened his mouth, then hesitated. The clerk rolled his eyes, "Policies are rules, Mr. Sherman. We will inspect your slave and set a price to start the auction. The bidders will signal that they accept the price and others will say that they will pay more. When enough time has passed, we will sell to the highest bidder, take our standard cut, and give you the majority stake."

"Fine," the driver said in a short tone. "Can I leave now?"

"No. The papers, Mr. Sherman."

"Um, say what, again?"

"Surely, Mr. Armand gave you his papers. It's no good selling him without them. Did he give them to you?

Clancy looked frightened, then searched his pockets. "Oh, yeah. Right here."

The worker snatched the paper out of Clancy's outstretched hand and scanned it. "Yes. These are them." He scribbled out some writing on a slip of paper and handed it to the driver. "Take this. It's a receipt. If you change your mind, you got to give that over and we'll give him back."

"Fine," Clancy said taking the paper. "Now can I go?"

"Yes. Be back tomorrow by noon. The auction begins at 10:30 and I expect they'll put up this one first."

The driver nodded and handed the clerk the key to Charlton's shackles. The young man motioned to two men on the other side of the building and they came over to assist. They removed Charlton's chains, to his relief.

"Take off your shirt," the clerk said to Charlton. Charlton obeyed. All three men stared at his well-toned muscles. Charlton flinched as the worker began pinching his arms, chest, shoulders, and back.

"This is something else," the clerk told the workers. "This is the most remarkable frame on a slave I've ever seen. He's going up first, all right. Could you men put Charlton into the barracoon? I'll return soon. I have to tell the boss."

The young man walked away. The workers allowed Charlton to put his shirt back on, then put the chains back on him. They led him to a cell in the back of the room where other shackled slaves waited.

***

All day, interested parties came to the slave market looking to inspect the merchandise. More than any other captive, Charlton had to come out of the cell to let the customers view and pinch him. The urge to fight kept pulling at him, but the thoughts of revenge on the master forced him to tolerate it. Before long, night fell and a new crew of workers relieved the daytime set. The night crew kept watch over the slaves and stayed silent, except for occasional snoring.

Charlton's heart ached for his fellow captives, who looked scared, concerned, and deserving of pity. One set of captives broke Charlton's heart more than the others: a whole family, mother, father, and siblings, huddled together on the floor. Their chattering centered on the father, who had to reassure his children and wife that they would sell together. He did that all day, attempting to talk to any customers who came to view them. He always chose the same topic; why the customer needed, not just him, but his whole family to work at their plantation. He promised to raise his kids to revere their new master and to work as hard as he did. When he pointed out his wife, he claimed extraordinary mammy skills for young looking prospective buyers, housekeeping skills for the well-dressed men, and planting skills for the rugged ones.

The young man from the desk strolled over and laughed a couple times as the man made his case with yet new skills attributed to his family.

One potential buyer who heard the man's laughter, turned to the desk clerk and asked, "What's so funny? Is he lying?"

The clerk's face turned mirthful, "I have no idea, but you should hear the yarns this boy's been spinning all day. Woo, boy, is he spinning them!"

The buyer looked from desk clerk to slave and back again. He waved his hand dismissing the slave and walked out of the mart. Charlton wanted to throttle the desk clerk. The clerk stood watching the customer leave. Charlton got as far as drawing breath to question the clerk's business practices, but decided against it. He didn't want to speak and appear too educated or smart. He chose to remain silent.

Chapter Thirty-Five

The barracoon's dimensions left enough room for the prisoners to lie down side by side for the night. The keepers tossed in some hay for mattresses, but the close quarters, the stench of sweat, and Charlton's shackles made sleeping difficult. Before light, he awoke to the sound of a key in the lock of his cell. A man with hunched shoulders stood near some brawny workmen. "You!" he said, pointing to Charlton. "Get up and come over here."

Charlton did as told. He sat up, then stood as fast as his weariness would allow. He wanted to obey to prevent suspicion. "Take him outside and hook him to the wall," the man said to the workers. One of the men took off Charlton's ankle shackles, then both grabbed him with firm grips, but not hard enough to make marks on his skin.

They hustled him outside and locked one end of his wrist shackle to a metal ring on the wall where riders tied their horses, leaving his other hand free. As he suspected, they made Charlton into the showpiece. He would sit outside and encourage potential buyers that they should come to today's auction.

From where they chained him, Charlton had plenty of space to maneuver. In the early dawn, he had enough light to write while disguising it from onlookers.

He had no stick or other tool and after trying with his finger and finding the ground too rough, he grabbed a loose stone and scraped away at the dirt. When anyone came out of the mart, Charlton stopped and hovered over the words. Few onlookers passed him at the early hour.

He knew that he could not write all the words, so he chose the most poignant. Finished early and relieved, he read the words he had written in his head, "All men are created equal and endowed with inalienable rights." He wrote the message in three stacked lines in a size and location that let him hide the finished words with his body as he wrote the next line. He looked natural and relaxed and the workers never told him to move.

As morning advanced, Charlton attracted crowds. He listened with disgust as they remarked between themselves about his body. His powerful legs, thick chest, and strong arms all got the crowd's attention. He hated them for judging him and anticipated how they would react when he moved.

***

The auction began. Prospective buyers crowded around the arch where the workers placed the table the desk clerk had used in the archway. Charlton assumed it would act as a stage to display the slaves.

A stocky man in a suit came out to the front and motioned for the workers to bring Charlton over to the table. Careful to keep his words intact, Charlton pivoted on his bottom, planted his feet on the ground and heaved himself up. No one noticed the words he had written, so with a flourish, Charlton rolled his palms and gestured at the words. "See the truth!" he said to the crowd in a booming voice. "I'm your equal! You take away my rights! Shame on you all!"

Gasps rang out from the crowd like chimes in the wind. Many of the onlookers stared down at Charlton's words. As the murmuring grew, Charlton continued to speak, louder and louder with the crowd shouting and cursing him. "We hold these truths to be self-evident, that all men are created equal, that they are endowed by their Creator with certain inalienable rights that among these are life, liberty, and the pursuit of happiness. That to secure these rights, Governments are instituted among men deriving their just powers from the consent of the governed." Charlton drew a breath to continue his memorized lines when the air came right back out of him.

He found himself yanked to the ground while his wrist pulled at the shackle attached to the ring on the wall, smothering his writing with his body as one of the burly workers struggled on top of him and the other stood above him. The worker on top of him pushed his hands into Charlton's face, trying to cover his mouth. Charlton fought him off, but couldn't get any more words out in the scuffle. The burly man spoke in a grunting voice the words "Shut it! Shut your mouth!" over and over again. The man who stood above them commanded the other to do the same, "Shut his mouth! Shut it!"

As the worker struggled, the crowd grew more hostile toward Charlton, cheering on his attacker. When he failed to subdue Charlton and his co-worker refused to help, two men from the crowd stepped forward and grabbed Charlton. With the odds stacked against a chained Charlton, he stopped struggling and let the three men straighten him up on his feet.

The worker who stood by and watched the struggle took the key from his pocket and unlocked Charlton from the wall, then cuffed his other wrist in front of him. The worker who had struggled with Charlton thanked the two men and asked them to step aside. Charlton allowed the workers to escort him back in the building. He could hear the auctioneer try to calm the crowd. The desk clerk paced inside the building and chattered in a high-pitched tone to himself. "Oh, this is not good. The boss will be mad. Very mad. He'll have my job. I know it." Meanwhile, the other slaves for sale stood to the side of the table, all staring at Charlton. The father of the slave family shot a menacing stare at him.

The workers marched Charlton past the desk clerk and to the cell he occupied before going outside. The worker in the lead unlocked the cell, swung the door open, and stood back as Charlton's escort shoved him inside.

Only after the lead worker locked the door and the two men backed away did the escort begin to talk. "You're done, boy. It's over for you. I don't know whether they going to hang you by your neck or whip your hide off you, but whatever it is, I want to be there. I want to see it and, damn it all, I want to help. I never seen such a display in all my life. Let's get out of here, Angus."

The two men turned around and headed back out to the auction. The clerk came to Charlton, who lay on the floor grinning. The lack of sleep, his sore muscles, his aching wrist, and the chafed skin around his metal confines all seemed like a distant memory after his triumph outside. Even the thought of punishment of death could not dissuade Charlton from his joy. So, he would die? Fine. He had his vengeance. His life's mission came to a close. He would find out the secrets of the afterlife or maybe he would die and cease to exist. Either way, he preferred death to life.

The clerk disrupted his thoughts. "You are just about the strangest creature I've ever laid eyes on. They're right you know."

Charlton furled his brow to prompt the desk clerk to explain. "Angus and Henry. They said you'd be put to death. You will. The laws are quite plain. Slaves can't read or write. They'll kill you."

Charlton stood up and looked the desk clerk in the eyes. "You think I care?"

"Of course you care. Don't you?"

"You ever been lashed?"

"No."

"You work for money?"

"Yeah."

Charlton continued. "I heard you over there when they threw me in here. You worried about losing your job. I want to have a job. I get lashed when I do the wrong thing. You get money for doing the right thing and if you lost your job, you'd get another one. It'd be one you wanted to do or not, but if you didn't like it you'd get rid of it and take another. Me? I can't choose. I just don't want to get lashed."

Charlton stopped there, the clerk looked thoughtful, then said "But, that's the way it is. You're black and I'm white."

Charlton's nerves fired up in unison at the words, but he took control of his breath and calmed himself. "Oh, I see, so the skin color I was born to wear made me deserve all this?"

"The law thinks so."

"You hear what I say out there?"

"No. Not all of it."

"The Declaration of Independence says I have rights. It didn't say, 'but only for white people.' It said for all. Jefferson tells me we should get rid of your government."

"You're a traitor, then!" the desk clerk said as he took a step back.

"No! It's your government. It ain't mine."

The desk clerk looked around wild eyed. "I can't talk to you anymore. You're playing tricks on me." He backed away from Charlton and headed toward the auction.

"Think about it," Charlton said.

***

A loud rattling sound woke Charlton. His eyes flung open to find the driver back again. He had a walking stick in between the bars of Charlton's cell and shook it back and forth. "Get up! Get up! Boy, get up!"

Charlton lifted himself off the cot making sure to take his time. The desk clerk nudged the driver out of the way to get the key to the cell into the lock. When he swung the door open, Charlton crept forward. The driver tensed his muscles and jerked forward. Charlton growled at him and the man backed away.

"Come on, we're going back to the carriage. I got to get you out of here and back to your master, or well, I don't know what they're going to do to me," the driver said.

"We're going back to the master?"

"Yeah, for some reason nobody wants you. You got nowhere else to go but back."

"All right, let's go." Charlton walked out of the cell and then the door of the slave mart with Clancy.

A couple of the faces from the auction stood waiting for them. They shouted at Charlton and Clancy, calling Charlton all sorts of names. He waved to them and smiled. Two of the party picked up rocks from the ground and threw them at Charlton and the driver. The driver didn't even secure Charlton to the carriage before he took the reins and got the horse to start up. Clancy got the horse up to full speed and left the young, catcalling men in the dust.

The trip back seemed to change the driver's mind about talking. He spoke to Charlton the moment they left Charleston behind.

"You know, boy, they was going to kill you back there. Well, turn you over to get hung at least."

"Yeah?" Charlton said. "Well, why didn't they?"

"They said it'd be bad for their business and they right. You can't be killing no one's slaves that don't belong to you."

After a while, when silence prevailed, the driver tried to engage with Charlton again. "You know your master, now there's a man that could kill you and I reckon he will when he hears what you done."

The driver looked back at Charlton with a wide grin. Charlton returned it. "You think I care, Clancy?"

The driver jutted out his jaw. "What you mean calling me that? I'm Mr. Sherman to you, boy. Don't you forget your place and what you mean by you don't care? Everyone want to live."

Charlton scoffed. "Everyone want to live? I don't see why a slave should want to live. Better to die than work for someone and get nothing for it."

"You're crazed," Clancy said.

"Maybe. What you think happens after we die, Clancy?"

"I told you not to call me that," Clancy said, turning around and sharpening his gaze at Charlton. Then, he softened his expression, turned around to look at the road again, and fell silent. At long length, he spoke. "I think our bodies, they stay down here on the earth, but our souls, they go to Heaven where we meet our divine Creator. Heaven is the place where the angels sing, you know. It's where everything is all right."

The simple man's words jammed an image of Angie, who Harriett had called their "angel," into his head. He saw her in her dress, still smeared with dirt from the fields. The image tore out of his mind when Clancy spoke again.

"Of course, only a white person, who's been good to others can make it," Clancy said.

Charlton's mixed feelings gave him a taste of indignation blended with one of pity for Clancy. The indignation went out to the whole South. Clancy didn't strike Charlton as a cruel man. His words didn't come out with any hatred behind them. He said them as fact. Yet, the cruelty of denying Charlton a place in Heaven after a life of suffering still stung.

"Clancy," Charlton said. Clancy's shoulders tensed, but he did not scold Charlton again. "I was with you until you said that. A white man has a different skin color than a black man. How can he make it to Heaven and the black man can't?"

If Charlton hadn't seen it, he wouldn't have believed that Clancy paused to consider his question. From the angle where Charlton sat, Clancy appeared to give it real thought.

"White men are your betters. God chose us," Clancy said.

"Why?"

"That's just the way it is."

"When someone says, 'that's just the way it is,' they mean, 'I don't know.'"

Clancy tried excuse after excuse, but could only refer to how The Good Book said men could keep slaves and facts about the way white people treated their slaves. He said whites must be better than blacks because they owned the whips and used them, they made the laws, and they could hunt down runaways. At every excuse Charlton pointed out that what Clancy said only meant white people had the power. He asked Clancy whether white people would have a worse time getting to Heaven when they did such bad things. Clancy had no answer.

By the time the horses pulled them into John Armand's plantation, Clancy and Charlton spoke on a first name basis without Clancy's protest. Charlton felt certain that he reached one person from the clouded darkness of the South. He looked with a gentle calm at the Big House and imagined the master's reaction when he found out what happened. A broad grin stretched across his face.

Chapter Thirty-Six

No one came out of the house when the carriage pulled up on the trackway. Clancy looked back at Charlton.

"Go ahead and tell him what happened, Clancy," Charlton said. "I know what you're thinking. You want to let me go and say I ran away."

"You could make it," Clancy said.

"Don't want to. I want you to tell the master what happened."

Clancy made a motion to shake Charlton's hand, but he looked around himself and withdrew his hand.

"You're a good man, Clancy," Charlton said.

Without another word, Clancy climbed the porch steps and knocked. A house slave let him in.

***

Charlton heard shouting from inside, then saw Clancy emerge from the house. The master appeared behind him and shoved Clancy out of the way to see Charlton in the carriage.

Charlton smiled as the master's face went from pale, to red, to purple. "So, it's true," he said in a hiss. He charged up to the carriage. "You vile, low-down, dirty devil! Do you deny that you wrote those words in the dirt?" The master paused waiting for an answer, his chest heaving.

"No," Charlton said.

The master pointed his finger at Charlton's face. "And did you speak to the white men and tell them out of your filthy mouth that they should be ashamed?"

Charlton grinned and said, "Yeah."

The master jumped up and down. "Don't you dare smile at me! You disgraced me and my family name!"

"You disgraced yourself, John," Charlton said.

The master's entire body shook. A tic in the master's face made his mouth twitch. He turned from Charlton and pointed an unsteady finger at Clancy. "You! Drive this devil to the slave quarters. Tell the cooks to put supper on hold. They are not to serve a single slave," the master said through his clenched jaw.

"Sir?" Clancy said.

"You heard me. Now do it!"

Clancy climbed into his seat and drove the horse and carriage to the slave quarters with Charlton still shackled.

A lump grew in Charlton's throat and another one settled in his stomach. He realized the master had something planned that would hurt the other slaves.

When they arrived at the slave quarters, Clancy dismounted and told the slaves preparing the meal to cover it up and not let anyone serve themselves. They did as instructed. Next, he spoke to the overseer who marched ahead of the returning slaves and handed over the key to Charlton's shackles. Clancy made eye contact with Charlton. They exchanged nods and Clancy fell back in with the overseer and a couple of the hired hands.

Before long, the master's carriage rolled into the courtyard and the master got out. He ignored Charlton and marched to the overseer. Charlton heard the chatter of the slaves returning for the day. The overseer nodded at the master, then gathered all the hired hands around him, explaining something as his arms cut through the air.

When the slaves returned, their eyes scanned the scene, including taking in Charlton confined in the beat-up carriage, the master's carriage, and the white field hands staring back at them. When they all stood inside the courtyard, the overseer spoke. "You will not get to eat your supper just yet. The master himself has ordered the women into the women's cabin and the men into the men's. Even if you don't live there."

The slaves exchanged glances with one another and chattered, not obeying at first. "Now!" the overseer said in a booming voice. Shouts of surprise and panic rose from the crowd. They hurried over to their designated areas, waiting in lines to go through the doors.

As the lines filed into the cabins, the overseer approached Charlton and without a word unlocked the shackles. Charlton sighed at the loss of his cuffs. "Get off the cart!" the overseer said. Charlton hopped onto the ground. He glanced in the direction of the Master's carriage and saw hired hands emerge with chains and two giant locks.

The field hand brought his bundle to the women's quarters, which now had the door shut and wove the chains through loops at the four corners of the door frame. The overseer pushed Charlton in the direction of the men's cabin. Charlton went to it and opened the door. The overseer shoved him inside and shut the door behind him.

***

Men and boys packed the space with multiple slaves sitting on the cots or standing shoulder to shoulder in between them. His fellow slaves stared with bewildered expressions at Charlton, who had his back pressed to the door. Out of the crowded mass, Archie emerged. He pushed through bodies to Charlton, hugging him tight. Charlton opened his mouth to speak words of comfort when he heard the master's voice through the walls.

"Those walls sure are sturdy aren't they? My father spared no expense to raise a quality set of quarters. I am a man of my word. You were told that you would be fed and you will, but not until Charlton is dead. You see, he has soiled my good name and for that there is only one fitting punishment. I am not going to do it, though. If he starves to death, you all starve to death, including the women. So you give some thought as to what you want to do. One of my hands will check with you every hour. When he is dead, you will eat."

Gasps and murmurs erupted from the men. Charlton peered through the slats in the door. He saw the master turn around and walk away.

When Charlton heard the words, he knew he would draw his last breath in this building. He looked at the faces of his fellow slaves. He saw some desperation, some bewilderment, and some anger. Not a single set of eyes looked away from him. Even Charlton couldn't help looking down at himself with Archie still clinging to him. Charlton saw the spots of missing skin on his wrists. The open wounds hurt and he resigned himself that his wrists would never feel better.

For what seemed a lifetime, no one made a sound or a move until Archie said in a trembling voice. "Charlton, what did you do?"

"The master tried to sell me at a slave auction. I told the crowd the truth," he told Archie in a whisper that echoed across the silent cabin.

Most of the other slaves turned to each other with looks of confusion. Phillip pushed his way to the front. "You done us all in, Charlton!"

"Phillip, you know I'm right."

"You was like a papa to me. And you taught me lots, but ain't no white man going to see we got rights. We going to die 'cause you a fool and think you going to learn them that?"

"You don't understand, I started to reach one of them."

"One? One white man and that make not a lick of difference. You want us dead, don't you?" While he spoke, Phillip approached Charlton and after his final words, shoved Charlton against the door. Archie fell back too as he clutched Charlton's side. "I ain't going to starve to death because you can't shut your mouth," Phillip said into Charlton's face.

A chorus of agreement rose from the rest, except for Archie, who whimpered. Archie got between Charlton and Phillip. He stood with his arms up and palms out. "Please, Phillip. Me and my sisters, we need him," Archie said in a choked, quiet voice.

Phillip's eyes softened as they rested on Archie. "We don't need him. We don't need him no more."

"Phillip's right, Archie. You don't need me no more," Charlton said. Archie let out a whimper of shocked protest, but Charlton silenced him with a warm smile. This time he spoke to Phillip and the crowd. "I know I got to die. Y'all going to do it too 'cause the master's going to make you. It ain't your fault. You got to eat."

Phillip made a motion to speak, but Charlton stared him down and he stifled it. "How about you let me talk to Archie? After that, I ain't going to stop you." Archie whined in protest. Charlton continued speaking. "Just give me time to say good-bye. All right?" he asked Phillip.

"Yeah," Phillip said. He crossed his arms and stared at Charlton.

Charlton crouched to speak with Archie, who no longer held back his tears. With little room to spare in the cabin for privacy, Charlton whispered into Archie's ear, determined to repeat his advice of the other night. "I know you won't see it this way, but this don't have to be sad. You and your sisters are going to make it out of here. Go on the Underground Railroad. It's the way out. You got to use it to escape. You know that big, old tree right outside here?" Archie nodded through his tears so Charlton continued. "Walk straight away from this cabin to the tree, take the path right behind it, and keep walking into the woods. Do it at night, so no one will see you. That path'll bring you to a broken-down barn. No one lives there, but there's wild crops growing there. You can eat that until the people come to help you. They'll take you up North."

"You come too, Charlton," Archie said.

"I can't. The master mean what he say. He'd see you all go hungry."

"I won't let them kill you, Charlton!" Archie said.

"You have to, but I don't want you to see it. You go to the back corner and you hold your hands over your ears and close your eyes. All right?"

"I…"

"Please, just do it?" Tears clouded Charlton's vision.

"But…" Archie said.

Charlton straightened up and called to Phillip, "I'm ready. Go!" he said to Archie and gave him a nudge toward the back of the cabin. Archie moved around everyone until they cleared a path. Charlton watched him disappear and sighed.

Phillip turned to the rest of the men who looked unsure of going forward. "Come on!" Phillip said to them. "He the one who got in good with the master and acted better than us 'cause the master like him. I know him. He talk to me all friendly like, just to get in my house and then made me leave," Charlton's neck muscles tightened, but he didn't correct Phillip. "He the one who killed Angie too. She didn't do nothing to him."

The longer the men listened to Phillip, the angrier they got, but they still seemed reluctant to become killers. Phillip looked flustered. He pivoted on Charlton. "What you do to the master anyway?"

Charlton's mind reeled. He had to get the men to hate him. They had to put an end to his life and resume theirs. Neither would happen without it. He needed to speak the truth. He looked Phillip straight in the eye. "I took the master's daughter in his house. It's my child she's carrying."

After a moment of awkward silence, Phillip spun back around to face the rest. "Now you see why the master want him dead. He put us in here to starve 'cause he can't do the right thing." He swung back toward Charlton. "You proud of it, ain't you?"

"Yeah," Charlton said and he grinned at the men.

Turning back to the rest, Phillip said, "He don't even care if we starve 'cause of what he did. He not just going to starve us. He going to starve the women too. We got to save them. Who'll help me?"

Two of the slaves Paul had broken stepped forward to offer their help. They advanced on Charlton while the others stood back to watch.

The two other men dove forward and grabbed one of Charlton's arms each, leaving his torso exposed.

Phillip stepped up to him, reared back, and connected his fist with Charlton's face. The blow stung and left a tremendous ache. He then swung into Charlton's stomach, making him double over. With his head lowered, Phillip gripped Charlton's neck with both hands.

At first, pain pervaded Charlton as his body begged for breath. Despite his effort to avoid resisting, Charlton pulled at the men who held him back, but they kept their grip. Desperation tensed his body and overwhelmed his mind. As he lost consciousness, the pain dissolved. His body longed for breath, but he didn't care and instead of the locked men's quarters at night, he felt the warmth of the sun on his head, shoulders, and back. Instead of Phillip, crazed and angry, inflicting the pain he had wanted to cause Charlton since he left his house, he saw the blue sky above him and the calm sea meeting a pale yellow beach at his feet. Instead of Phillip's curses, he heard gentle waves lapping the sand and the calls of seagulls. He stretched his arms above his head and took off running toward the water. His feet splashed in the ocean and changed the course of the waves. He dove into the sea.

Charlton's spirit soared when he came back to the surface and noticed familiar, happy faces bobbing in the water with him. First, he passed his mother and next to her, a youthful man who swayed in the current. He recognized his father at once. To the right, Mr. and Mrs. Zutter beamed at him. William floated next to them, but not quite there. Charlton could see through him as though he did not yet belong to this new world.

Charlton swam strong and further into the water. Ole Joe floated on his back with his hands behind his head. A splash caught Charlton's attention and he turned to see Paul jump out of the water and dive back in, laughing like Charlton had never heard him do in life. Charlton squinted beyond where Paul dove to see the faded shapes of three childlike figures close together, but far from him.

He kept swimming away from the shore. Further along, the translucent head of Belle as a child beamed at him in the water. Near her, a young darker-skinned woman of stunning beauty looked at him with admiration, the blue sky visible through her. Charlton's heart skipped a beat as he looked into the face of his daughter. A tear of joy fell from his eye.

He wanted to stay and speak with his loved ones, but he looked up and saw in the distance, an island rising from the water. A slender woman with long dark curls and a gleaming white gown stood waving to him. Charlton swam faster. Every stroke clarified Angie's face. She ran up to the end of the land and into the water. A smile spread across his face as his feet found the ground under the water and he pushed against it to sprint into her embrace.

OTHER ANAPHORA LITERARY PRESS TITLES

The History of British and American Author-Publishers
By: Anna Faktorovich

Notes for Further Research
By: Molly Kirschner

The Encyclopedic Philosophy of Michel Serres
By: Keith Moser

The Visit
By: Michael G. Casey

How to Be Happy
By: C. J. Jos

A Dying Breed
By: Scott Duff

Love in the Cretaceous
By: Howard W. Robertson

The Second of Seven
By: Jeremie Guy

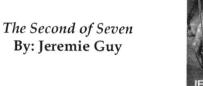